Networks of Power

Networks of Power:

Corporate TV's Threat
to Democracy

Dennis W. Mazzocco

Foreword by
Herbert I. Schiller

South End Press   Boston, MA

*To my mother
and the memory of my father.*

Cover design by John Moss
Text design and production by South End Press collective
Printed in the U.S.A.

Library of Congress Cataloging-in-Publication Data

Mazzocco, Dennis W.
    Networks of power : corporate T.V.'s threat to democracy / by Dennis W. Mazzocco : foreword by Herbert I. Schiller.
      p. cm.
    Includes bibliographical references and index.
    ISBN 0-89608-473-6 : $30.00. — ISBN 0-89608-472-8 (pbk.) : $14.00
    1. Mass media—United States—Ownership. 2. ABC Television Network. 3. Mass media—Political aspects—United States. 4. Communication, International. 5. Broadcast journalism—Political aspects—United States. 6. United States—Politics and government—1981-1989. 7. United States—Foreign relations—1981-1989. I. Title.
    P96.E252U655   1994
    302.23'0973—dc2094-9165
    CIP
South End Press, 116 Saint Botolph Street, Boston, MA 02115
    01 00 99 98 97 96 95 94 1 2 3 4 5 6 7 8 9

Table of Contents

Exposing the Networks of Power • Media Ownership Reflects Power • Earlier Warnings about the Media Cartel • What's Ahead?

Serving My Country • The Reality of Broadcasting • Lesson on Labor • The "Creative" Assembly Line • Third World Broadcaster • Political Awakening • Manufacturer of Consent • Growing Disillusionment • Changing Networks • Broadcasting for the Few • Conclusion

Roots of Oligopoly • Going Hollywood • Leonard Takes Control • The Sun Never Sets... • Is This News? (The FBI Network) • KGB and CIA Cooperation • Simon Says, "Takeover!" • ITT and Howard Hughes • "Number One"

Secrets of Success • Frank Smith • Lowell Thomas • The Dulles Connection • Dewey and the CIA • Murphy, "The Pope" • William Casey, "The Fixer" • "Spinning" the Adolf Eichmann Trial • Decentralizing • "Burke's Law" • Lean and Mean • Building the Empire • Who's the Boss?

ABC Becomes a "Dinosaur" • Unfit to Lead? • The End Is Near • A Not-So-Free Market • The New Right • Wall Street Moves • Making Its Peace • The 900–Pound Gorilla • A "Friendly" Merger?

The Capital Cities Workplace • Cleaning Up • Controlling the Working Class • Top Management Rewards • Pressure to Perform • Political Lobbying and Public Relations • Capital Cities and the FCC • Losing Money? • Interlocking Corporate Ties • Home Shopping • In the Sponsor's Interest • When Sport is Not Competitive • Cable / Video Enterprises—The U.S. and Beyond • ABC

News Bends Right • News Competition? • ABC Radio—More Monopoly • Limbaugh, Farber, and Harvey = Reagan Radio • Warren Buffett—The Most Important Director

The Democratic Illusion • So, What's a Better System? • What You Can Do • Media Literacy • What Government Must Do • "Corporatizing" Public Broadcasting • C-SPAN—Funded by a "For-Profit" Cable Industry • Paying for an Alternative System • Toward a More Democratic Media

Acknowledgments

This work is dedicated to my mother and the memory of my father, Martha and William Mazzocco, who together with my grandparents spent over a century working for U.S. corporations. They always worked hard and supported the system, even when it deceived and exploited them. And they never lost faith in me. I will always be grateful to them.

There are many others who have helped me. Rossy woke me up politically and I appreciate her efforts. My aunt and uncle, Lena and "Red" Bruni, regularly encouraged me with kind words, thoughts, and wisdom. Lena died in March 1994, just before this book went to press. I will never forget her.

My friends, former colleagues, and many other current U.S. media workers continue to show me through their hard work and dedication that it is the U.S. broadcasting system which needs reform, not the people who work for it.

Many thanks to Rita Atwood, my graduate advisor at California State University, Fresno, who in 1990 first urged me to write this book. Thanks to other faculty and staff at CSUF: R.C. Adams, Phil Lane, Joel Fowler, Paul Adams, Don Priest, Jeanne Tempesta, and Kathie Vander Mere. I also acknowledge my former CSUF classmate and Norwegian journalist, Margaret Oglaend, who passed away in 1993.

At the University of California, San Diego (UCSD), I thank Herb Schiller, Dan Schiller, and Michael Bernstein, who have all found time to graciously offer me their advice, counsel, and encouragement. I am particularly indebted to my senior mentor, Herb Schiller, for writing the Foreword to this book, and for teaching me (and countless other students over the forty-plus years of his distinguished academic career) to always question authority in the struggle for greater social and economic justice, and to never trade one's ethical or moral principles in return for greater bureaucratic power over others. There are other professors (not all at UCSD) whose scholarship has guided me: Michael Cole, Jack Banks, Susan Davis, Bill Drake, Yrjo Engestrom, Dee Dee Halleck, Dan Hallin,

Val Hartouni, Robert Horwitz, Robert McChesney, Vincent Mosco, Michael Schudson, and Harley Shaiken. I should add, of course, that any errors of fact remain my responsibility. Although not all of those I have mentioned share my particular interpretation of these complex issues, their work has nevertheless informed my research.

Fellow graduate students at UCSD have also been generous with their time. David Smith read early drafts of this manuscript and thoughtfully offered guidance. Isaac Mankita, Carol Christopher, and Sara Waterman were always available for scholarly debate and friendly discussion. Other graduate students at UCSD also made suggestions or comments: Dianne Bartlow, Tedi Bish, David Bradvica, Virginia Escalante, Paul Fotsch, Judy Gregory, Alex Halkias, Meighan Maguire, and Doug Williams.

Thanks to Groundwork Books, the UCSD student book cooperative, for lending me books and articles that I used in completing this book. I am also grateful to Eliot Kanter in the UCSD Central Library for providing vital research leads and assistance.

Cecilia Ubilla of the UCSD Oasis Language Program has been a trusted friend and advisor. Besides reading the entire manuscript, she has taught me much about the struggle for equal rights and social justice.

A special note of thanks to Ben Bagdikian, Jeff Cohen, George Gerbner, Ed Herman, Ralph Nader, and Michael Parenti for responding with thoughtful comments and critical suggestions on preliminary drafts of this book. While I remain indebted to each of them, I must absolve them from any shortcomings within the book.

I acknowledge my co-editors, Karin San Juan and Dionne Brooks, at South End Press. Not only have they scrutinized the text, they have also offered invaluable suggestions and research materials. I want to thank Cynthia Peters for her expert assistance on the production phase of this project. I will always appreciate their deep and genuine commitment throughout the development of the final manuscript.

Finally, and most importantly, I thank Emiko Tanioka. Emi's love, friendship, and steadfast support helped me most to realize that there is life outside of the U.S. networks. Without her, this book would very likely not have been written.

D.W.M.
La Jolla, California
September 1993

Foreword

by Herbert I. Schiller

We cannot begin to understand, much less cope with, the social breakdown that overhangs our age if our alarm system is not functioning. When our informational apparatus and its sources are unreliable, the communication principles that have served as guides to, and guarantees of, our security become reduced to rituals or apologetics.

Who in the United States, and how many, for example, possess meaningful freedom of speech in the 1990s? Where, other than in a journalism textbook, can one find a truly free press? While these questions are troubling many people, their consideration should be—but at the present time is not—a high priority on the national agenda.

An honest assessment of how the national information supply is produced and distributed could be a natural starting point. How do these processes actually work? Who puts them in operation? Why are they organized as they are? To whom do the benefits accrue? Who bears the costs?

Of course, getting the answers would constitute only the first part of a long overdue inquiry into the national information condition. Equally important is to imagine other possibilities, alternatives to the existing arrangements. This would be a formidable assignment. The debris of obsolete and self-serving rationales blocks the way. Anything that suggests a different course is labeled either unrealistic or dangerous to what once may have been unassailable, bedrock principles.

So why another book about the media? Stacks of such volumes already strain our book shelves. To be sure, they are witness to the now widely recognized centrality of the information process to the entire texture of contemporary existence. Yet, with a few worthy exceptions, most ignore the basic relationship of the media to power. And power, whatever its nature, today includes a crucial media component.

Contemporary politics are unthinkable without access to TV and print. So, too, the corporate engines that run the U.S. economy rely on the uninterrupted transmission of their marketing and ideological images and messages to a national audience. The governmental machine is no less dependent on available, and accommodating, informational networks to present its policies and actions in attractive and acceptable formats.

In short, how, and for whom, the informational processes operate in daily life are matters that go to the heart of U.S. capitalism. No theory of contemporary social control can ignore the interplay and impact of the informational apparatus on economic, political, and cultural activity.

How independent, for example, are the message and image enterprises that dominate the informational landscape? Are the media merely a profit-making industry, or are they integral parts of the governmental apparatus and the corporate economy overall? How much autonomy is possible for individual journalists, broadcasters, and editors within each media enterprise? Are there limits set on their work and creative efforts? What form do these restraints take? Does enterprise size matter, and how important is the question of ownership?

Finally, why and how does Washington's foreign policy secure almost unfailing media support, however reprehensible it may be—e.g., the invasion of Panama, the missile strikes on the center of Baghdad, and the Gulf War—to list but a few recent scandalous episodes.

Every imaginable, and often unimaginable, rationale is employed to suggest that the U.S. informational system actually is what it claims to be—information-supplying, competitive, and diverse. Individual news and cultural workers are supposed to perform their tasks in a relatively uninhibited environment. If restraints are acknowledged at all, they are the result, it is said, of the general complexities of a large-scale enterprise.

These are some of the questions and concerns that Dennis Mazzocco's *Networks of Power* addresses. The book is especially illuminating because it represents the experiences of a skilled information worker who was employed for several years by a powerful player in the TV broadcasting industry, Capital Cities/ABC, Inc.

In meticulously examining the establishment and expansion, as well as the business and programming practices, of a broadcasting heavyweight, Mazzocco uncovers a comprehensive and startling pattern. It is one which characterizes in a vivid way cultural information production in the age of super-conglomerates. The reality that Mazzocco uncovers renders totally unsustainable the all-too-familiar claims of the media industry, and of much academic work as well, about the role and function of global media enterprises.

Objectivity of the news process, insulation of the media enterprise from external governmental or corporate authority, pluralism and diversity in programming content—these are the cherished qualities that never fail to be invoked by those who defend and extol the prevailing institutional arrangements.

Mazzocco's personal encounters, along with his research findings, point instead to widespread and systematic departures from these standards and criteria. What now exists, contrary to general and dominant assertions, is an almost unaccountable, privately directed, giant message and image machine. This apparatus possesses strong, though usually unacknowledged, links to certain nuclei of coercive governmental power. It recognizes little responsibility to the public.

The existence of this increasingly closed circuit of information and cultural production, if it were fully known and publicized, would call out for public discussion and action. It would also generate a popular willingness to imagine and utilize significantly different means of organizing the nation's creative talent, and of disseminating information and entertainment. No one formula would be adequate to this task, but Mazzocco has some plausible suggestions to offer.

If there is a linchpin in the enormously intricate U.S. economy, it is the information component. The rapidly developing electronic information highway adds to its significance. At a time when a few dozen giant companies are striving to take over and direct the electronic circuits now being built into America's living rooms, studies of key players—one of which is Capital Cities/ABC—are especially relevant and valuable.

How we perceive our social condition and what we (may) prescribe for its repair or improvement depend largely on the quality and interpretation of our basic data. *Networks of Power* powerfully focuses on these vital matters.

Herbert I. Schiller
La Jolla, California
July 1993

Preface

The 1976 movie *Network* vividly reveals many of the inner workings and power dynamics of U.S. network television. Written by Paddy Chayefsky, an award-winning television writer from the 1950s, the film exposes the anti-democratic potential of the advertiser-supported U.S. television system and the "free-market" society.

Some may say that the movie is only like the stuff of fiction. But after working for nearly 20 years as an insider for the ABC and NBC television networks, both as a management executive and as a producer-director-writer on several hundred programs, I can say that *Network* does not exaggerate when it describes corporate media as an extension of state power.

Network reveals that the "for profit" U.S. media system exists first and foremost to capture an ever greater share of the $120 billion (or more) spent annually by U.S. corporations on advertising. Commercial and "public" media largely funded by corporate sponsors remain vital instruments for corporate domination of U.S. political power at home and abroad.

During the 1980s, U.S. media corporations were bought and sold with little concern for the political, economic, or social consequences of concentrated media ownership. At the same time, corporate power remained unchecked. Today the U.S. broadcast media, both private and public, must continue to please a small group of banks, insurance companies, and giant institutional investor groups that also control billions of dollars in U.S. pension funds through their inter-locking ownership of corporate stock and government securities. Their profit pursuits largely influence a corporate media culture that treats profits as if they were the root of all that is good.

When government, corporate, or military power remain out of the control of ordinary citizens, no matter how profitable or efficient that may appear when "packaged" for the public's consumption, it is tyranny—whether it appears "friendly," "patriotic," "lawful and orderly," or "economically necessary." Media ownership remains the private domain of a privileged few in corporate America.

This, of course, does not mean that all of those who work in the media are aware of this, or are able to do something about it. Like most U.S. media workers, I did not learn about the full extent of corporate control over global media production and distribution until after I resigned from ABC in 1988. To succeed in the competitive world of U.S. broadcasting (in which corporate structures increasingly resemble the top-down, tightly ordered hierarchy of a military organization), I enthusiastically endorsed the basic tenets of the system. I claimed that it was democratic, open to all citizens, and under the basic control of the audience through the ratings.

Only now do I realize that my continued ignorance and denial of the history of Capital Cities and ABC (and of the background of the top executives who managed those corporations) were an asset and not a liability to the company. U.S. media workers are paid to subtly (and at times not so subtly) influence public opinion. They learn to adopt the owners' views in order to succeed, even when their paychecks or political and social connections may be those of ordinary citizens. No media worker who wants to keep his or her job will ever admit this publicly. Nor will anyone who wants to succeed in U.S. broadcasting publicly confirm that management investment decisions are made to protect the firm's political-economic power and inevitably affect their company's on-air programming.

Introduction

Exposing the Networks of Power

This book is an exposé of the history and current state of concentrated media ownership and monopoly prominent within U.S. network television today. Although I focus my inquiry on the rise and current power of Capital Cities/ABC, Inc., much of what I write applies to other global communications conglomerates as well, since before too long, most of them will be joined through multifaceted business partnerships.

Today, Capital Cities/ABC, like the rest of the networks, continues to protect its power, privilege, and profits through the classic techniques used by big-business monopolies in the automobile, steel, railroad, and oil industries: slashing wages and staff, fixing prices, and restraining trade to limit competition. At the same time, Capital Cities/ABC officials, in their efforts to gain even more freedom from government regulation, publicly deny that the network is a member of a U.S.-based, transnational media cartel.

While I do focus on the "before," "during," and "after" of the 1985 takeover of ABC by Capital Cities, I also see the rise of a media cartel as a logical outgrowth of the buildup of the private corporate state underway since the end of the Civil War. Much like the trusts and monopolies that dominated earlier eras of U.S. economic history, Capital Cities/ABC, like its partners in the U.S. media cartel, has set out to become "one of 'the six or so integrated companies' that compete in the global communications" industry by the year 2000.[1]

During the four years following the 1985 Capital Cities/ABC merger, CBS was acquired by the Loews corporation, NBC by General Electric, and Time, Inc. merged with Warner Communications. These companies' cooperation in generating programming and new business development undermines independent corporations and limits competition. All of these 1980s media mergers demonstrate that U.S. cultural and information products have become critical U.S. commodities and exports within the global economy.

Capital Cities, with a quarter of the annual revenues of ABC, required the support of the highest government and financial powers to both finance and gain regulatory approval for the $3.5 billion takeover. At the time, Capital Cities/ABC represented the largest non-oil merger in U.S. history.

Media Ownership Reflects Power

The networks, through vast corporate holdings and diversified profits, still represent U.S. political and economic power in the world, and will continue to do so in the years to come.[2] In many respects, today the U.S. networks are a far more potent political, economic, and social force in the U.S., and throughout the world, than they were at the end of the Vietnam War or during the Watergate scandals. The Reagan administration did more to help the networks expand their profits and power than any other administration in the history of U.S. broadcasting.

William J. Casey, Reagan's CIA director, who later benefited both personally and politically from the Capital Cities/ABC takeover, was considered the second most powerful figure in the Reagan administration.[3] As one of Capital Cities' founders, long-time counsel, board member and largest stock holders, he put enormous pressure on ABC and all of the major U.S. news organizations to become more supportive of the Reagan conservative agenda. In November 1984, he asked the FCC to revoke all of ABC's TV and radio licenses in retaliation for the network's airing of an ABC News report suggesting that the CIA had attempted to assassinate a U.S. citizen. Casey's challenge marked the first time that any U.S. government agency had tried to intimidate the U.S. networks with the 1949 Fairness Doctrine. The next month, Capital Cities made its first offer to buy ABC. Two months later, Casey again asked the FCC to reconsider his Fairness Doctrine complaint against the network. The following month, Capital Cities bought ABC. Casey's pressure on the U.S. networks (and particularly ABC) was in line with other Reagan administration attempts to manipulate the U.S. media for its own political and economic advantage.

After the merger, it became public knowledge that William Casey owned 34,000 shares of Capital Cities stock, worth about $7 million at the time of the announced takeover of ABC.[4] As Capital Cities' corporate counsel and tax attorney, with continuing ties to the CIA through his years on Wall Street and in Washington, Casey had owned 68,000 shares of Capital Cities stock at the time he became Reagan's CIA director in 1981. Yet he refused to place them in a blind trust.[5] While legal, Casey's refusal only seemed to reinforce his nickname, "The Fixer." From 1981 to 1985, about a dozen of Casey's top deputies at the CIA were provided with regular updates of his private stock investments to protect him against charges that "he was using the CIA as his own private investment-research arm."[6]

Capital Cities made its greatest political advances during Republican administrations. In 1960, Senator William Proxmire (D-Wis.), a longtime critic of Casey's willingness to profit at the taxpayers' expense, stated that Capital Cities' political connections represented "political payola at its worst." Proxmire, who later was Casey's toughest congressional critic, charged that Eisenhower's press secretary, James Hagerty, had influenced the FCC to grant Capital Cities channel assignments in Albany that were not available to others.[7] Hagerty also had served as press secretary to Thomas Dewey (another one of Capital Cities' original owners) during his unsuccessful runs for president in 1944 and 1948. In 1960, Eisenhower gave ABC permission to hire Hagerty as the first president of ABC News while he was still serving as press secretary. Later, Hagerty became ABC's head of worldwide public relations at a time when the U.S. networks were secretly helping intelligence agencies such as the CIA and FBI in domestic and foreign propaganda and intelligence-gathering.[8]

One of Capital Cities' greatest political supporters was Richard Nixon, Casey's political hero and mentor for many years. And Nixon later threatened the so-called "liberal" networks with economic sanctions while serving as president. In 1973, Nixon nominated James Quello, a former Capital Cities vice-president, to the FCC to represent broadcasters' interests. Quello worked for continued media deregulation to support the growth of global media conglomerates such as Capital Cities/ABC. A Nixon and Reagan supporter, he was named interim FCC chair by the Clinton administration in 1993.

In 1978, 1980, and 1987, several reports described the familial and earlier business ties between Capital Cities and the gambling and real estate conglomerate Resorts International and its mysterious predecessor, the Mary Carter Paint Company.[9] Resorts, which allegedly had ties to the CIA, organized crime, Howard Hughes, and former fascist leaders in Chile, Nicaragua, and Iran, also owned Intertel, a subsidiary that was described by *Rolling Stone* in 1976 as a U.S. "private CIA for hire." Intertel specialized in assisting corporate leaders in "sizing up" potential takeover targets. In his 1978 book *Spooks: The Haunting of America—The Private Use of Secret Agents*, Jim Hougan characterized Intertel's service to government and corporate clients (and private intelligence operations) as "guarding proprietary information at home, encoding communications, infiltrating governments in the Middle East, or funding counter-revolutions in Latin America."[10] None of these details were ever revealed at the time that the 1985 Capital Cities takeover of ABC was being announced to U.S. citizens. If they had been, the "friendliness" of the Capital Cities takeover of ABC might have been seriously questioned.

Yet, Capital Cities' historic links to U.S. power centers do not fully explain its success in taking over ABC after far larger transnationals such as ITT, Hughes Tool, and GE, with equally strong ties to U.S. power, had failed to do so before 1985. Capital Cities and other corporations became the beneficiaries as the Carter and Reagan administrations pursued deregulatory initiatives that later led to massive corporate restructuring and leveraged buyouts that increased the federal debt—not to mention repeated allegations of criminal misconduct.

As the United States declined into debtor status in the 1970s, the information culture industry emerged as a prime source of economic growth. Through the power of U.S.-based transnational corporations, the Pentagon, and U.S.-dominated financial groups such as the International Monetary Fund and the World Bank, U.S. financial leaders were able to maintain their leadership role in the postwar international political economy and domination over other nations' affairs in the name of U.S. "national security." The closer ties between the U.S. networks reflected the growing fusion of government, industry, and financial institutions which threatens a self-governing citizenry in the global, corporate-dominated economy. In 1975, the Trilateral Commission, composed of high-level bankers and industrialists from North America, Japan, and Western Europe, urged its members to promote oligarchic integration and greater press controls as a means to protect themselves against the "the excess of democracy" and the widespread political participation by "the general population."[11] By the end of the Carter administration, the

U.S. networks began to face increased pressure from bankers and creditors to become more profitable and more supportive of global economic stability.

During the Reagan-Bush era, U.S. media ownership became more concentrated as corporate leaders moved to limit public knowledge and criticism of their decisionmaking by exercising their substantial financial control over mass-media corporations.

Earlier Warnings about the Media Cartel

Fellow media critic and analyst Ben H. Bagdikian, a Pulitzer Prize-winning journalist and former editor at the *Washington Post*, observed in *The Media Monopoly* (1983) that 50 dominant media corporations controlled the production and distribution of most U.S. mass media products—magazines, radio and TV programs, books, motion pictures, cable offerings, and recordings—for profit and influence. In the 1992 edition of his book, Bagdikian lamented that the number of media companies had shrunk to twenty as a result of Reagan-Bush trust-building policies and a silent Congress. He believes it is possible that by the year 2000, just five or six media conglomerates will remain.[12]

Despite the compelling force of Bagdikian's research, however, many government policymakers, scholars, and journalists vigorously dispute the "totalitarian potential" of a global media cartel. They argue that "modern and objective" journalistic practices, the "free market," and an enlightened citizenry provide checks and balances to the power of corporate media owners. Some even dare to boast that the giant media conglomerates of today are able to provide citizens instantaneously with more up-to-date information than at any previous time in U.S. history—as if increasing the quantity of information automatically empowers citizens to be more politically active. There are also those who dismiss macro or systemic explanations for the global media cartel as "conspiracy theory."

But as Edward S. Herman and Noam Chomsky make clear in *Manufacturing Consent: The Political Economy of the Mass Media*, concentrated corporate media ownership works to narrow the limits on what is considered reasonable, responsible, or so-called objective reporting by journalists. Herman and Chomsky state that most of the censorship by mainstream U.S. media organizations is self-censorship exercised by media workers who have been selected for their willingness to conform to the established rules and the existing political culture. Such behavior is encouraged among the rank and file within mainstream media organizations. Acting as an extension of state power, workers and managers learn not to question the system or status quo.[13]

My inquiry into the political, economic, and social implications of the rise of giant global communications conglomerates is guided by five questions. First, how do those in the U.S. power elite exercise their control over the media? Second, how is this hidden so that subordinate groups will cooperate in their own political disenfranchisement? Third, how do media techniques systematically serve the interests of those who have power? Fourth, what are the connections between economic forces and political decisionmaking that seem to create a belief among those who work in the media, and those in the audience, that the media serve the public interest? Lastly, how can the present media system be transformed into one that is more democratic and open to citizen access and participation?[14]

I rely upon several sources: popular and academic books, mainstream and alternative media periodicals, academic journals, U.S. government publications, mainstream and alternative media broadcasts, and over 500 "on-the-job" contacts with staff and freelance employees at ABC, NBC, ESPN, and various local broadcast stations in the United States, Latin America, Europe, and Asia. The employee contacts run the gamut of the broadcast corporate hierarchy: technicians, secretaries, producers, presidents, and vice-presidents.

I have avoided using the actual names of individuals with whom I have worked over the years to protect them from harassment.

Although all of these employee contacts have provided me with valuable insight into the culture of both ABC and Capital Cities, and the other U.S. networks, I have not used any information from former or current broadcast workers that has not been corroborated by at least two additional published sources.

This book questions many of the undemocratic relationships between the U.S. media and government while providing the reader with substantial, previously published documentary evidence. All of the source material cited in the following pages has been publicly available for several years, but rarely mentioned in mainstream media. This should not come as a surprise to anyone who has studied the U.S. propaganda mill. Media self-censorship protects the illusion of democracy and the capacity for widespread citizen thought control through the "state-corporate propaganda system."[15]

What's Ahead?

Chapter One provides details regarding my own experience as a student intern and 20-year employee with ABC, NBC, and various public and commercial broadcast stations. Chapters Two and Three describe the corporate histories of ABC and Capital Cities before they merged in 1985. In both cases, the powerful, inside connections of their corporate leaders were crucial to their company's success during the three to four decades leading up to the takeover. The generally conservative practices and profit-making interests of both corporations, protected by the government's endorsement of U.S. oligopoly in broadcasting, played a major role in creating the United States national security state and the Cold War. The rash of media takeovers in the 1980s that followed the Capital Cities/ABC merger further ensured that the international and domestic propaganda role of the U.S. networks would continue in the years to come.

In Chapter Four, I probe more deeply into the actual merger details of the 1985 Capital Cities/ABC takeover. In the years that followed, published reports from some former ABC executives implied that there may have been an organized political and economic campaign to "destabilize" ABC in the minds of Wall Street investors and Washington political officials. While these allegations will probably never be conclusively proven, the Capital Cities/ABC takeover seems to have been far less friendly than it has been previously described.

Chapter Five looks at the post-merger performance of Capital Cities/ABC. Despite continued denials by network leaders that a U.S. media cartel exists and aims to dominate information and cultural production in the United States and throughout the world, I look at evidence that suggests otherwise. To show how Capital Cities is taking the lead in driving down costs, turning its back on labor, and protecting its markets, I track some of its corporate practices over the seven-year period following the takeover.

Finally in Chapter Six, I conclude with some suggestions as to how the media might be induced to work for more democratic aims and widespread citizen knowledge of government and corporate affairs. To promote an alternative, citizen-dominated U.S. media system, I offer a two-fold plan for what the average citizen can do, as well as what the government must do, to reduce corporate domination of the media. That domination, I believe, continues to threaten democratic societies worldwide.

To reshape media power to favor of democracy, I propose that media corporations and their sponsors be taxed for their government-protected "right" to monopolize the publicly owned airwaves and cable channels for their own profit. The proceeds of this tax would be used to fund a decentralized system of "free speech" media in which average citizens would play a major role. Eventually, however, I would like to see the majority of U.S. broadcast media placed under the ownership of nonprofit foundations serving a government in which power is truly vested in average people. Anonymous (and largely unaccountable) corporate media insiders survive only through the singleminded pursuit of power and profits. Their success has little to do with empowering citizens to remove political, economic, or social injustices and imbalances. Democracy remains an illusion for many in the United States and throughout the world. Control of the media must be returned to average people for genuine democracy to thrive.

Chapter One

The Unmaking of a TV Worker

Serving My Country

As a "television child" of the 1950s and 1960s, much of what I learned and believed about the world was filtered through the corporate myths and illusions of U.S. commercial radio and television. I grew up believing that one's "status" was measured by material consumption.

In 1972, I enrolled in classes at Seton Hall University, and the sobering reality of U.S. foreign policy began to affect me. Two years earlier, four student protestors had been killed at Kent State University while demonstrating against the U.S. invasion of Cambodia. In the months before my high school graduation, President Richard Nixon ordered heavy bombing attacks on Hanoi and the mining of Haiphong's harbor in North Vietnam as he tried "to bring peace with honor for the U.S." Since I did not want to be drafted to fight in a war I did not understand, I chose to study medicine so I could avoid mandatory military service but still serve my country.

Although I didn't realize it then, I had selected a university that also enjoyed a national reputation in college radio broadcasting. WSOU was an unusual public university station. From the time it first signed on the air in 1948, Seton Hall's administration had empowered students to take an active role in WSOU's management. Juniors and seniors held the key leadership positions of news director, program director, and station manager. Students and faculty, as well as volunteers from the towns surrounding the campus, worked at WSOU without fear of commercial-sponsor control or retaliation. The university paid the station's operating expenses as an expression of its commitment to the local community. I discovered the school's radio station during freshman summer orientation.

After working at WSOU for two years and learning more about the public service aspects of broadcasting, I began to think about pursuing a career in the media. By that time, the military draft had been suspended,

and the Vietnam peace treaties had been signed. With the Nixon administration under increasing attack for its crimes and attempted cover-up of
the Watergate scandal, the U.S. media were perceived as the "guarantor
of democracy," while public confidence in government and big business
had reached an all-time low.

In 1974, my best friend and I produced a feature on "The Lone
Ranger," a legendary radio program of the 1930s and 1940s. Shortly after
our special broadcast, I received a telephone call from a top executive with
ABC Television in Manhattan. A regular WSOU listener, he requested a
copy of our feature. A few weeks later, the same executive (whom I will
call "P.") invited us to meet in his office and to tour the ABC studios. Over
dinner at the Hotel Dorset in Manhattan, P. explained to us that it was not
money that made people better broadcasters, it was something else—
"commitment, enthusiasm, and public service." He also advised us to
enjoy our days in college radio. But he warned, "When you graduate and
start looking for a job, you will learn that broadcasting is a business." In
my naiveté, I could not see the contradiction in P.'s remarks.

Despite his advice about the realities of broadcasting, his vote of
confidence led me to think that I might have the talent and perseverance
to succeed in a media career. Considering his other comment that "WSOU
was perhaps the finest U.S. college radio station," I decided, a few months
later, to formally change my major to Communication Arts.

Later that summer, in July 1974, the House Judiciary Committee
recommended three articles of impeachment against Richard Nixon for
conspiracy to obstruct justice, abuse of power, and refusal to comply with
congressional subpoenas. The Watergate scandal, and the continued widespread lack of confidence in government stemming from the Vietnam
War, led me to think that I could serve my country by working in the
media. I was mistaken.

The following year, the historical links of broadcast ownership to
U.S. intelligence, espionage, and propaganda efforts became public when
the U.S. Senate Select Committee on Intelligence revealed that the CIA
and the FBI had used U.S. and foreign media organizations for "cover"
and for secret information gathering. The Church Committee also found
"hard evidence" that the CIA had been involved with organized crime
figures in assassination plots against foreign heads of state.[1] The 1975
Rockefeller hearings disclosed that the CIA and FBI had engaged in
"illegal and improper" domestic spying on 300,000 U.S. citizens and

organizations—involving the use of secret dossiers, wiretapped telephones, surveillance, and break-ins—under six presidents, from Roosevelt through Nixon.[2]

The Reality of Broadcasting

In the summer of 1975, largely through P.'s urging, I competed for a coveted spot in the International Radio and Television Society (IRTS) summer internship program, hoping to experience firsthand how commercial broadcasting operates. Member organizations—all the major television and radio networks, advertising agencies, sales representative firms, and ratings agencies—were to host six students for eight weeks during July and August of each year. IRTS selected me and other interns on the basis of an essay we wrote, about the FCC's 1949 Fairness Doctrine. Following P.'s advice, I argued that the Doctrine was a "burdensome regulation" and unnecessary since broadcasters were already committed to fairness and objectivity.

In 1975, the IRTS summer internship program became part of an on going industry public relations effort to force Congress and the FCC to repeal the Fairness Doctrine, which required every broadcaster to present a balanced presentation of controversial issues of public importance. Such industry campaigns meshed well with later bipartisan efforts in Congress to allow "market forces" to rule broadcasting. The Fairness Doctrine was ultimately eliminated as a "burdensome government regulation" by the Reagan-Bush FCC in 1987.

At the beginning of the internship, we spent a few days in the headquarters of Grey Advertising, Benton and Bowles, and John Blair and Katz Television—national advertising and sales firms that represent hundreds of radio and TV stations in deals with major corporate sponsors. IRTS also scheduled time with executives at Arbitron and Nielsen so we could learn to interpret the broadcast ratings through which advertisers and broadcasters sell air time to sponsors. In White Plains, N.Y., as guests of the transnational corporate foods conglomerate General Foods (GF), we were told by its director of advertising that "what gets on the air is largely determined by huge sponsors like GF." At that time, GF was the second largest national advertiser in the United States (Procter & Gamble was the largest), with total annual advertising expenditures that exceeded $140 million in 1974.[3]

My IRTS indoctrination with the "corporate-think" of the broadcast industry was, unfortunately, effective. Following my college graduation, I contacted some of the industry people that I had met the previous summer on the IRTS internship. After a few weeks, I was granted an interview with ABC personnel through P., who also helped several other graduates get entry-level jobs with ABC and other media firms around the nation.

In August 1976, I was hired as a clerk-typist by the ABC television network to work in its commercial scheduling department. Commercial schedulers assisted the various advertising agencies around the country that purchased air time on the ABC-TV network. The task was to ensure that each network program carried the designated advertisements and promotional announcements as decided by sponsors, advertising agencies, and ABC's promotion department. The pressure in commercial scheduling was high since one mistake could cost ABC thousands of dollars in lost ad revenues. Each scheduler was responsible for five or six network programs, every day, and directed the placement of commercials and promotional annoucements that were worth anywhere from $100,000 to $500,000. Since the department was not unionized, most personnel were paid just above the minimum wage.

A few months after I started at ABC in commercial scheduling, I made an error that caused ABC to broadcast the eastern version of an automobile commercial in a western region of the United States. When the sponsor requested compensatory time, I was told that my 30-second error had cost ABC $30,000. Although I knew that there was a great deal of money for ABC and its sponsors riding on my job performance, it was the first time that I had been threatened by the commercial realities of the broadcasting world.

Lesson on Labor

My next lesson in how power was distributed in the network came in 1977 when ABC was faced with a four-month strike by its largest union, the National Association of Broadcast Employees and Technicians (NA-BET). The striking workers—some 1,800 at ABC's television network; television stations in New York, Los Angeles, San Francisco, Detroit, and Chicago; its Washington news bureau; its own TV and radio stations—included engineers, technicians, telephone operators, news writers, and make-up artists.

NABET called the labor action to stop ABC from implementing plans to hire freelance news-camera crews. Though there were several other minor interests at stake, the focus was on changes in the network's hiring practices that would have dramatically altered the union-management balance of power, had ABC won. As management attempted to gain greater control over all phases of worker output, freelance workers were often used by companies in an effort to exploit a two-tier workforce of permanent and temporary workers. Employers often pitted one group against the other to drive down wages and reduce the voice of employees in the workplace.

Many of ABC's union work rules had been negotiated in earlier years when human labor was vital in broadcasting, and when advanced electronic technology had not yet enabled management to automate jobs and lay off workers. During the 1950s and 1960s, ABC's union rank-and-file gained considerable power over scheduling and disciplinary measures in the workplace. At that time, the unions also won the right to determine how compensation for workers' contributions to the company's profit-making goals should be handled. Many of NABET's demands in 1977 were centered on job security, while ABC argued that NABET's intransigence would "impair ABC's ability to compete with CBS and NBC."

With the stakes very high for both ABC and NABET, the network embarked on the most elaborate anti-strike preparations in its history. For several months before the strike, "volunteer" management and non-union employees, from vice-presidents to mailroom workers, were bussed daily to a temporary facility in a remote location and taught how to keep ABC on the air in the event of a NABET work stoppage. The company made no secret of its "war plans" in an attempt to force NABET into submission at the bargaining table and to warn non-union employees about the consequences of questioning top management's power.

One of my friends from Seton Hall, whom I will call "C.," was a NABET technician for ABC's radio network. Although most of the issues addressed through the strike of May 1977 concerned television news-gathering, C. supported the strike because he understood that ABC's tough line was aimed at weakening NABET as a bargaining unit pursuing workers' rights. It was the first time that I was forced to think about the way in which C. and I were different. He was a union member; I was not.

Because of my friendship with C., I refused to work "strike duty"—a euphemism used by ABC to refer to serving as "scabs." But many of my colleagues in commercial scheduling worked overtime as "replacements" at night and on weekends. This activity represented a temporary step up for these non-union and management workers in the ABC corporate hierarchy. Encouraged by the upper brass, many were led to believe that the temporary strike duty would lead to higher paying and more exciting jobs after the strike. In the event, many of my departmental colleagues did not get the jobs that they had hoped, and all of them returned to commercial scheduling. They had helped defeat NABET as an organizing force for higher wages and more workplace democracy. ABC's victory also fragmented NABET since many union members thought they had been sold out by the union leadership. Rumors circulated that the top NABET officials were corrupt and had been bought off, induced through under-the-table payments from management to settle the strike in favor of ABC. The union leadership was ultimately forced to accept the offer made by ABC four months earlier.

The Management's right to hire, fire, or "release" workers at will was demonstrated at all of the networks after the NABET strike of 1977. In 1987, General Electric forced a confrontation with NABET workers at NBC and won, just as ABC had in the summer of 1977. After 17 weeks, 2,800 striking NABET workers at NBC returned to their jobs, and the network gained the right to hire freelance workers. By 1989, 12 years after the 1977 NABET strike, ABC, CBS, and NBC had cut their workforces by at least 7,000 (both union and management ranks.)[4]

The "Creative" Assembly Line

In 1978, after 18 months in ABC-TV's commercial scheduling department, I was promoted to a position as operations manager with ABC Sports, where sports is considered a matter of life and death. For many of my colleagues, nearly all white males from middle- and upper-class families, sports participation was often considered an essential proof of masculinity. Failure to know who played quarterback for each NFL team was enough to immediately put one's gender under suspicion.

ABC Sports producers developed programs that primarily could serve as commercial vehicles for sponsors. As it became known worldwide for its many highly rated and highly marketable programs, Sports continually reinforced this image by closing every telecast with the corporate positioning statement, "ABC Sports—recognized around the world as the leader in sports television."

My department coordinated in-house production resources—videotape machines, technical crews, satellite feeds, and editing rooms. We also worked with the sports syndication division, which marketed and distributed programming to broadcast stations located on six continents.

For two years, I routinely worked 80 hours per week, on holidays, and through my vacations. At the 1980 Lake Placid Olympics, I worked as a key assistant in ABC's Main Broadcast Center where the network's Olympic programming was assembled and sent on to the network's audiences at home. A few months later, I was promoted into the ABC production ranks as an associate director (AD). ADs are the low-profile, behind-the-scenes workers who keep track of timing and coordination, primarily to ensure that the company's commercials get on the air. I also became a union member since ADs are represented by the Directors Guild of America (DGA), which also represents most film and television directors working in New York and Hollywood.

In 1982 ABC Sports transferred me to a less glamorous part of the company—the AD staff pool—to make room for those with "more advancement potential." The pool supplied workers to other programming divisions within ABC in order for them to become more professionally seasoned. ADs transferred to the pool were sometimes asked to resume working for ABC Sports whenever it was short-handed.

A few weeks after being transferred from the full-time ranks of ABC Sports, I was awarded my first Emmy for work as an AD on ABC's "Wide World of Sports." The Emmy Awards are given annually to network and local media workers by the National Association of Television Arts and Sciences for excellence and outstanding achievement in television programming, production, or performance. As with the IRTS, the Emmy Award selection process is often dominated by elites already working for the U.S. networks and local broadcasters. While an Emmy can denote significant accomplishment and stature within the U.S. television industry for media employees, it is almost impossible to earn one if you are not working for a "recognized" network or local station.

The DGA contract, containing a negotiated seniority clause that mandated a "last hired, first fired" policy, forced ABC to retain me as an AD. Through the years that followed, I realized that the DGA was saving me my job. I became more committed to the union than I had ever been before in my career.

Following my departure from the full-time ranks of ABC Sports, I worked in the Network Operations AD pool, supervising ABC's telecast of its primetime programming in the studio and editing the network's commercials into its shows for later playback on the air. On other days, I directed talent auditions for ABC's primetime "made-for-television" movies and soap operas. Casting decisions were exclusively made by the Casting Department and by talent agents who set up the auditions almost exclusively based on looks, sex appeal, and similarities to famous movie and television stars. Acting talent had very little to do with network casting practices. I also worked on ABC News programs and worked for the network's soap operas, "Loving" and "One Life to Live," which were (and still are) a large source of profits for the network. My work on the entertainment and news side taught me still more about how much of a business network television really is.

Third World Broadcaster

In 1983, I was contacted by a representative of a Latin American media magnate who had visions of becoming a international syndicator of Spanish-language programming. I had met him and his programming assistant on a vacation trip to Latin America in 1979. Only on that trip did I really become aware of the immense political, economic, and social inequality that exists in the Third World.

I saw for the first time the wide disparity between average working people and the few privileged families who control government, business, and the military system. My contact owned a private network of television stations, his country's leading national news magazine, and numerous other interests in its publishing and oil industries.

After agreeing to work for him on a freelance basis during my vacations from ABC, I was hired as an "adviser" to teach the staff "U.S.-style network television production techniques and secrets" that would "upgrade the quality of the company's television production and syndication capability."

At the time, I was not fully aware of ABC's or the other networks' extensive broadcast holdings throughout most of the Third World. In the 1950s and 1960s, ABC, CBS, and NBC controlled 64 television stations in 16 Latin American countries. ABC established the Central American Television Network, and then later consolidated stations throughout the continent into the Latin American International Network Organization. From the 1960s to the 1980s, about 80 percent of all Latin American programs were produced in the United States, with about 70 percent of the advertising coming from U.S.-based transnationals that controlled much of the Latin American advertising market.[5]

The political and economic foreign policy of the United States, shaped by the militarism, imperialism, and racism dominant in U.S. transnational corporate history, had had a significant impact on the lives of those ordinary people whom I saw on the streets during my stay in Latin America. The television system that I was being hired "to refine" was essentially directed at making peasants and the middle classes better consumers, less politically knowledgeable, and more intolerant of radical political and economic change.

In the months that followed my first consulting trip, I realized that despite the fact that my advice was given solely in the area of technology and programming, my contact was making decisions and changes at a completely different level. He put all of his station's resources behind the conservative presidential candidate running for office at the time. This candidate had been educated in the U.S. and was a strong supporter of Reagan's so-called free-market, transnational-based political economy.

On a second trip in March 1984, I was asked to cause the "forced retirement" of a well-respected vice-president of news who opposed U.S. intervention in Latin American political and economic affairs. My contact was attempting to install his twenty-four-year-old nephew, whom he said had "tremendous potential to modernize news-gathering practices," as the network's director of news. When I refused to support the management decision, I was never called back.

Political Awakening

In the months leading up to my first trip to Latin America in 1983 as a paid broadcast consultant, there were several stories in the news that increased my awareness of the way that mainstream journalism in the United States worked.

First, there was the Soviet shoot-down of Korean Airlines (KAL) Flight #007, killing all 269 people on board (including the daughter and granddaughter of an ABC colleague). The Soviet government alleged that the KAL flight had been on a spying mission, a claim the U.S. government denied. Then there was the suicide car-bombing of the U.S. Marine barracks in Lebanon that killed 241 soldiers in the U.S. peacekeeping force. Finally, there was the U.S. invasion of the small Caribbean island of Grenada to depose a government that had earlier ousted a tyrannical U.S.-backed government. I could see that the mainstream media were simply parroting the government propaganda line. And I knew that there had to be much more to these stories than the usual "us versus them" framed by the vast majority of U.S. reporters—both broadcast and print.

After working in Latin America, I realized that I knew very little about world politics. Yet, I also became aware that my credentials as a representative from ABC—one of the most powerful media conglomerates in the world—guaranteed me instant respect and credibility wherever I went abroad. My affiliation with ABC, whether I personally agreed with its foreign and domestic policies or not, also identified me as an representative of U.S. aggression and imperialism abroad. By working for ABC, I had been indirectly complicit in its transactional control and support of U.S. foreign policy.

The 1982 film *Missing,* directed by Costa Gravas, further opened my eyes to U.S. domination of Latin America. The film details the true story of an American freelance journalist who was tortured and killed in Chile by the U.S.-sponsored, fascist Pinochet regime in 1973. The young journalist disappeared when he asked too many questions about U.S. involvement in the coup, in the course of which Chile's democratically elected president, Salvador Allende, was assassinated. Between 1974 and 1990, Pinochet's military forces, nearly all of whom had been trained by the U.S. military, were responsible for the disappearance and execution of well over 2,000 people who were perceived as a political threat.[6]

Even though the 1975 Senate Intelligence Committee hearings documented U.S. corporate and governmental complicity in the coup, few Americans learned that Allende's assassination came about as a result of close cooperation between U.S.-based transnational corporations and the U.S. government acting through the CIA. The hearings were not given much attention by the broadcast networks. Many of the corporations involved, such as the transnational advertising agencies of J. Walter Thompson and Kenyon & Eckhardt, controlled hundreds of millions of dollars in advertising billings in the United States and around the world.[7]

Manufacturer of Consent

In the summer of 1984, I worked with 5,000 other employees to cover the Los Angeles Olympics for ABC Sports. The Olympics coverage, like most other U.S. programming, promotes national and corporate interests around the globe with a form of advertising propaganda. The Olympics celebrate "heroes" so that transnational advertisers may sell more products as audiences temporarily escape from daily pressures.

Four years earlier at Lake Placid, I had witnessed the U.S. hockey team's victory over a more experienced and seasoned Soviet team. The U.S. team later won a gold medal. At the time, 52 hostages were being held by Iranian student militants at the U.S. embassy in Teheran. The victory seemed to temporarily lift U.S. citizens out of the national malaise that had overcome them during the Carter administration. However, since Carter failed to bring the hostages home, deal with spiraling inflation (that pushed the prime rate to over 21 percent by the fall), and stand up to the Soviets following their invasion of Afghanistan, an Olympic gold medal in hockey provided only short-term relief.

In Los Angeles, the Herculean task of broadcasting well over 180 hours of programming to the United States (and the world) over the course of three weeks forced every ABC employee to work long hours to make profitable ABC's investment of more than $400 million in production costs and the acquisition of broadcast rights. As a result, ABC's revenues exceeded $2 billion for the first time in network history in 1984, mostly due to its overwhelming financial success with the Olympics.

A few months later, in the fall of 1984, I was invited to work with ABC Community Relations directing, co-producing, and co-writing a new network children's series, "ABC Notebook." Community Relations is the department within the network's public relations unit responsible for building the network's public service image in the eyes of public service organizations, schools, and educators across the country. It also dealt with public criticism of the network's highly commercial and profitable kiddie programming on Saturday mornings.

A key part of ABC's public relations strategy during the early 1980s was aimed at influencing the Reagan-Bush FCC and the Congress to forgo further regulation of children's programs. Through ABC's government relations office, staff attorneys and lobbyists coordinated congressional,

White House, and regulatory agency campaigns to support the network's case for further broadcast deregulation so it could make more profits.

Because of the possibility that all of the networks might be penalized if a proposed children's television bill passed in 1984-1985, Community Relations was directed to develop "educational" programming that could be used by ABC executives and lobbyists to prove that the network was, at last, producing worthwhile programming for children. At the time, in the more than 70 hours of national programming that ABC offered to its affiliated stations, it did not have even one program that the FCC would call educational.

Six programs, labeled the "ABC Notebook" series, were funded by ABC in early 1985 to highlight the role of children and young people in various activities. It mandated that these programs be 30 minutes in length, and that they be broadcast on the network at 4:00 PM, just after the soap opera "General Hospital." Four times per year, they were to alternate with the "ABC Afterschool Specials."

Shortly after ABC announced "ABC Notebook" as a network series, the merger of ABC and Capital Cities was announced in March 1985. Because the project was already in the planning stages and deemed necessary to stop the children's television bill from being enacted by Congress, production of "ABC Notebook" was allowed to continue.

Because of the pressing cost-containment and profit-making objectives, the series was structured to be both promotional and educational. Its continuing success would depend on its ability to promote ABC's other entertainment, news, and sports programs. The network was in business to make money, and the only way to do that was by gaining the highest ratings possible.

Due to limited promotion and low ratings, the series ended in October of 1986 with "ABC Notebook: Learn to Read," a program that showed U.S. teenagers were combatting the growing problem of adult illiteracy. Corporate and government leaders from the Reagan White House had targeted adult illiteracy as a contributing factor to the poor competitive position of the United States in the global economy. At the time, one out of every five adult Americans could not read road signs, directions on a medicine bottle, or other simple messages.

The Reagan White House had been actively pushing private-sector funding of volunteer efforts as the most cost-effective means of addressing the nation's pressing social problems. In program meetings, ABC executives talked openly about how important it was that Barbara Bush, the vice-president's wife, was leading the Reagan national campaign for voluntary adult literacy efforts. This close working relationship between the White House and ABC became increasingly important following the 1985 takeover by Capital Cities when ABC needed regulatory waivers from the Reagan FCC to continue operating its highly profitable local broadcast stations.

This kind of financial pressure to support the government line could also be seen in ABC's censorship of "ABC Notebook." A few weeks into the planning of "Learn to Read," Notebook staffers met with PBS and ABC's principal liaison with the Reagan White House to coordinate release of public relations materials on the Reagan literacy campaign. This ABC speechwriter cautioned us against interviewing anyone who might be perceived as an enemy by the Reagan White House. Jonathan Kozol, author of *Illiterate America*—a sobering book on the causes of illiteracy in America—was at the top of the speechwriter's list. The speechwriter told staffers that it would be better not to focus public attention on Kozol, since he was considered "angry and radical" by the Reagan administration. In his book, Kozol had criticized Reagan's massive 25 percent cut in federal funds for education in 1981 as one of the factors that would help push up U.S. adult illiteracy levels. Furthermore, Kozol opposed private-sector action to correct pressing social problems.[8]

The "ABC Notebook" series won one Emmy and was nominated in several categories of writing, directing, and producing during its two year run. In addition, it was the only ABC "educational" program produced at a fraction of the cost of most ABC half-hour shows. But the series was canceled in November of 1986 largely because its original purpose, to persuade government officials and the public to oppose reregulation of network television, had been served. Public relations efforts such as "ABC Notebook" were now considered to be of limited value, given the fact that Capital Cities already had strong ties to the Reagan White House and the FCC.

No new children's television legislation or regulation affecting the networks was adopted by Congress or the FCC at the time. Congress ultimately passed the Children's Television Act of 1990 in a half-hearted attempt to force the networks and local stations to provide more educational programs for young audiences. But as a result of the U.S. broadcast industry's lobbying efforts, television continues to exploit children by airing commercial and violent fare in its search for corporate profits.

Growing Disillusionment

By 1988, changes in the workplace arising from the Capital Cities/ABC merger became apparent. I resented Capital Cities' public declarations that ABC employees who did not like cost-cutting and efficiency measures should leave. Workers were also being scheduled solely by the time clock. Those who objected to the growing management control seemed to be singled out for disciplinary action by the company. Workers who questioned the rules faced the constant threat of harassment by management and even dismissal.

At the 1988 Calgary Olympics, for example, ABC Sports workers were told that because ABC's former management had spent over $300 million to acquire the broadcast rights for Calgary, strict cost-efficiency measures would have to be put into place in order to protect the company from taking a "paper loss of $100 million."[9] Workers faced tremendous pressure from Capital Cities to boost productivity. Union employees seemed to be more closely monitored than others, in part because they were contractually entitled to receive extra pay and other overtime bonuses for working the 12-18-hour days that were common in a marathon-like Olympics telecast. However, ABC transported "a total of 1,200 advertisers to Calgary" and provided them with "free room, board, and $300 worth of custom-fitted cowboy boots and hats," as well as tickets to the Olympic sporting venues of their choice.[10]

Changing Networks

After working on the Calgary Olympics, I decided to end my network career with or without the promise of another job. Working at the networks had absorbed me and was quite addictive. Like a powerful drug, the intensity of working in the most popular form of popular expression in society is difficult and quite unsettling to abandon. For a long time, I thought that I was doing important work. Yet, I could see that I had frequently been helping to make people become more disillusioned and politically alienated, as ABC and the other networks broadcast themes that could be sold to advertisers.

A few weeks after making my decision to leave ABC, I was offered a freelance position with NBC to work in its broadcast center at the Seoul Olympics. I accepted because I knew it was only a two-month assignment.

In South Korea, I saw NBC employees subjected to many of the same new "efficiency measures" being instituted at Capital Cities/ABC. Veteran NBC employees told me in Seoul what several of my former fellow union members had told me in Calgary: "Get out of the business. Here, they want machines, not people."

I was again immersed in world politics while I spent two months in South Korea. The Seoul games became a showcase for the emergence of the country as a vital Pacific Rim economic power. In the same way that the 1984 Los Angeles games had served U.S. propaganda aims, Seoul's games became another misleading display of what "free market" economic policies could achieve. In addition, South Korea was a police state, but that did not seem to matter during the Seoul Olympics.

The Pentagon also seized upon the Seoul games for their public relations value. The U.S. Army organized daily press junkets for all NBC workers and some international journalists who wanted to travel to the "demilitarized zone" on the North Korean border. The Pentagon wanted to convince world opinion that U.S. ground forces should remain in South Korea. Due to the constant threat of military aggression from North Korean troops, U.S. military officers escorted us directly to the 38th parallel to face the "enemy" all the while warning us of the possibility "that [we] could be shot at any time by the North Koreans who wanted to provoke an international incident."

As I toured Panmunjon where the peace treaty that ended the Korean conflict was signed in 1953, I realized that Cold War tensions had eased very little. Working for the U.S. networks, I was "used" to promote U.S. foreign policy goals through my association with NBC. The Seoul Olympics was just another battlefield, and propaganda was a weapon being used by both sides.

Broadcasting for the Few

In October 1988, I was hired to work in a local radio station in a small California town near Fresno. My duties included making occasional on-air announcements, running the control board, and preparing commercials for the station's automation system that came in from local and regional advertising agencies.

The station had moved away from local music programming by signing a contract in 1984 to receive national music programming from the Satellite Music Network (SMN). By 1989, however, it was still losing money due to developments in the broadcast industry. The strength of local radio stations, which for years had supported the economy of area businesses and other community interests, was falling under the control of national network companies, thus placing editorial power in the hands of national sponsors and large media conglomerates. In 1990, SMN was purchased by Capital Cities/ABC.

By joining SMN, the California station adopted an adult-contemporary program format (mostly Top 40 music) from its Chicago network studios. This was followed around the clock, except for four hours during the morning drive period, 6 a.m. to 10 a.m. All the local commercials came from a prerecorded tape, which also included prerecorded "local station identifications" from the network's announcers. This production technique, used at most of SMN's more than 1,000 affiliated local stations, creates the illusion that all of the station's programs are coming from the local community.

At my small FM station, the only news came out of SMN's Chicago studios for five minutes every hour. During the "locally originated" morning program, the station's announcer would literally read topical items out of the local newspaper or *USA Today*. There were no truly local newscasts. The station's management had canceled a contract with Associated Press a few years earlier in order to save money.

As innocuous as this station seemed to be, however, other aspects of its operation reminded me of my earlier experience in Latin America as a "consultant." For example, this was the first station I had ever worked for that had an expensive shredding machine in the front office to destroy office memos and station records. I often wondered who was paying my salary and why a small station in a rural area needed a shredder. After talking to other employees, I found out that the station was owned by a wealthy sugar baron in the Philippines, who also owned a network of radio stations there. The owner was apparently using this California station as his personal "offshore tax shelter" for his considerable wealth and income in the Philippines.

The station was purchased in 1982, apparently through a "front company," at a time when wealth was legally and illegally being transferred out of the Philippines. Although majority-owned by foreign interests, the station was legal under U.S. broadcasting laws. The Philippine owner, citing his wife's U.S. citizenship, had used his family's connections in Washington to purchase it. I never met the owner or his wife, the people who were supposed to be paying my salary. Few of the station's listeners in the local community, except some of the major advertisers, knew that all programming and management decisions were made in Manila by officials of the owner's major broadcasting company. In order to maintain further control over local operations and perhaps to avoid serious questioning of their practices, the absentee owners hired a former beautician to manage the station.

After reviewing my experience as a media consultant in Latin America in 1983-1984, I knew that I had to resign from this station and did so in 1989. In particular, I was concerned that if rumors at the time were true, I might be working for the Philippine oligarchy which had been assisted by CIA agents to secretly and illegally invest Philippine money—some of it stolen from the national treasury by President Marcos and his cronies—in the United States and other friendly countries.[11]

When an FCC investigation was prompted by a former employee's threat to expose the station's curious tangle of foreign ownership and control, the Philippine sugar magnate forced the beautician to retire. The owners sent in a freelance journalist from Manila to manage and upgrade the station so that the Philippine owners could sell it (in 1991, it was finally sold to new owners). The new manager was a U.S. citizen and had been a former newswriter and correspondent with the U.S. networks and with a major West Coast newspaper. He was one of only a handful of journalists allowed into Malacanang Palace (the Philippine presidential quarters) to make live reports for the U.S. broadcast networks while the Marcos family was negotiating its exile with Reagan administration emissaries. The regime was forced out of power in February 1986.

The televised images of the Benigno Aquino assassination by the Philippine military, when he returned from exile to oppose the U.S.-sponsored Marcos regime in 1983, were vivid in my mind. I knew that the regime had managed to silence enemies and to maintain its power in the Philippines over the years. And I understood the pattern of arbitrary detention, torture, disappearances, and executions ordered against those who opposed the dictatorship. In 1979, a U.S. Senate investigation found that the Marcos government—protected by U.S. intelligence agencies—had conducted "systematic campaigns inside the United States to spy on, harass, and, in some cases, plan assassinations" of U.S. citizens and Philippine nationals.[12] In 1981, the Marcos family was implicated in the Seattle assassinations of two Filipino labor officials—both U.S. citizens.[13]

I was never able to confirm the true extent of the radio station's owners ties to the Marcos family or to gather details as to how they had been able to buy the station. But the secrecy that surrounded its operation was a clear indication of dubious activities. In October 1988, a U.S. grand jury in New York indicted Marcos, his wife Imelda, and eight others, including international arms merchant Adinan Kashoggi, on charges of embezzling more than $200 million from the Philippine government. Although the case later ended in an acquittal, rumors persisted about the Marcos's secret holdings, which were allegedly laundered through a network of "front companies," foreign banks, and Marcos cronies in the United States and around the world. Imelda Marcos was sentenced to an 18 to 24-year prison sentence for graft by a Philippine court in September 1993. The Philippine government continues to believe that the Marcos family looted the national treasury while in power, and deposited the funds in so-called legal investments and bank accounts around the world.[14]

A few weeks after I left the station, a woman who prepared the station logs and was still working there told me that a personal emissary from the owners—rumored to have been an assassin in the Philippines—visited the station and persuaded the former general manager to remain silent about the station's foreign ownership. This coercion was a new twist in owner-staff relations that I had not experienced during my 12 years with ABC and NBC. Out of concern for the employees who still worked there, I naively and anonymously alerted the FCC, the FBI, and the *Fresno Bee* to the possible improprieties at the station. At the time, I didn't fully realize that foreign intelligence services were allowed to operate in the United States with impunity to eliminate opposition to their anti-democratic regimes overseas. Two weeks later, I was approached by the new general manager about a possible job offer that involved producing an exclusive television interview with deposed President Marcos, then living in exile in Hawaii. A similar offer ostensibly for work directing music videos came from the former program director of the station, then on good terms with the Philippine owners. I did not accept either freelance assignment because I did not know who would be paying my salary.

This was not the only radio station in the town that had dubious ownership and ties. I began to work at another station, one of the new FM operations licensed by the Reagan FCC supposedly to encourage competition and diversity of ownership in broadcasting. The owners had received a special minority-status permit—even though they did not seem to be minority members and did not put any programming on the air that would qualify as minority-oriented. Like the Philippines-owned station, this one appeared to have been acquired through a "front company" to hide its real ownership from the FCC. It actually belonged to a wealthy Republican landowner from a nearby town, who had purchased it for his son. Eventually, the station went bankrupt and left the air in 1991 as a result of financial mismanagement, a "soft" local advertising market, and rumors of drug and alcohol abuse by the owner's son.

Conclusion

U.S. media ownership reflects U.S. power. It always has. After 20 years of experience, I know that corporate elites reap the principal benefits of profit-making, social privilege, and political influence from the advertiser-supported media system operating today. When you work in broadcasting, it is very hard not to become an agent for the political-economic interests of those who employ you.

I do not regard my work experiences with the networks, or with local broadcasting stations in the United States and abroad, as exceptional or extraordinary. There is little room for independence on the job or off, due to the tremendous competition for the ever-decreasing number of jobs available in the broadcast industry. For the most part, organized labor in broadcasting has been defeated in its role as a bargaining agent for workers. Rank and file media employees are relatively powerless to resist management political-economic decisions aimed only at profit-making whenever possible.

Both at the national and local levels, media policies today are, more than ever before in the history of U.S. broadcasting, shaped by transnational media conglomerates. The massive propaganda campaigns launched by these vast networks of power during their cheerleading coverage of the 1989 Panama invasion and the 1991 Gulf War are glaring examples of how U.S. media companies allow little independent criticism of government policies. One study, for example, found that heavy viewers of Gulf War TV-coverage had less knowledge about the fundamental causes and issues of the war than those who watched television less frequently.[15]

All of this is true not only for the networks. In the majority of small U.S. towns and cities, so-called independent local broadcasting has ceased to exist because of the crushing economic power of national media companies and advertisers—another casualty of U.S. media cartelization.

Over the next two chapters, I will describe the histories of ABC and Capital Cities before their 1985 merger. This analysis will illustrate the point that media ownership has always been the province of the wealthy and powerful.

Chapter Two

The History of ABC: Always Be Conservative

ABC was founded when Edward J. Noble, a wealthy and conservative entrepreneur, purchased the National Broadcasting Company's (NBC) "Blue" radio network in 1943. Nicknamed the "Almost Broadcasting Company," until the late 1960s ABC was often on the brink of bankruptcy or takeover by other more capitalized corporations.

Despite its financial problems, ABC managed to survive because the FCC traditionally awarded the most lucrative broadcast licenses to those with wealth and elite social connections. Moreover, the FCC's unofficial policy of restricting access to the airwaves enabled large corporate sponsors and advertisers to encourage widespread consumption of their products and services by the U.S. industrial population.

Due to Noble's influence, ABC became known as the most conservative of all of the U.S. networks. In order for it to survive as America's fourth television network in the 1950s (behind CBS, NBC, and DuMont), ABC's leaders learned not to rock the boat for fear of jeopardizing regulatory favors and continued access to operating capital from Washington and Wall Street, respectively. Most of the leadership came from the ranks of the Republican party, and were able to maintain their protected status by rarely challenging U.S. political-economic global expansion or social injustice at home.[1]

Roots of Oligopoly

In 1919, U.S. corporate control of radio broadcasting dates back to the establishment of the government-sanctioned Radio Corporation of America (RCA). This partnership later allowed General Electric (GE), Westinghouse, American Telephone & Telegraph (AT&T), and United Fruit to jointly monopolize almost all U.S. electronic patents for an "American-dominated system of world communication," although there was often significant opposition to the for-profit, commercial broadcasting system that later evolved.[2]

While network-dominated, corporate broadcasting has never been officially codified by Congress, charges of monopoly against the four companies led, in part, to the formation of the NBC in 1926.[3] NBC's owners--RCA, GE, and Westinghouse--purchased AT&T's broadcasting outlets and expanded network for-profit broadcasting service in the United States.

NBC established Red and Blue radio networks. The Red Network, eventually the NBC Radio Network, became the larger of the two with many powerful stations in the largest U.S. cities and a huge roster of star performers and profitable programs. Blue Network shows could only be heard in smaller cities.[4]

The most important use of NBC's two networks, however, was to maintain RCA's domination in national broadcasting and a competitive advantage over CBS, which had only one network at the time.[5] NBC, in 1941, after the monopolistic effects of its operating two networks became apparent, considered renaming the Blue Network the United Broadcasting System—perhaps to convince the public that this second network was independent.[6]

The Roosevelt administration forced NBC to divest itself of its two networks when the FCC ruled that no one company could operate more than one national radio network.[7]

After this 1941 ruling, 42 companies representing powerful investor groups—including the Mellon family, Marshall Field, Dillon, Read & Co., Paramount Pictures, and the American Type Founders—competed to buy the Blue Network, which gave a sale price of $8 million.[8]

In 1943, Noble, a former transit advertising salesman, bought the Blue Network and renamed it the American Broadcasting System. Noble had influential connections to the U.S. power elite, and was most respected in Washington and on Wall Street for developing the Life Savers candy roll. In 1913, he had purchased a failing candy company for $1,900 and 15 years later he had sold it for $28 million.[9] Noble's corporate empire eventually encompassed Beech-Nut Foods and substantial portions of Bristol-Myers, Sterling Drug, Vicks Chemical, and United Drug.[10]

The first chairperson of the Civil Aeronautics Authority, Noble later served as an undersecretary of commerce in the Roosevelt administration. In 1940, Noble resigned his government post to campaign for Wendell

Wilkie, the Republican presidential candidate of that year. Wilkie was a rich Wall Street financier whose campaign rhetoric labeled Roosevelt's New Deal business and labor policies "Socialist" and "un-American." When Noble formed ABC, he surrounded himself with conservative managers like Justin Dart, his protégé at Life Savers. Dart later helped form Ronald Reagan's "Kitchen Cabinet," the group of wealthy, right-wing Southern California industrialists who bankrolled Reagan's successful runs for the California governorship (1966 and 1974) and the U.S. presidency (1980 and 1984).[11]

Noble also hired Robert Kintner, another conservative, as ABC's vice president in charge of news, special events, and publicity. Kintner became president of ABC in 1950. He supported Republican political figures and also argued for more corporate control over media and less government regulation.

In 1946, Noble moved ABC into television by obtaining federal licenses for the frequency labeled Channel 7 in five of the largest U.S. cities: New York, Los Angeles, Chicago, San Francisco, and Detroit.

In 1948, before any ABC-owned TV stations began operating, Noble signed up his first network affiliate, WPVI-TV in Philadelphia.[12] WPVI was owned by publisher Walter Annenberg, an influential Republican party contributor with strong ties to U.S. conservative politics.[13] Annenberg owned the *Philadelphia Inquirer* and the *Philadelphia Daily News*. He also published the magazines *TV Guide, Seventeen,* and the racing publications the *Morning Telegraph* and the *Daily Racing Form.* After accepting this post in 1970, president Richard Nixon appointed Annenberg as U.S. ambassador to England for his loyal Republican support. Annenberg sold his nine broadcast stations to Capital Cities Communications and Gateway Communications, the latter formed by Annenberg's former employees.[14]

By 1950, ABC was nearly bankrupt due to the considerable capital investment required to establish a national for-profit television network. Noble started negotiations with Leonard Goldenson in May 1951, the head of United Paramount Theatres (UPT), to sell a portion of the company.

Leonard Goldenson had been searching for a way to build UPT into a media power when he learned of Noble's financial problems at ABC. Noble, who had already invested $5 million of his personal fortune to retain control over the network, wanted $25 million from Goldenson's

UPT before agreeing to its merger with ABC, about $15 million over its market value at the time.[15]

Goldenson eventually agreed to pay Noble's asking price, but the merger talks repeatedly broke down over the issue of who would control the amalgamated corporation, American Broadcasting-Paramount Theaters (AB-PT). Noble was insistent that the combined corporation be called a merger and not a takeover, and even managed to extract a promise from Goldenson not to interfere in ABC's operations for three years.[16]

The ABC board of directors, largely a rubber-stamp committee serving Noble's personal interests, quickly approved the creation of AB-PT. The Paramount Theaters board was not convinced of AB-PT's chances for success, since Paramount already owned a major financial stake in the DuMont network--America's third most watched television network behind NBC and CBS.[17]

Goldenson gained approval after he revealed his plans to develop new television programming in cooperation with the Hollywood studios. Although most television programs at the time were done live in New York City in front of a studio audience, Goldenson argued that by moving television production to Los Angeles, the entire network television industry would realize expanded profits. In L.A. it could rely on Hollywood's well-developed star system and film production services. Goldenson's plan also aimed at saving the Hollywood studios from the growing threat of television and possible extinction.

Goldenson and various supporting members of the PT board brought their plans to Harry Hagerty, vice-chairman of the Metropolitan Insurance Company, one of the largest and most powerful institutional investors in the United States. As the biggest lender in the country at the time, Hagerty had lent money to CBS, and held a seat on the RCA board of directors. He gave his blessing to the AB-PT merger and promised to back it with his own funds if necessary.[18]

The remaining obstacle was obtaining federal regulatory approval for the merger from the FCC. But the commission challenged the AB-PT merger. The American Civil Liberties Union, along with one dissenting FCC commissioner, argued that an AB-PT merger would represent a threat to democracy, since it would put U.S. media control into fewer corporate hands. ABC, using the same argument that had been employed to defend network monopolies during the 1920s, argued that ABC could only become fully competitive if it got the added capital funds that would be provided by merging with UPT.[19]

During the hearings, Paramount Pictures' past predatory practices were continually referred to. Between 1920 and 1951, some 531 anti-trust cases were filed against Paramount, 234 of which took place after August 1948. Despite opposition, the FCC voted five to two in favor of the AB-PT merger in February 1953. The two dissenting commissioners said that the merger would eventually create a "monopolistic multimedia economic power" that would not serve the public interest.[20]

Going Hollywood

Despite Goldenson's many ties to Hollywood (he was a former division vice-president of Paramount Pictures and president of United Paramount Theaters), he initially encountered great difficulty in obtaining new programming from other Hollywood film moguls. ABC was blamed for Hollywood's rising labor costs and dwindling theatre audiences that resulted, in large part, from the increased competition from the four U.S. television networks.[21]

NBC tried to make an arrangement with ABC and CBS to destroy the DuMont network. According to Leonard Goldenson, RCA Chairman David Sarnoff approached Goldenson with an offer for ABC to broadcast "second-run" hits after they had aired on NBC and CBS. Although Sarnoff's offer suggested an attempt by a network leader to control costs and fix prices for network programming—a violation of U.S. anti-trust laws—Noble and Goldenson did not report it to the Justice Department. This was apparently for fear of being portrayed as uncooperative members of the U.S. broadcast oligopoly.[22]

Another major factor standing in the way of ABC's parity with NBC and CBS in the 1950s was its poor network distribution system and limited number of station affiliates. In 1953, ABC had just 14 primary affiliated stations scattered across the United States, while CBS had 74 at the time, and NBC had 71. DuMont had slightly more affiliates than ABC. This meant that one hour of network time on CBS and NBC, for example, brought in five times more advertising revenue than one hour on ABC or DuMont.[23]

After a great many initial rejections from the Hollywood studios, ABC signed an exclusive agreement with the Walt Disney studios, one of the most conservative, anti-labor, and patriarchal studios at the time. In this first major corporate alliance with a Hollywood film company, ABC bought thousands of shares in Disney's still-to-be-built dream amusement park, Disneyland. In return, ABC received a one-hour, weekly film series program and access to Disney's 600-title animated-feature library. Also part of the package was ABC's promise to give one free minute each week at the end of the Disney program to promote Disney's latest feature film release.[24]

Goldenson could arrange this deal because CBS, NBC, and nearly all U.S. banks and institutional investors, had refused to lend Disney money for Disneyland. To get the money, Goldenson contacted Karl Hoblitzelle, a theater owner, oil company executive, and chairman of the Republic Bank in Dallas. In 1946, Hoblitzelle had persuaded Goldenson's Paramount Theaters to make a $10,000 political contribution to Lyndon Johnson, then running in his first congressional race.[25]

As an apparent payback for Goldenson's earlier financial support of Johnson (who won an election marred by ballot-box stuffing and Democratic dirty tricks, and went on to become the Senate Majority Leader in the 1950s), Hoblitzelle agreed to lend $5 million for Disneyland. Soon after, other banks followed Republic's lead. With this additional capital in hand, ABC put up another $500,000 and guaranteed all the loans that Disney needed to build Disneyland ($17 million was then spent in the first year alone of operation). In exchange for this financial help, ABC received all of the profits from Disneyland's food concessions for 10 years, and an eight-year agreement to purchase Disney programming for $40 million.[26]

The ABC-Disney deal represented the largest programming agreement signed in 1954. The next year, Disney produced the "Mickey Mouse Club" for ABC, and a few years later "Zorro."[27]

After completing the Disney deal, Goldenson approached Warner Brothers to produce a weekly, filmed, episodic television series for ABC. In return, along with its fee, as a bonus, Warners would receive one free minute of broadcast time each week to promote the latest Warner Brothers feature film release.[28]

ABC also signed Lawrence Welk to do two big-band music shows a week. The ultra-conservative sponsor J.B. Williams, who had forced liberal commentator William Shirer off CBS in 1947,[29] citing his alleged communist sympathies, wanted to use Welk's program to sell his controversial product, Geritol, a liquid that Williams touted as having "fountain of youth" properties. Even though the FTC had earlier warned Williams about false Geritol advertising claims, ABC accepted the commercials without apparent concern.[30]

ABC also aired religious shows during its early years, offering themes that were frequently mixed with conservative ideas and politics. Catholic Bishop Fulton J. Sheen was given 30 minutes a week on the network to talk about whatever was on his mind. Later, because of the high ratings of Sheen's program, ABC gave the Reverend Billy Graham a half-hour program in which to extol "anti-communist politics and fundamentalist Christianity." ABC eventually reversed its policy of selling network time for religious programming due to pressure from some of its sponsors. After signing programming agreements with Walt Disney, Warner Brothers, and national religious figures, ABC also exploited the fear of the cold war by developing the detective and crime genre. Programs like "77 Sunset Strip," "Bourbon Street Beat," "Adventures in Paradise," "Hawaiian Eye," and "Naked City" were able to attract important audiences and sponsors.

Many of ABC's new programs came out of the networks' relationship with Dr. Paul Lazarsfeld, a Columbia University television professor, who had advised CBS on how to develop larger audiences for its radio programming in the late 1930s. Lazarsfeld, while still working with CBS, became an advisor to ABC and suggested that the network do more programs for younger audiences. He felt that viewers between the ages of 18 and 49 would be "more open to change" and more easily influenced to try new products from ABC's advertisers.[31]

Leonard Takes Control

In 1956, the nearly bankrupt DuMont television network was forced by owner Paramount Pictures to sell its television stations so it could concentrate on its television manufacturing operations. In this way, Paramount enabled ABC to move by default into the number three spot among the U.S. networks. That year also marked the end of the three-year "hands off" period that Goldenson had negotiated with Noble.

Goldenson took control of ABC by forcing a top-level battle with Robert Kintner, Noble's heir apparent. At first, Noble objected and threatened a proxy fight to maintain control over ABC's future, but

Goldenson ultimately prevailed. Kintner was forced out of ABC in 1956 and later became the president of NBC.[32]

After his victory over Noble, Goldenson continued to build ABC by staying close to the levers of U.S. corporate power, by courting wealthy and prominent U.S. industrialists. In 1957, for example, Goldenson met with Henry Kaiser at the Waldorf Towers in New York City. Kaiser, one of the largest and most powerful government contractors, owned the Aluminum Corporation of America (ALCOA), the third-largest aluminum company in the world, and half the hotels on Honolulu's Waikiki Beach.

Kaiser wanted weekly exposure on ABC in order to raise the value of his company's stock on Wall Street. ABC again turned to Warner Brothers to develop a one-hour Western series for Kaiser called "Maverick" (ABC, Warner Brothers, and Kaiser each owned one-third shares in the program). It became a hit series for ABC, and Kaiser raised the value of his corporate holdings through his increased visibility as a national television sponsor.[33]

In 1959, pending congressional investigations into network and advertising agency rigging of quiz shows caused ABC, indeed the entire broadcast industry, to try to project a public service image to Washington regulators and Congress. Although ABC did not produce any of the network quiz programs that led to the investigation, it did have major problems with its popular daytime teen music show, "American Bandstand." Dick Clark, the host of "Bandstand," had financial interests in record companies whose artists were featured on his program. Some people in Congress believed that Clark had participated in the "payola" system. He denied that he had ever taken payola for artists appearing on "Bandstand," but confirmed that the companies he invested in had paid bribes to have their artists' records played on other television and radio stations-- which was legal. Because congressional investigators concentrated on those who had received bribes and not those who had offered them, Clark's career was saved.[34]

With a friendly Eisenhower administration in the White House, ABC managed to hold onto its valuable teen program franchise. In later years, Clark contributed to ABC's success by serving as a host and producer of primetime specials and made-for-television movies, as well as "American Bandstand."

Through his spirited defense of Dick Clark and of the network practice of programming for the lowest common audience denominator, Goldenson endeared himself to the rest of the network television industry, which needed justification for its practice of programming for the largest possible audience. Goldenson later defended U.S. network commercial television in his 1990 autobiography:

> Of course there are lousy programs—perhaps 40 percent of what's on the schedule at any given time is junk. But that leaves 60 percent that isn't... This isn't a Tiffany business. It's Woolworth and K-Mart. There's a place for the articulate minority—on public broadcasting (which I have long supported).[35]

The Sun Never Sets...

Since the 1951 ABC-UPT merger, Goldenson had envisioned a worldwide television empire that would mirror the global theater holdings of Hollywood studios that had worked since the 1930s to export U.S. motion pictures overseas. In 1956, Goldenson bought a 6 percent interest in Rupert Murdoch's Australian television syndication company, News Limited, and also worked with a group of Costa Rican businessmen to set up new television stations.[36]

Beginning in 1959, Goldenson began to buy television ownership interests in nations throughout Central and South America, the Middle East, and Asia. ABC established La Cadena Centroamericana (the Central American Network), operating with both affiliated and owned stations in Guatemala, Honduras, El Salvador, Nicaragua, Panama, and Costa Rica. Later, these stations were linked in a global network partnership, World-vision. ABC sold air time on these stations to U.S.-based transnational advertisers such as Exxon and General Motors, and bought U.S-produced programs for Worldvision. These purchases gave ABC more leverage with the Hollywood studios and other syndicators when bargaining to sell its domestic lineup of television shows.[37]

CBS and NBC had already gained a foothold in foreign television. Seeking to blaze its own path through the foreign syndication field, ABC set its sights on establishing a worldwide network of stations that would be patterned after the network system in the United States. Because ABC had so many foreign television interests in parts of the world that were considered prime targets for U.S. colonial domination, it became an instrument with which the State Department and the CIA could promote U.S. foreign policy and capitalist expansion. This was not at all extraordinary. Since the 1940s, CBS's chairman, William Paley, had permitted CIA operatives to screen news film, to eavesdrop on conversations between CBS news officials and their reporters, and to masquerade as CBS news employees. He also used his personal philanthropic foundation to hide overseas money transfers for CIA-sponsored projects abroad.[38]

When ABC aligned itself with the business elites who typically own and operate broadcast outlets, it and its foreign partners were obliged to support (publicly and privately) repressive political and military leaders—many who had strong ties to the United States—in order to maintain control over their media properties abroad. For example, in the early 1960s, ABC became partners with a Venezuelan businessman, Diego Cisneros. Through his connections, ABC managed to obtain a 35 percent interest in the Venezuelan television network. Cisneros, "the Pepsi-Cola King of Caracas," had invited ABC to become his partner.

In Venezuela, ABC and its local partner screened every employee for communist affiliations, used the Venezuelan National Guard as its security force, and installed machine guns on the roof of its Caracas station to protect it against rebel attack. Rebel forces had apparently targeted the station as a symbol of increasing U.S.-based transnational control over Venezuela's political economy and U.S. interventionist policies in Latin America, applied through transnational corporations like ABC, which protected the wealth and privilege of a small number of wealthy families at the expense of the lower and middle socio-economic classes. Probably the largest Pepsi bottler in Venezuela, the Cisneros partnership with ABC was not viewed positively by the Venezuelan labor unions that formerly had controlled the network.[39]

With marketing help from Pepsi-Cola, ABC's station in Caracas soon drew more viewers than did the Venezuelan government station. Joan Crawford, the vice-president of corporate public relations for Pepsico, had made a celebrity appearance at the station's grand re-opening.[40]

ABC also became a 25 percent partner with the Latin American Jesuits, who operated one of Argentina's few television stations. It brought in one of its semi-retired executives from Chicago to watch over its assets in Buenos Aires, and established relations with the Argentine military to keep the station on the air in the event of military takeovers.

Paraguay and Bolivia were the only Latin American countries in which ABC did not have television stations. Paraguay did not allow foreign investment in its media, and Bolivia was so poor that Goldenson saw little benefit in developing a transnational advertising market there.[41] ABC also invested in television stations in Japan, Hong Kong, and Lebanon, and worked aggressively to set up a network covering the Arabic-speaking countries. Goldenson approached the Emir of Kuwait for permission to open a broadcast station there. Besides his connections to Arab countries, he came to know Golda Meir, the prime minister of Israel. He sponsored luncheons in New York for Meir with the heads of top multinational corporations seeking corporate favors and expansion in the Middle East. In his *de facto* role as a U.S. diplomat in the 1970s, Goldenson was asked to carry diplomatic messages between Pope John Paul II, Anwar Sadat, and Menachem Begin, and was involved once in efforts to arrange a Middle East peace accord.[42] He also tried to enter the European market, but many countries were opposed to private investment in their media. ABC's international role was, however, drastically cut back when a rising tide of nationalism and charges of U.S. cultural imperialism spread throughout the industrialized and developing worlds.[43] By the 1970s, ABC had reduced its foreign holdings to a few properties in Guatemala, Panama, Bermuda, and Japan.[44]

Is This News? (The FBI Network)

ABC was so undercapitalized in the 1950s that it could not afford the worldwide public service and news operations maintained by CBS and NBC. Conservative commentator John Daly became ABC's vice-president in charge of news, special events, and publicity, and ABC's only staff on-air news anchor from 1953 to 1961. He was legendary for his stubborn refusal to accept criticism, announce sponsors' products on the air, or to include liberal views within his largely conservative news broadcasts.[45] While he served as ABC's news VP, Daly also hosted the weekly game show "What's My Line?" on CBS.

ABC was forced to rely on newsreel suppliers like Hearst-Telenews and Fox-Movietone for film of news events.[46] These services were also consistently conservative in the selection of stories, and served as a prime vehicle for the delivery of government and corporate public relations messages to the American public. In addition to raising money, ABC news executives were later forced to find potential sponsors before starting work on journalistic projects.[47]

Because of limited budgets, ABC sometimes relied on freelance news commentators. In the 1940s and 1950s, syndicated newspaper columnists Drew Pearson, Walter Winchell, Louella Parsons, and George Sokolsky were given radio and television slots to attract cross-over newspaper audiences. This policy, though cost-effective and profitable, brought ABC closer to elements of the U.S. Right. Winchell, Sokolsky, and Parsons were virulent anti-communist conservatives, who used their ABC air time and newspaper columns to encourage the blacklisting of actors, directors, producers, and other performing artists during the Joseph McCarthy-led witch-hunts of the House Un-American Activities Committee (HUAC). During this period, anyone with real, or even alleged, progressive ties was subject to blacklisting.[48]

ABC's right-wing tilt was especially evident in its support of Walter Winchell and George Sokolsky. A close personal friend and confidant of FBI Director J. Edgar Hoover, Winchell routinely attended social functions with Hoover and became one of the Bureau's most vigorous defenders in the press. Sokolsky, a columnist for William Randoph Hearst's newspaper chain, sought FBI advice on what to write. Winchell and Sokolsky regularly received from Hoover confidential FBI information, which they both later used in their newspaper columns and ABC broadcasts to accuse suspected communists.

The relationship between ABC and the FBI was not limited to Winchell's and Sokolsky's activities, but was also based on Noble's ties to Hoover.[49] Noble had broadcast Hoover's "This Is Your FBI," in 1945 on his radio network, and it served as Hoover's "official" conduit to the American public from 1945 to 1953.[50] ABC became an indirect but crucial channel for Hoover's propaganda aimed at promoting him and the Bureau throughout the United States and the world. At the same time, Hoover was able to divert public attention away from the FBI's domestic role as the country's "national political police."[51]

In the 1960s, ABC's affiliation with the FBI brought it high ratings and revenues through the primetime program "The FBI." Hoover had reportedly received 600 offers to produce a TV program about the FBI, but was persuaded to choose ABC's by his trusted friend, James Hagerty. Hoover was also encouraged by the fact that "The FBI" would be produced by its Hollywood partner Warner Brothers, a strong supporter of the 1950s anti-communist purges in Hollywood.[52] (Walt Disney, also one of ABC's partners, served as a secret informer for the FBI. In return for his information on alleged communist infiltration of Hollywood labor unions, Hoover allowed him to film in the FBI headquarters in Washington. Disney in turn also allowed Hoover access to movie scripts at his studio, and Disney was reportedly made an official Hollywood contact for the FBI in 1954.)[53]

In making the TV series "The FBI," Hoover retained complete control over all scripts, personnel, and sponsors. He even assigned a special agent to spy on everyone on the Warner Brothers set where the programs were filmed each week. In addition to reading and correcting every script, Hoover made filmed appearances to introduce the premiere episode of each new season of "The FBI." After the show premiered in 1965, and began a nine-year run, he received financial royalties from the series. In addition, Hoover received a $500 consultant's fee for every program broadcast. Over the course of "The FBI"'s nine-year run, this fee arrangement netted him approximately $200,000, which he reportedly turned over to the FBI Recreation Fund. Before the TV series began, James Hagerty purchased the rights to Hoover's book, *Masters of Deceit*, for $75,000.[54] But ABC never produced a film adaptation of the book, a fact that adds to speculation that this sum may have been a bribe to secure Hoover's involvement in the "The FBI."

After Hoover's death, an official investigation revealed substantial criminal conduct and abuse of power while serving as FBI director, and that thousands of dollars had been diverted from the FBI Recreation Fund for his personal use. In actuality, only 20 percent of the revenues from *Masters of Deceit* ever went into the FBI Recreation Fund, while the rest went to Hoover, Clyde Tolson (his assistant), and a few other journalists who polished up the final draft. Because of Hoover's influence, the book became an immensely popular best-seller, selling 250,000 copies in hardcover and two million in paperback. It also became required reading in many public schools after it was first published in 1958 and widely touted as a manual on "Communism in America and How to Fight It."[55]

"The FBI" became Hoover's most important public relations vehicle at a time when the Bureau was actively involved in a systematic, domestic campaign to harass and intimidate various political and minority activist groups. The series on ABC conveyed an image of "unfailingly polite, white, male, middle-class agents to whom the FBI was family, men

protecting a public that responded with gratitude and respect." Forty
million U.S. viewers watched on Sunday nights. In addition, the program
was also syndicated to some 50 nations around the world.[56]

KGB and CIA Cooperation

In the 1950s, all of the U.S.-based networks became partners with
the U.S. government in its campaign to repel communism and foster free
market policies throughout the world. ABC's efforts to establish a global
network of stations that accepted U.S.-created programming and portrayed the advantages of U.S. multinational corporate domination played
a prime role in Washington's foreign propaganda operations.

After John F. Kennedy was elected president in 1960, Goldenson
was summoned to Washington by Senator John Pastore, then Democratic
chairman of the Senate Communications Subcommittee which oversees
regulation of the broadcasting industry. Pastore told Goldenson that ABC
needed to build a more competitive news and public affairs operation in
order to enhance its public image.[57]

Following his Washington meeting with Pastore, Goldenson asked
President Eisenhower for permission to hire former presidential press
secretary James C. Hagerty as ABC's first president of news. As president
of ABC News, Hagerty played a role in resolving the 1962 Cuban missile
crisis. Four days after the Kennedy administration insisted publicly that
the Soviet Union remove its offensive nuclear missiles from Cuba,
Hagerty's top diplomatic correspondent John Scali was contacted by a
"deep-cover KGB colonel" based in the Soviet Embassy. Scali was asked
by the colonel to convey to Kennedy a Russian offer to break the
diplomatic deadlock. According to Goldenson, the Soviets contacted Scali
because they apparently thought that he was a secret U.S. intelligence
agent with ties to then Secretary of State Dean Rusk. Alexandr Fomin, the
KGB colonel, was director of all Soviet espionage activities in North
America.[58]

Following Scali's meeting with the KGB, Goldenson placed Scali
on an official leave of absence from ABC to avoid possible conflict-of-
interest charges. Leonard Goldenson later reported in his autobiography
that he and James Hagerty knew about the Soviet Union's overtures for a
peace settlement even before the White House did.[59]

After the crisis eased, Scali, a Republican, returned to ABC News as a top correspondent. He was later appointed special assistant to President Nixon and succeeded George Bush as the U.S. ambassador to the United Nations. After his government service, Scali returned to his former post as an ABC diplomatic correspondent. In 1989, Scali signed a four-year contract with ABC News making him the oldest working television journalist at the time.[60]

During hearings of the Senate Select Committee on Intelligence in 1976, Sam Jaffe, a former ABC News correspondent, admitted in public testimony that he had secretly served as an FBI spy while working as a correspondent for ABC News during the 1960s. He told Senate investigators that his association with the FBI began while he was working at *Life* magazine and CBS News in the 1950s. He continued his double career as spy and ABC News correspondent from 1961 to 1968. Jaffe later came to suspect that a portion of his travel expenses were deposited directly into his ABC News bank account by the U.S. government. In an interview with *The New York Times,* Jaffee later said that "he had never knowingly worked for the CIA in this country [the U.S.] or abroad."[61]

In a 1977 article in *Rolling Stone*, investigative reporter Carl Bernstein reported that CIA officials had said that Jaffe had "performed clandestine tasks" for the agency, although they "refused to say whether the agency was continuing active relationships with members of the ABC News organization. All cover arrangements were made with the knowledge of ABC executives," according to Bernstein's CIA sources. While other mainstream news groups like CBS, *The New York Times*, and Time, Inc., were reported to be even more widely used as CIA cover organizations, ABC surely did its part to fortify national security. One CIA insider told Bernstein that "business is nice, but the press is a natural. One journalist is worth twenty [secret] agents. [The journalist] has access, and the ability to ask questions without arousing suspicion."[62]

Simon Says, "Takeover!"

When advertisers found in 1964 that color television increased the sales of their products, ABC found it needed $134 million not only to construct new studios, production facilities, and transmission plants for color conversion, but also to acquire the latest Hollywood motion pictures it needed to compete with CBS and NBC. Because of this pressure to expand and to acquire new sources of capital, ABC became vulnerable to takeover. In 1964, noting its nearly five million shares that were outstanding on the New York Stock Exchange (almost half of which were held by large, outside investor groups), many on Wall Street lost confidence in ABC's ability to keep up with changing technology; and its stock prices fell below the market value of its total assets.[63]

The first businessperson to mount a serious takeover bid for ABC was Norton Simon. A collector of art and companies, Simon owned the giant Hunt Foods & Industries, and the popular *McCall's, Redbook*, and *Saturday Review* magazines. He had additional important interests in meatpacking and soft-drink production. When Simon began his attempted ABC takeover in 1964, the *Wall Street Journal* called him an "industrialist," a "financier," and a "rugged corporate proxy in-fighter." And trade journals wrote that Simon wanted a "voice in, if not outright control of, ABC's affairs."[64]

Simon was not alone in wanting to take over the network for his own political and economic advantage. There were also public reports circulating in the summer of 1965 that the arch conservative Texas millionaire H.L. Hunt had purchased 100,0000 shares of CBS in order to control its news and public affairs policies. Allegedly, Hunt was attempting to influence other conservatives to buy up CBS stock as well, although the brokerage house that reportedly handled the sale refused to comment on these allegations.[65]

As many hostile corporate raiders often do, Simon denied he wanted to control ABC when his McCall Corporation began to acquire many shares. After he obtained nine percent of ABC's outstanding shares, he requested a seat on its board through the Wall Street investment firm of Goldman Sachs. Like Noble, who had used ABC to further his personal business interests, Simon said he wanted to use it to boost profits at his corporate subsidiaries.[66]

To stop Simon, Goldenson went to George Jenkins, a member of the ABC board and chairman of the finance committee of the Metropolitan Life Insurance Company—the same company that had supplied the funds for the AB-PT merger in 1953. When Simon demanded a seat on ABC based on the number of shares he had purchased, Goldenson stopped this takeover bid by secretly changing ABC's Cumulative Voting Law, which allowed stockholders one vote for every share owned. Although he failed to take over ABC, Simon continued to buy up available ABC stock on the open market.[67]

ITT and Howard Hughes

After successfully repelling Norton Simon, ABC searched for the funds it needed to compete with CBS and NBC and to protect the corporation from a future hostile takeover. Goldenson was next approached with a serious merger offer in 1965 by Harold Geneen, chairman of ITT. The company was a major defense and military contractor that had worldwide sales of nearly $2 billion and profits of $76 million. With 60 percent of its revenues coming from its overseas operations and 6.5 percent of its shares owned by foreign interests, ITT had more power than many nations. Officials from ITT said that they wanted to use ABC's distribution networks to gain domestic prominence while boosting the company's image among America's smaller investors.[68]

When the press was notified of the pending ABC-ITT merger in December 1965, the merger was promoted by both companies as one that would provide a real economic opportunity for ABC to compete against CBS and NBC. They believed that the arrangement would also allow ABC to "broaden its base by joining forces with a company with greater capital resources, more diversified earnings, and broader technical experience." But ABC's receptiveness to ITT's offer apparently also rested on ABC's desire to spurn Simon's continuing takeover bids. ABC cited its lack of parity with CBS and NBC in television outlets in the top 100 markets, the heavy costs required to convert to color broadcasting, and the increasing costs of network programming. Based on the optimistic public relations statements from ABC and ITT, the only obstacle to the merger seemed to be gaining federal approval from the Johnson-led Justice Department and the FCC.[69]

At the end of two days of hearings on the merger in September 1966, there was dissension at the FCC, the Justice Department, and in the Congress about the impact of such concentrated media power on the public's right to know. The principal concern was that ITT would pressure ABC News to censor its news coverage in those countries in which ITT did business and had political connections. To reach an agreement, three FCC members opposed to the merger co-authored a letter to ITT requesting more information on the full extent of its worldwide empire where ITT earned 60 percent of its revenues in 118 countries.[70]

ABC controlled 17 owned-and-operated radio and television stations, as well as the ABC television and radio networks. It also ran the largest U.S. theater chain and owned substantial interests in foreign television outlets and film distributors. ITT, on the other hand, operated the largest overseas telegraph network, had 180,000 employees, and was the world's largest manufacturer and supplier of electronic and telecommunication equipment, including satellites. Clearly, an ABC-ITT merger would have radically altered the domestic and international media picture. CBS and NBC would have been dwarfed almost overnight by such a conglomerate.[71]

During the FCC-Justice review, three veteran Washington reporters revealed they had been pressured by ITT to write favorable accounts of the ABC-ITT merger. (They refused and alerted their editors.) It was also learned that an ITT official secretly taped a closed Justice department hearing about the merger, although these tapes were later destroyed by ITT attorneys. The woman who made the recordings, Dita Beard, was later implicated in another public ITT scandal involving the Nixon administration in the early 1970s when it attempted to bribe federal officials to settle an antitrust suit in its favor, and offered the CIA $1 million to prevent the democratically elected government of Salvador Allende from coming to power in Chile in 1970.[72]

In December 1966, when the FCC failed to act, the Justice Department and two Senators charged that the FCC had acted improperly. After the FCC voted in favor of ABC-ITT, the Justice Department moved to stop the merger in the Federal Courts in 1967. ITT called off the merger to avoid exposing its myriad foreign operations in public court on January 1, 1968. However, ITT did manage, through its increased visibility, to raise its stock price to earnings ratio threefold at the public's expense. Norton Simon, who had earlier tried to takeover ABC, made $10 million as public interest in ABC-ITT mounted.[73]

ABC also considered other corporate merger partners during this time: Sears, Transamerica, Walter Kidde, and General Electric. A serious takeover bid was also made by Monogram Industries, the largest manufacturer of aircraft chemical toilets. None was successful, however, due to increasing elite concerns that the U.S. networks already had too much power.[74]

On July 1, 1968, Howard Hughes offered to buy 43 percent of ABC through his Hughes Summa Corporation for $150 million. The reclusive Hughes had numerous secret links to the CIA and organized crime, and his top aide, Robert Maheu, had conspired in CIA-Mafia attempts to assassinate Cuban President Fidel Castro in 1960-1961. Realizing that Hughes wanted to buy ABC in order to promote his radical right-wing views, the entire ABC board of directors rose up against him.[75]

ABC fought the Hughes takeover vigorously. Hill and Knowlton, the world's largest public relations firm, was enlisted to spread the word throughout the financial and government community that Hughes wanted to buy ABC to further his conservative political-economic interests. He was later defeated when ABC's lawyers forced the FCC through the U.S. Court of Appeals to demand that he appear in person at the Commission's hearings on the proposed merger. The reclusive Hughes refused. Apparently, several of the liberal commissioners on the Johnson FCC were also disturbed by Hughes' many defense contracts with the U.S. government and his ultra-conservative political beliefs.[76]

"Number One"

After failing to complete the ITT merger, Goldenson brought in Elton Rule from ABC's top-rated Los Angeles affiliate, KABC-TV, to run ABC in 1968. A reported common practice among the all-Jewish network chiefs at NBC, ABC, and CBS was to hire managers with Anglo-Saxon names to court the U.S. financial leaders on Wall Street.[77] But ABC's failure to obtain regulatory approval for the ITT merger was viewed in Washington and on Wall Street as a sign of its waning influence and power. Soon Goldenson's promotion of Rule brought positive results. Rule installed a cash management system to control costs and better manage the network's growth. With Rule at the helm, ABC's profits increased 10 percent in just his first year as president.[78] As his reward, he was named second-in-command and in 1974 promoted to serve as ABC's corporate president and chief operating officer (COO). Frederick Pierce, a 20-year employee and head of ABC's television research unit, succeeded Rule as the manager of ABC's broadcast operations.

In 1976, ABC lead the Nielsen ratings for the first time among the three U.S. broadcasting networks, with programs such as "Happy Days," "Laverne and Shirley," "Charlie's Angels," "Starsky and Hutch," and

"The Bionic Woman." Though the network was sometimes criticized for becoming the top U.S. network by offering a program lineup based mainly on sex, violence, and nostalgia, U.S. corporate sponsors focused only on the high ratings that ABC achieved.

In its quest to become Number One in the ratings, ABC often accepted programming and financial risks that the other U.S. networks would not. At the time, both Rule and Goldenson commented that network leadership entailed a social responsibility that extended far beyond profits or ratings. Thus, in 1977, ABC presented the primetime entertainment mini-series "Roots," which attracted some of the largest audiences in television history. With 130 million in the United States watching the series comprising 12 hours spread over eight consecutive nights, "Roots" remains one of the most watched programs in U.S. television history. While "Roots" is still considered breakthrough programming, it does not make up for the 20 years of ABC and other network shows that glorified crime and war, and reinforced racial and gender stereotypes.

In 1977, ABC's television revenues for the first time exceeded $1 billion. So its television operation was finally able to catch up and enjoy the extraordinary success of ABC's other divisions: the radio network, its owned-and-operated radio and television stations, and the sports division, all of which had earned high ratings through most of the 1960s and 1970s. In 1977, ABC jumped from 170 to 152 on the list of Fortune's 500 largest industrial corporations. As it headed into the 1980s, the network had 9,400 employees and assets of well over $1 billion.[79]

But when the Reagan administration decideed to aggressively pursue a radical privatization of the U.S. broadcast networks in 1981, ABC again became vulnerable to takeover. Its stock price fell in relation to its assets because of an economic recession and declining profits resulting from failed ventures in cable and pay-per-view television.

Over almost 30 years, Goldenson's skill in repelling powerful predatory raiders became legendary. Yet even his skill and commitment were no match for the determination of Capital Cities' top leaders to become network owners. With its excellent credit rating and business reputation— based primarily on its well-publicized 30-year history of earning 40-50 percent profit returns at all of its local broadcast stations— and its ties to the highest levels of U.S. power, Capital Cities became the darling of Washington and Wall Street. ABC, known for many years within the broadcast industry as "Leonard's candy store," was forced to the selling block almost on the day Ronald Reagan's so-called free-market policies were enacted. In Chapter Three, Capital Cities' rise to power will be detailed as the corporation became one of the most powerful communications conglomerates in the world.

Chapter Three

The Rise of Capital Cities (1954-1978)

Capital Cities was born in 1954 with the purchase by Frank Smith of a failing UHF television station and a 5,000-watt AM radio station in Albany, New York. Over the next 31 years, until it purchased ABC, Capital Cities succeeded in developing unprofitable, or nearly bankrupt, broadcast properties and so enjoyed an excellent reputation among U.S. financial investors.

Secrets of Success

Behind a carefully crafted public image as a "mom-and-pop" media operator, Capital Cities made maximum use of the wealth, privilege, and social connections of its early founders and executives—Lowell Thomas, Frank Smith, Thomas E. Dewey, and William J. Casey, among them—who preferred to keep their business affairs out of the public eye.[1] All were well trained in constructing public images; most had previous experience with U.S. intelligence and propaganda agencies, political institutions, or corporate public relations/advertising firms.

Capital Cities became a dominant U.S. media power by purchasing stations that had shown signs of business failure, management ineptitude, or creditor dissatisfaction. By exploiting the sales and marketing potential of failing stations, while keeping its operating and labor costs low, Capital Cities was able to invest in station improvements and acquire programming that its competitors often could not match.

The success of Capital Cities, like that of all the dominant U.S. broadcasting powers, was buttressed by bold and aggressive business practice, the maintenance of key relationships with U.S. government and corporate leaders, and a carefully controlled plan to dominate every business market in which it operated.[2] Though Capital Cities' leaders supported "free-market" policies in U.S. broadcasting, they apparently saw nothing contradictory in demanding, and receiving, corporate tax breaks and regulatory waivers from the government to protect the broadcasters' freedom to make windfall profits at the public's expense.

Frank Smith

Smith, as Capital Cities' first CEO, was not afraid to take on substantial debt to build the company. But it was his knack for acquiring inside information that most contributed to Capital Cities' success as a media power. One of Smith's managerial challenges at WROW-TV in Albany, the first Capital Cities' television station, was to compete with two other stations: a CBS-affiliated UHF station owned by the Stanley-Warner theater chain and an NBC-affiliated VHF station owned by General Electric. After buying WROW-TV, Smith canceled the affiliate agreement with ABC and signed with CBS. He also bought two more UHF stations in fringe areas, and set up a *de facto* UHF network that extended WROW-TV's broadcast range to match GE's VHF coverage of the larger Albany-Troy-Schenectady market. By improving WROW-TV's signal and attracting more highly rated network shows from CBS, Smith significantly increased WROW-TV's value to national and local commercial advertisers. He could now offer them a higher percentage of Hudson Valley's television audiences.[3] His efforts to counter GE's dominance of the Albany market were later extolled by Thomas S. Murphy (Smith's successor as Capital Cities' CEO): "Anyone with less guts would have folded his tent and quietly stolen away. What Smitty did was to compete with a 'V' [VHF station] the way nobody else had tried before."[4]

When Smith originally found the nearly bankrupt UHF station in Albany, he had also discovered, perhaps through Capital Cities' close ties to the Eisenhower White House and FCC, that there was a "white spot" just 10 miles outside of Albany—an area where a new VHF station could be added. He also knew that the FCC was likely to grant Capital Cities permission to make use of the area to improve WROW-TV. This probably was the decisive factor that led to Smith's decision to buy WROW-TV in the first place, since it was a cornerstone of Smith's sales talks to investors for additional capital funds. Given that most home television sets could not receive UHF signals at the time, attaining VHF status helped to make WROW-TV a full competitor to GE's VHF station almost overnight.[5]

This was the kind of inside information that would also later play a crucial role in the Capital Cities takeover of ABC. At the time of the original WROW-TV purchase, Smith reportedly knew of the FCC's willingness to add a VHF station in Albany just as Tom Murphy "seemed to know" in December 1984 of the FCC's intentions to reduce federal broadcast ownership limits when he first approached ABC about a merger with Capital Cities. In 1985, the FCC changed the rules allowing one company or individual to purchase up to 36 radio and television stations, a big increase from the previous limit of 21.[6] This Reagan FCC "7-7-7" rule change enabled Murphy and Capital Cities (and other Wall Street favorites) to buy ABC with the profits from its expanded owned station line-up.

Smith's passionate belief in "free-market" economics was tempered by his understanding of how the federal broadcast regulatory apparatus worked. In an industry where hostile buyouts were frowned upon by the FCC, Smith was particularly skilled in convincing the owners "bought out" by Capital Cities to later testify before the FCC that such purchases were indeed "in the public interest."

By frequently agreeing to pay more than the market value of the stations he purchased, Smith's generosity was also useful in deflecting potential public criticism of Capital Cities' formidable influence in Washington and on Wall Street. While this policy was used to great advantage by Smith and his successors to gain support from the former owners of the media properties they purchased, Capital Cities' future competitors did not always agree it should be continued.

After the purchase of WROW-TV in 1954, its UHF competitor in Albany alleged that Capital Cities made a secret, binding agreement to affiliate with CBS pending FCC approval of its purchase, a possible violation of FCC rules. In a civil suit, Stanley-Warner, the other UHF owner in Albany, accused CBS and Capital Cities of conspiring to revoke its previous affiliate agreement.[7] While these allegations were never proven in court (Capital Cities won the case), it is true that CBS president Frank Stanton had urged Smith to enter the television ownership ranks in 1950.[8] Just a few years earlier, Smith and Stanton had signed an exclusive agreement that brought the highly profitable Lowell Thomas program to CBS from NBC. Smith's links to major U.S. corporate leaders were so formidable that General Electric, his principal VHF Albany competitor, apparently did not object to his moves to change WROW-TV into a VHF station. In fact, GE regularly purchased air time on Capital Cities through Smith's long-time friendship and business relationship with the J. Walter Thompson Advertising Agency, according to Lowell Thomas.[9]

Smith, a graduate of the Harvard Business School and the son of a prosperous Tennessee banker, had been a long-time corporate advertising and public relations executive before starting Capital Cities' broadcasting operations. Because of his outstanding business reputation and connections, he was sometimes asked to serve as personal manager and financial advisor to rich and famous personalities. Two of Smith's best known clients were the flamboyant Broadway producer Mike Todd, and millionaire broadcaster, newspaper reporter, raconteur, entrepreneur, and world traveler, Lowell Thomas. In his autobiography, *So Long Until Tomorrow: From Quaker Hill to Kathmandu*, Thomas called Frank Smith a genius for saving him from personal bankruptcy in 1946. The Hudson Valley Broadcasting Co., Capital Cities' original corporate name, was formed by Smith and Thomas eight years before they purchased WROW-TV and WROW-AM in Albany. In April 1946, Hudson Valley Broadcasting became a New York state corporation through which Smith began to reorganize Thomas's financial affairs.[10]

Smith signed Thomas to an exclusive sponsor arrangement with Procter & Gamble, then the second largest radio sponsor in the United States. This business deal also moved Thomas' radio program from NBC to CBS and rescued Thomas from considerable debt to the Sun Oil Company. Sun had been Thomas's NBC sponsor and major creditor, bankrolling most of Thomas's losing real estate ventures.

Lowell Thomas

Thomas first met Smith during World War II when Smith was packaging "Victory Is Our Business" for the Trans-American Broadcasting & Television Corporation (TAB). A syndicated program that celebrated American war triumphs during World War II, "Victory" was paid for by conservative radio sponsors such as General Motors and *The Reader's Digest*.[11]

Thomas remained the most famous of the original twenty-two Capital Cities investors, largely because of his reputation as a media celebrity. He had narrated the Fox-Movietone newsreels during the 1930s and 1940s, before becoming a commentator on NBC radio. His written and oral accounts of his widely publicized world-travel exploits earned him access to national and world leaders.

Although he was often associated with "objective journalism" by his audiences, Thomas's ties to the advertising community were so strong that he was once elected president of the Advertising Club of New York. One of the most influential and powerful media organizations, the club comprised elite advertisers, media owners, and government leaders. Thomas was also a member of the Bohemian Grove—an annual retreat of "one of the most exclusive men's associations in the U.S."[12]

Earlier in his career, after attending graduate school at Princeton, Thomas enlisted in the Creel Commission's propaganda campaign to support U.S. intervention in World War I. He toured the nation and delivered speeches on the issue to wealthy industrialists. Working indirectly with Edward Bernays, who many have called the father of modern public relations, Thomas, according to his autobiography, raised $100,000 from 18 U.S. millionaires in a two-week period to fund World War I domestic propaganda efforts. The Creel Commission had been set up by President Wilson to "create war fever among the generally pacifist U.S. population," and "to support the righteous conquest of foreign markets [by the U.S.]."[13] Since the government had no public relations budget at the time, the Commission was instrumental in encouraging U.S. citizens to support the war effort.[14]

After the country entered World War I, the Commission also managed U.S. government news and information with "the cooperation of loyal media and the intellectuals."[15] Thomas continued to work for the Commission through his authorship of several exaggerated accounts of the Middle East "conqueror" Lawrence of Arabia.[16]

The Dulles Connection

Before World War I, while in graduate school, Thomas had been a classmate and friend of Allen Dulles.[17] It was apparently at Princeton in 1914-1915 that what would be continuing ties between the Capital Cities' founding fathers and U.S. intelligence agencies began, although Dulles was not a member of the original Capital Cities investment group.

Dulles was hired by the State Department and became involved in secret U.S. espionage efforts in Western Europe. During World War II, he was drafted by "Wild Bill" Donovan to work with the Office of Strategic Services (OSS), principally because of his many connections to the Nazi government, developed as a foreign service officer in Europe in the 1920s and 1930s. After World War II, Dulles became a Wall Street corporate lawyer, but continued to work publicly and privately for the establishment of the Central Intelligence Agency (CIA), which was to continue the work of the OSS to maintain U.S. dominance overseas. He worked with his brother John Foster Dulles, Republican presidential candidate Thomas Dewey (another Capital Cities investor), and others to convince the Truman administration to fund the CIA and protect U.S. [corporate, financial, and military] interests abroad "by whatever means necessary," according to investigative reporter Howard Kohn.[18]

Throughout their careers Allen and John Foster Dulles, along with Lowell Thomas, supported Republican candidates, and served as top advisors on international affairs when Dewey made his bids for the presidency.

Allen ultimately became Eisenhower's CIA director (1953–1961). He not only developed propaganda programs as the head of foreign intelligence early in the Cold War, but also managed the overthrow of governments in Iran and Guatemala. Then he helped the Pentagon plan the unsuccessful Bay of Pigs invasion of Cuba in 1961, which led to his dismissal as CIA director by President Kennedy.

Thomas's ties to Allen Dulles and his brother John—a powerful Wall Street corporate lawyer and secretary of state in the Eisenhower administration—gave rise to rumors that Thomas had often acted as a secret intelligence agent for the OSS and the CIA. The Soviets accused him of being an intelligence agent because he often showed up at U.S.-USSR espionage-intensive sites with his photographic and film crews. Though he always denied being a spy, Thomas was a vigorous anti-communist. He once appeared in a film, sponsored by the John Birch Society, with John Wayne and several U.S. military generals denouncing those weak on communism, according to a 1987 report in the alternative newspaper, *L.A. WEEKLY.*[19]

Dewey and the C.I.A.

Between 1945 and 1947, Thomas Dewey, a former Wall Street lawyer, worked with other elite Washington and Wall Street conservatives

to persuade Congress to pass the 1947 National Security Act through which the CIA was created. During the 1948 presidential election, "the CIA funneled more than $1 million from its secret budget to Dewey's campaign," according to *Rolling Stone*.[20]
Earlier in his career, before his rise to political prominence, Dewey became famous as New York's Mafia-fighting special prosecutor in Manhattan by successfully putting the organized-crime boss Lucky Luciano in prison. As governor of New York, Dewey reportedly worked with Allen Dulles to arrange Luciano's parole in exchange for help in organizing Italian dock workers to support the Allied invasion of Sicily. Luciano and his deputy Meyer Lansky also were instrumental in the OSS's efforts to infiltrate the New York waterfront with undercover dock workers to prevent Nazi sabotage against civilian and military vessels stationed there. Luciano's later release was rumored to have also been arranged in exchange for secret campaign contributions to Dewey when he ran for governor.[21]
According to Howard Kohn, an investigative reporter for *Rolling Stone*, the Luciano deal led to a long and secret association between the OSS, the CIA, and the Mafia. Kohn reports that "much of this association passed through Dewey." In later years, the CIA and the Mafia also passed money and information to Dewey's later political protégé, Richard Nixon. All of these Republican supporters were connected to Resorts International, rumored to have suspicious ties to the mob.[22]
Before World War II, Dewey threatened New York publishers with costly litigation if they attempted to publish books that exposed U.S. intelligence operations. As an influential Wall Street lawyer, he made many contacts that helped him receive the Republican nomination for president in 1944 and 1948.
In 1976, *Rolling Stone* reported that Allen Dulles had given Dewey and Thomas $2 million in 1958-59 to set up a CIA front company, the Mary Carter Paint Co. Although the company did manufacture paint and painting supplies, according to several sources, Mary Carter's primary purpose was to launder money for anti-communist insurrections in the Caribbean, Central America, and South America.[24] This Tampa, Florida-based company was probably also aiding and abetting terrorist activities, such as Operation Mongoose, "a major terrorist program carried out against Cuba under the Kennedy administration in 1962-1963." The program included "sabotage raids, contamination of food supplies, bombings, boycotts by

intimidation, and assassination attempts against [Cuban president] Fidel Castro."[25] In 1968, Mary Carter became the gambling and real estate conglomerate, Resorts International.

James Crosby, an executive with a Wall Street brokerage firm, was alleged by *Rolling Stone* to have been named as the first CEO of Mary Carter by Allen Dulles, Dewey, and others. Crosby's father reportedly had also been "a member of the secret circle that lobbied for the establishment of the CIA" after World War II to protect U.S. interests abroad.[26]

In 1977, when Resorts sued for libel, *Rolling Stone* was forced to retract the part of Kohn's story that alleged that the CIA had set up Mary Carter Paint as a front company in 1958-59. Since then, two published reports in 1980 and 1993 appear to support Kohn's original allegations that the mysterious Mary Carter Paint company had ties to the CIA and organized crime.[27]

Mary Carter Paint had other interesting connections. In 1963, the company loaned $100,000 to stock promoters with alleged organized-crime connections. Later, it invested in a 1,300-acre tract of land on Grand Bahama Island, intending to subdivide it and sell plots to wealthy, retired Americans who could take advantage of the island's strict bank-secrecy laws. Then in 1968, James Crosby, Mary Carter's CEO, sold the paint operation and changed the business and the company name to Resorts International.

Resorts established a new subsidiary, International Intelligence, Inc. (Intertel), in 1970. This subsidiary, managed mainly by ex-intelligence and espionage officers from the U.S. government and military, was set up as a private police force to keep gangsters away from the casinos that Resorts owned in the Bahamas. Intertel eventually became the largest U.S. investigative agency outside of the CIA and FBI, with clients like Howard Hughes, ITT, the Shah of Iran, Augusto Pinochet, and Anastasio Somoza, among others. Resorts' and Intertel's activities were cited in the left-wing press as evidence of a front for secret CIA operations that sometimes involved the Mafia.

Through Intertel, the Shah fled Iran and went to the Bahamas, Hughes left Las Vegas for the Bahamas, and Somoza fled the United States for Paraguay (Somoza was later assassinated there by a car bomb). In the last years of his life, billionaire Howard Hughes and his fortune were placed under the protection of Intertel's worldwide security network.[28] During the Watergate scandal, federal investigators learned that Resorts had laundered an illegal $100,000 campaign contribution to Richard Nixon through his crony Bebe Rebozo's, Key Biscayne bank. Rebozo served Nixon as a courier and money launderer.[29]

When Crosby died of a heart attack in 1986, Thomas and Henry Murphy, his brothers-in-law through marriage, oversaw the sale of Resorts to Donald Trump with several other investors. Henry, a Trenton, New Jersey, mortician, and Thomas, CEO of Capital Cities, both married Crosby's sisters.[30]

Murphy, "the Pope"

In 1954, Thomas Murphy was hired by Frank Smith and Lowell Thomas to manage WROW-TV and WROW-AM in Albany. Before this, Murphy had graduated from Cornell, worked for Texaco Oil, and was later accepted at Harvard Business School.[31]

After receiving his MBA in 1949, he began working for the Kenyon & Eckhardt agency in Manhattan, where he became a product manager on the Dove soap account.[32] Smith believed that Murphy, despite his lack of television experience, possessed the right credentials and "people skills" to become a success in Albany. Like Smith, Murphy believed that broadcasting did not require any special skill, and so managed Capital Cities with the guiding assumption that "good broadcasting is good business."[33] To save costs, Smith and Murphy began operating in a 125-year-old building that had once been a home for retired nuns.[34] Eventually, Murphy earned the nickname, "the Pope" from his business associates.

While Murphy ran the Albany stations, Smith remained in New York City looking for media properties to add to his business network. In 1957, Smith bought another troubled television station in Raleigh, North Carolina, at a time when the Albany stations were still in the red. In 1959, the name was changed to: "Capital Cities Broadcasting, Incorporated."

William Casey, "The Fixer"

In 1954, William J. Casey became an investor and partner in Capital Cities. As a corporate attorney with a New York law firm that ultimately became known as Hall, Casey, Dickler, and Howley, Casey also began to advise Capital Cities on tax matters. His advice saved the company thousands of dollars in operating capital, which Smith used to acquire additional stations. Through Casey's financial craftiness, Smith and Murphy capitalized on a $1 million tax loss from the early years of the Albany operation.[35] Capital Cities reportedly did not have to pay any taxes until 1960, nearly six years after its first broadcast.

In the company's first public stock offering in 1957, Casey bought a block of 51,000 shares at 13 cents per share according to Casey's biographer, Joseph E. Persico.[36] By 1966, when Capital Cities began trading on the New York Stock Exchange, the share price had increased to some $37 per share, placing his stake in the firm at just under $2 million.[37] In 1981, when Casey was appointed Reagan's CIA director, his 68,000 shares were worth $4.7 million. From that until 1985, Casey sold a portion of his block of Capital Cities shares. Once the Capital Cities/ABC merger took place, Casey's 34,000 shares were worth over $7 million ($215 per share at time of merger).[38]

Casey's hard bargaining tactics proved profitable to Capital Cities over the years. With his advice and counsel on how to minimally satisfy tax and investment laws, the company was set to play a leadership role in broadcasting.

Nicknamed the "Cyclone" in his youth and later the "Fixer," Casey was known as someone who could obtain results, even if it often meant bending the law to do so.

Casey later became a key Reagan strategist in political-economic affairs. The first CIA chief to hold cabinet-level status, Casey once boasted that he was heading up the action arm of Reagan's foreign policy machine. He identified two areas in which he would focus as CIA chief: "technology transfer and subversion."[39]

Casey, as advisor to Capital Cities or as director of the CIA, was a reactionary Cold Warrior who saw nothing wrong with using public office to further his own conservative political interests. George Shultz, Reagan's secretary of state, later accused Casey of providing "faulty intelligence" to Reagan and others to bolster his own policy ideas.[40]

After leaving the OSS, Casey—as a Wall Street attorney, author, and advisor to numerous companies, including Capital Cities—maintained his intelligence contacts. He also became a dominant player in Republican party politics, always siding with the party's most rabid anti-communist and reactionary Cold War political factions. As a close associate of President Nixon, Casey held several government posts in the administration: chair of the Securities and Exchange Commission, president of the Import-Export Bank, undersecretary of state for economic affairs, and member of the president's Foreign Intelligence Advisory Board.[41]

While he was not publicly implicated in the Watergate scandal, Casey did achieve notoriety for his secret role in helping to arrange the Iran-Contra arms-for-hostages deal while serving as Reagan CIA director. At the time of this incident, many Washington insiders said that Casey's breaking of the law was merely a continuation of his usual shady dealings.

During World War II, Casey had managed OSS tactical support for the French resistance during the Normandy invasion. His work is said to have resulted in many deaths and injuries due to Casey's willingness to take unnecessary risks. After Germany's surrender to the Allied Forces in 1945, he faced charges of having aided Nazi war criminals fleeing Europe after the war. Casey later resigned from the SEC in the face of widespread allegations of insider trading among his colleagues and his refusal to place his private investments into a blind trust.[42] Before serving in the Reagan administration as CIA director, he was linked to organized crime as a counsel to a waste disposal company and as a co-founder of an agribusiness company.[43]

Besides his questionable government and corporate practices, Casey was continually involved with far-right extremists. During the Nixon years, Casey founded the Citizens' Committee for Peace with Security, which backed deployment of the Antiballistic Missile (ABM) system. The committee placed newspaper ads around the country, claiming that the results of a scientific public poll showed overwhelming support for the ABM.[44] As Reagan's director of the CIA, Casey became responsible for the design of a Nicaraguan policy manual that told the U.S.-sponsored Contras how to "neutralize" (assassinate) political opponents.[45]

Casey also endorsed propaganda campaigns that encouraged wealthy industrialists to support U.S. interventions abroad. Later he set up a funding operation for Reagan's secret war in Central America during the 1980s. This effort closely mirrored Lowell Thomas's World War I propaganda efforts for the Creel Commission. Casey and marine Lt. Colonel Oliver North, a Reagan aide with the National Security Council, organized a series of briefings to encourage American conservative war-backers to support the Reagan administration's secret war in Nicaragua and other Central American nations.[46] Like Thomas's war boosterism, which mostly supported the conquest of foreign markets by American business, Casey and North were intent on reversing the Nicaraguan revolution.

By 1991, persistent reports circulated throughout world diplomatic circles and among arms dealers that Casey had used his intelligence connections in the Middle East to secretly broker a deal with the Iranians in 1980 while serving as Reagan's campaign manager. Casey wanted Iran to keep the U.S. hostages a while longer so that the Carter secret negotiations to gain their release would appear unsuccessful, and Reagan could defeat Carter in the November presidential election. While the existence of a so-called October Surprise has yet to be proven with absolute certainty, it was certainly not the first time that Casey had been accused of using dirty tricks to get his way. During that election, he was also implicated in the theft of Carter's debate book.[47]

Indeed, when the Capital Cities takeover of ABC was announced in 1985, allegations were made that Casey had used his intelligence connections to profit on his sizeable holdings of Capital Cities stock. When the takeover of ABC was revealed, one senior CIA officer reportedly teased Casey by saying, "I understand Sam Donaldson's working for you now."[48]

There were other indications that Casey may have wanted more than just profits from Capital Cities. Acting as the intelligence agent he was, especially in his business and legal dealings, he had long wanted the CIA to step up its use of U.S. corporations to provide cover for its potentially illegal, covert intelligence-gathering and propaganda operations.[49] Even though in the 1970s congressional committees and the Securities and Exchange Commission had criminalized unreported corporate liaisons with the CIA, Casey did not mind continuing such links. Casey said to his CIA aides that despite the rules, he "knew many businessmen who would be happy to do favors for the CIA."[50]

"Spinning" the Adolf Eichmann Trial

In 1961, despite its ownership of only a few U.S. broadcast stations, Capital Cities was chosen over many competing film and television companies to become the world producer and distributor of film coverage of the Adolf Eichmann trial by the government of Israel.

Capital Cities used Odyssey, Lowell Thomas's personally owned film company, to gather and distribute footage of the trial proceedings in Jerusalem to other stations around the globe each day. By serving Israel's public relations needs, Capital Cities gained considerable respect as an international broadcaster in the United States. Its selection as the world-pool producer for the Eichmann trial coverage came at a time when the company was in the midst of rapid corporate expansion and needed federal regulatory leniency for its project to purchase broadcast stations in the top 10 U.S. markets. Later, Capital Cities announced that it was donating the profits generated by coverage of the Eichmann trial to an Israeli charity.[51]

Capital Cities CEO Frank Smith later "persuaded" the three U.S. networks, which had competed and lost out in the pool-producer selection process organized by the Israeli government, to share Capital Cities' initial costs of $1.5 million to cover the trial. He did this by "threatening" to reveal publicly that Capital Cities had provided footage of the trial to the networks for broadcast in the United States and around the world.[52] In effect, the U.S. networks paid Smith to maintain the illusion that they were actually covering the trial in Jerusalem.

There was significant Israeli government concerns about how the world would react to its clandestine pursuit and kidnapping of a Nazi war criminal within the sovereign nation of Argentina (without Argentina's knowledge or consent). The choice of Capital Cities over other more recognized journalistic organizations is revealing. Thirty years later, the 1961-1962 Eichmann capture, trial, conviction, and subsequent execution for Nazi war crimes remains one of the greatest triumphs of the Israeli intelligence service, the Mossad. It is quite unlikely that Capital Cities would have been selected to cooperate in Israel's attempt to manage world public opinion against charges of violating international law had it not enjoyed the right contacts and political influence in the U.S.

The value of serving U.S. interests in the Middle East by covering the Eichmann trial should not be underestimated, in explaining Capital Cities' rise to prominence as a U.S. media power. By serving as Israel's public relations arm, Capital Cities became one of the first U.S. corporate public relations organizations to "spin" news stories for profit. In the 1990s, video public relations releases have become standard corporate public relations tools that are routinely used by government and businesses to persuade television stations to see and present things their way.

Decentralizing

On the surface, Capital Cities' business style seems to largely reflect individual employees. However, the company's success of the top managers has been mostly ensured by hiring those who share Frank Smith's commitment to decentralized management practices.

Decentralization is a prominent feature of most transnational corporations such as General Motors, General Electric, ITT, and IBM, among others. For corporations that are spread over five or six continents, it has become a management necessity. Aside from making it possible to better integrate a large, diverse workforce, decentralization allows large corporate organizations to become more responsive to changes in the marketplace:

> Given the advantages of modern communications and computerized information systems, conglomerate managers are supremely confident that they can run a widely diversified organization by continually monitoring certain performance variables and pulling on a few control strings as conditions warrant. One conglomerate executive boasts that his central staff of ninety experts can run any company in the world, any company.[53]

Indeed, some corporate leaders have become so passionate about decentralization that they claim it is a form of workplace democracy. When General Electric, for example, developed its model of modern decentralized corporate practice in the 1950s, GE president Ralph Cordiner described it as "people's capitalism":

> [It's] a way of preserving and enhancing these contributions of the large enterprise, and at the same time achieving the flexibility and the human touch that are popularly associated with—though not always attained by—small organizations...[54]

Decentralization worked at GE to improve corporate profits because, in Cordiner's words, "Each employee of the company had, in his position, full responsibility, authority, and accountability for a certain defined body of work and teamwork." More accountability at the local level, of course, also assured corporate leaders of higher productivity levels and profits for the parent conglomerate.

Thus, decentralization has also become a major element in corporate-labor relations. As local managers solve employee problems and become more responsive to employees' concerns, decentralized management structures help to discourage employees from relying on trade unions to work for better wages and improved working conditions. It is a form of "internal" public relations aimed at convincing employees that they are in charge of their destiny. Again, quoting Raph Cordiner, the former CEO of GE:

> Responsible decentralization—as a philosophy—makes it possible to provide at once the big results that come from big enterprises, with the human freedom that comes from respecting the competence and dignity of every individual in the enterprise. This philosophy must prevail if freedom is to survive in the world.[55]

Decentralization allow GE and Cordiner's successors the freedom to develop eight priorities for ensuring continued success: profitability; market position; productive utilization of human, capital, and material resources; product leadership; personnel development; employee attitudes; public responsibility; and balancing of corporate long-range and short-term goals.[56]

Indeed, increasing revenues and profits are top priorities for GE and other transnationals. Public responsibility falls near the bottom of the list. GE, of course, remains one of the most anti-labor and ultra-conservative corporations in U.S. history. It also is a corporate felon with multiple convictions.[57]

Some companies, in the name of decentralization and to enhance overall profits, pit subsidiaries against each other. "Kaiser Industries brags that its nine major subsidiaries are urged to 'beat the other's brains out' in a struggle that, says one company officer, 'tightens and toughens.'"[58] Making managers more accountable also helps corporate leaders to achieve higher productivity levels and improved profits.

Furthermore, decentralization protects upper-level corporate leaders from responsibility for the mistakes made by local management. It provides them with "plausible deniability," through which top executives can protect their image as responsible business leaders in the event of scandal or misconduct by lower-level employees. It also allows others to perform the often unpleasant task of cutting costs, while upper-level leaders claim that employee layoffs and firings are a result of consensus. Decentralized management practices only survive when lower-level managers continue to ensure profits and unconditionally endorse top management's political and social beliefs. As an example of this, when Dan Burke was hired to succeed Tom Murphy at the Albany Capital Cities station in 1961, Murphy is reported to have given Burke an hour's introduction and did not contact him again for several weeks. To stay in touch, Burke began to mail weekly memos to New York where Murphy was working with Smith on building the Capital Cities empire.[59]

"Burke's Law"

Dan Burke's older brother James, later CEO of Johnson & Johnson, was a close friend of Murphy, whom he met in the Harvard Business School class of 1949. After graduation, the elder Burke and Murphy shared a bachelor apartment in New York City until their respective marriages. Murphy is said to have been impressed with the Burke brothers, who had been raised in a traditional Catholic home, much like his own in Brooklyn.

Daniel B. Burke graduated from the University of Vermont and then earned an MBA at Harvard in 1955. Following a stint with the U.S. Army in Korea, he worked for General Foods before Capital Cities hired him to manage the Albany stations in 1961. Ironically, Burke had been raised within the signal range of WROW-TV. His father was an executive with the New York Life Insurance Company, and his mother was a Wellesley graduate whom Burke has described as an "early feminist."[60]

Unlike Ed Noble, Leonard Goldenson, William Paley, David Sarnoff, and Allen DuMont, all former U.S. network leaders who chose to run their companies as their personal empires, Capital Cities chose a shared-management model system that was handed down directly from Frank Smith and Lowell Thomas. This structure sent a message to would-be takeover artists that Capital Cities' business stability rested not on one executive's shoulders, but several.

Murphy and Burke continued to cultivate ties to U.S. power. Burke became a summer neighbor and friend of Vice-President and eventually President Bush at his vacation retreat in Kennebunkport, Maine. Although he was offered top national posts as the commissioner of major league baseball in 1984 and on the staff of the *Washington Post*, Burke chose to remain at the helm of Capital Cities as president and chief operating officer, while Murphy remains chairman of the board.[61] (Dan Burke retired as president of Capital Cities/ABC in February 1994 when he reached the Capital Cities mandatory retirement age of sixty-five.)

An important factor in Capital Cities' rise to power has been its ability to maintain an impeccable public image, despite its ruthless cost-cutting and tough labor policies. Both Murphy and Burke have been described as "models of pleasant rationality who know how to motivate managers without brandishing bludgeons or setting financial specific goals."[62] Nicknamed "the Pope" by fellow Capital Cities executives and members of the board, Murphy is also good friends with other millionaire investors—CBS chairman Laurence Tisch, Warren Buffett of Berkshire Hathaway, and *Washington Post* publisher Katharine Graham.[63]

Burke, nicknamed "the Cardinal," is said to be generous with compliments and often sends thank-you notes to those he visits in the Capital Cities empire. His annual management retreats in Phoenix, Arizona, for all high-level managers are designed to publicly recognize achievement, and to provide Burke and Murphy with an early warning about those local managers who are not measuring up to the company's profit expectations.[64] For Capital Cities' managers, image has always been as important as profit-making.

Lean and Mean

Burke and Murphy are both successful followers of Frank Smith's management style, which not only features decentralization and strict attention to cost controls, but also encourages a *bottom-to-top*, corporate hegemony. "[Capital Cities] doesn't like to have more personnel than it needs. Too many people with too little to do lead to 'office politicking' and other behavior that's 'destructive' for an organization," Murphy has said.[65]

While it developed a reputation for being "lean and mean" early in its corporate history, Capital Cities was well known for its success in motivating lower-level employees to adopt corporate objectives. According to *Fortune* magazine, the company has fired few managers over the years, and many have served for more than 20 years.[66] For top executives who follow the rules, Capital Cities can be especially rewarding. Its management stock-and-bonus system is tied to executive performance and profit-making. For example, a single share of company stock purchased for $18 dollars in 1974 was worth $200 in 1984, a more than 1,000 percent increase in 10 years.[67] In 1983, Murphy and Burke earned (with stock options) $6 million and $4.3 million, respectively.[68]

Because executive salaries and bonuses are tied to performance, profit and market dominance are the perennial goals of Capital Cities managers. For example, the company took an early lead in developing sensationalist "shoot-em-up sensationalist local newscasts" that exploit crime, violence, and government waste and corruption.[69] This earned the company a substantial profit.

Building the Empire

Frank Smith died of a heart attack in 1966 at the age of 56.[70] Murphy became Capital Cities' CEO and concentrated on acquisitions, while Burke became president and made the day-to-day operating decisions. Through all of their expansion, Murphy and Burke never paid any dividends to stockholders, preferring instead to reinvest profits to generate greater corporate growth. From 1974 to 1984, Capital Cities never had a down quarter and enjoyed nearly a 20 to 1 earnings ratio on its investments—one of the highest in the industry. The individual broadcasting stations remained the most profitable asset in the Capital Cities portfolio of holdings. Profit margins at its owned TV stations reached 55 percent in 1984.[71]

Over three decades of growth, management ran all of the media empire with a relatively small staff from a suite of offices in a brownstone building on New York's East 51st Street, near St. Patrick's Cathedral. The usual corporate accoutrements—a company jet, a legal department, a public relations staff, and other expensive, overhead items—were conspicuously rejected by Capital Cities in favor of cutting costs and increasing profits.[72] These items, quite crucial to the operation of a major corporation, were acquired on a temporary basis when necessary.

By 1966, Capital Cities acquired five VHF television stations in media markets that ranged from the 11th to 56th largest in the United States, as well as numerous radio stations. In 1970, Capital Cities bought three more television stations; WPVI-TV, Philadelphia; WTNH-TV, New

Haven; and KFSN-TV, Fresno—from publisher Walter Annenberg's Triangle Broadcasting Group for $100 million. This purchase made Capital Cities one of the largest and most powerful U.S. local-station group owners outside of ABC, CBS, and NBC.[73] On reaching the federal limits on broadcast ownership, it later sold its stations in Albany and Huntington, West Virginia.[74]

In 1973, the company changed its corporate moniker to Capital Cities Communications, Inc., to reflect its widening ownership of print and broadcast properties. In 1968, Capital Cities moved into the publishing arena with the purchase of Fairchild Publications, Inc., which at the time owned eight trade publications, including *Women's Wear Daily*. By 1981, Fairchild owned a news service, a book publishing company, *Editor and Publisher*, and a division that publishes newspapers for specialized professional readers.[75]

When it acquired Fairchild, Capital Cities retained the services of John B. Fairchild, its owner and a major player within the U.S. power elite. Not only was he allowed to preside over this new division, but Burke and Murphy also provided him with a seat on the Capital Cities board that he continues to hold in 1993. Fairchild has been a major arbiter of world fashion trends and was the one who coined the term, "The Beautiful People."[76] During the Reagan years, a close friend and admirer of Nancy Kissinger and Nancy Reagan, he reportedly "banned from his newspaper pages any designer whose words or works offended him."[77]

In 1969, Burke and Murphy expanded into newspaper publishing when they bought their first daily newspaper, the *Oakland Press* in Pontiac, Michigan. They later acquired the *News-Democrat* in Belleville, Illinois (1972); *The Fort Worth Star Telegram*, Fort Worth, Texas (1974); and *Kansas City Star* and *Kansas City Times* in Kansas City, Missouri (1977). In 1978, they purchased the *Times-Leader* in Wilkes-Barre/Scranton, Pennsylvania; and in 1980, they acquired two daily newspapers and six weekly publications in Oregon with the purchase of the Democrat-Herald Publishing Company.[78]

Capital Cities, during its expansion into broadcasting and publishing, also aggressively invested in cable television. Enjoying a monopoly in the cities where it was franchised, Capital Cities Communications owned 54 cable television systems throughout the United States by 1984.[79] Capital Cities was also one of the first U.S. communication companies to establish cross media partnerships with other companies. In Belleville,

Illinois, the *News-Democrat* began providing daily newscasts for its local cable outlet. Additionally, in Fort Worth, Capital Cities also entered into an information retrieval partnership with the *Fort Worth Star Telegram* and the Tandy corporation, the owner of Radio Shack. Tandy has become one of the largest manufacturers of personal computers in the United States.[80]

Burke and Murphy also began their own TV-production company, Capital Cities Television Productions, which developed special program packages for their local stations and for the national syndication market. Several of the programs put together by this subsidiary were developed in association with Paulist Productions, a Roman Catholic enterprise.[81]

By 1983, Capital Cities had enjoyed 28 consecutive years of increasing net profits, high ratings, and circulation. Its success was largely dependent on the monopoly status it enjoyed in nearly all of its markets. Its "frugal management style" contributed to the high profit ratios and was a principal reason why 80 percent of its 13.2 million shares were held by institutional investors.[82]

In 1981, the top 71 stockholders of Capital Cities included the most prominent U.S. mutual funds, banks, insurance companies, and pension funds. The company was largely "a creation of outside investment capital" unlike some other publishing companies that had a central, founding family who controlled most of the shares and who lived in the local communities where they publish.[83]

Among Capital Cities' major institutional investors were the Capital Group, Inc., Morgan Co., and the Prudential Co. Capital Group, Inc. has also had other holdings in Knight-Ridder, MCA, *Time,* and Times-Mirror. Morgan held top-20 investment stakes in Gannett, Metromedia, RCA, Time-Life, Times-Mirror, and the *Washington Post.* Prudential controlled holdings in CBS, Knight-Ridder, MCA, Metromedia, and RCA. The Capital Group and Prudential, in particular, held major interests in ABC before Capital Cities purchased it:

> Thus as the linkages among the various companies that constitute Capital Cities' top twenty owners are traced out, the ties become so complex, dense, and overlapping as to make it virtually impossible to describe one owner in isolation from the entire system of [U.S. media] ownership.[84]

In its tangle of ownership links to other major U.S. media corporations, Capital Cities especially reflects the kind of modern corporate media clout that Ben Bagdikian describes in *The Media Monopoly*.[85]

Who's the Boss?

The most controversial element in the history of Capital Cities—and perhaps the most politically explosive—has been its repeated defeat of union requests for higher wages and improvements at its varied media subsidiaries. These conflicts have been handled with a minimum of negative publicity, with one exception.

After successful rejection of union demands at its Michigan, Kansas City, and Fort Worth newspapers, Capital Cities bought the failing *Wilkes-Barre Times Leader* in 1978. Despite the formidable union rank-and-file support at the *Times Leader*, Capital Cities was from the beginning, convinced of its substantial profit potential. Murphy and Burke decided that all of the *Times Leader* unions would have to bow to their requests for more flexible work rules, higher standards of employee productivity, and more "objective" journalistic practices.

Thomas J. Keil describes the company's conduct during this labor dispute in his excellent book, *On Strike! Capital Cities and the Wilkes-Barre Newspaper Unions*. Largely overlooked in New York, the U.S. major-media capital, Keil's book is the first scholarly work to document Capital Cities' aggressive labor policies against its union employees.

In the company's view, the *Times Leader* had to "control costs, increase productivity, improve the quality of the paper, and expand its market" in order to raise profit levels.[86] To improve worker productivity, Capital Cities applied various types of internal and external pressure to motivate the *Times Leader* workers.

Union members at the paper, however, saw things quite differently. They charged that Capital Cities was trying to use its new editorial power to change the northeastern Pennsylvania region, politically as well as economically. The union charged that by moving the editorial policy and news agenda in a more conservative direction, management was attempting to lower the level of wages and working conditions throughout the heavily unionized region.[87] After decades of dealing with oppressive coal mining companies, many Wilkes-Barre residents could easily draw parallels between Capital Cities employment practices and those of the local coal mines that generally exploited the area's workers.

Nevertheless, Capital Cities did eventually improve the quality of the *Times Leader,* but failed to settle its union problems in a way that enhanced its public image:

> A local Capital Cities official, reflecting on the situation, stated that the company should have come into Wilkes-Barre and shown itself to be a good citizen, signed contracts with the unions, made whatever changes it could in the paper's format and the like, and, then, when the contracts expired, taken an aggressive stand.[88]

Instead, the company used warlike tactics against the union rank-and-file to force them to accept management demands at the bargaining table.

During the contract negotiations, Capital Cities installed surveillance cameras, hired guards, and built a 12-foot high fence around the *Times Leader* building. It also hired Wackenhut's Security—one of the largest private investigative firms in the U.S.—to coordinate security and intelligence operations against the union. Many Wackenhut top executives had been with the FBI, CIA, and other intelligence-gathering organizations. Wackenhut has had extensive contacts with military juntas and governments throughout the world—in Argentina, Ecuador, the Dominican Republic, Guatemala, Colombia, Canada, Bermuda, Italy, South Korea, and Saudi Arabia, among others. It also serves corporate clients and the U.S. government.[89]

William Casey was a key participant in the *Times Leader* labor dispute. While serving as Capital Cities' corporate counsel and a member of its board, he also served as the Wackenhut's corporate counsel during the Capital Cities purchase of the *Times Leader.*[90]

In the months leading up to the *Times Leader* strike, Wackenhut employed mostly black guards to oversee the nearly all-white union rank-and-file—a favorite practice that U.S. coal companies had often used to break strikes. These guards served to intensify racial tensions and to exacerbate labor-management conflict. The *Times Leader* employees viewed the security procedures as an act of intimidation by Capital Cities during contract negotiations; but the managers believed that they were operating in defense of their assets and stockholders, since union members had threatened violence and vandalism against the company in order to win the strike.[91]

The Capital Cities management team was said to be appalled by the power that the union members had at the *Times Leader*. The managers demanded workplace changes that would allow them to hire part-time workers and introduce a merit system. By setting up management as the sole workplace decisionmaker, Capital Cities intended to boost productivity, and also to make the employees grateful to the company, rather than to the unions. It also insisted on changes to enhance the journalistic ethics of the paper, charging that several conflict-of-interest cases involved *Times Leader* reporters and a number of companies in the community. These outside relationships also interfered with the power of Capital Cities to become the sole economic support of its employees, according to author Thomas Keil.[92]

After labor negotiations broke down, management decertified the union, and hired replacement workers. The company then put into effect the "war plans" that Wackenhut had designed to keep the *Times Leader* publishing. It was playing to win in an economic system that is antagonistic to workers' demands for a greater say in workplace decisionmaking.

As soon as the strike went into effect, the unions retaliated. The *Times Leader's* "windows were broken, buildings were defaced, a considerable number of company vehicles were destroyed," and Wackenhut's guards were brutalized by militant union members.[93]

However, the unions enjoyed widespread support among the local citizenry, especially after Capital Cities threatened to permanently lock out striking union members who would not cross the picket line. The union rank-and-file had significant political support as well and that seriously undercut Capital Cities' ability to enlist the local police force to intercede on management's behalf. Pennsylvania politicians refused Capital Cities' repeated requests to deploy the state police or national guard to quell the violence or force the unions back to the bargaining table.

Finally, after state and local authorities had continually refused to break the strike, Capital Cities printed a story in the *Times-Leader* about a pending FBI probe of the Wilkes-Barre police department for its failure to protect the civil rights of Wackenhut's guards and *Times-Leader* replacement workers. The FBI reportedly looked into the matter and sent agents to Wilkes-Barre to investigate Wackenhut's and Capital Cities' charges. Ultimately, however, "the FBI took no formal action against the police department or any of the unions."[94] Nonetheless, when the federal investigation began, many in Wilkes-Barre became convinced—whether accurate or not—that Capital Cities was "the corporate evil incarnate, a practitioner of 'the worst form of corporate exploitation imaginable.'"[95]

The unions decided on economic retaliation. Realizing that monopoly was the key to successful newspaper publishing in many cities, they directly challenged Capital Cities' position as the only major daily newspaper in the Wilkes-Barre market by beginning to publish their own daily, *The Citizen's Voice*, which is still being published.

Thus the Wilkes-Barre newspaper unions taught Capital Cities valuable lessons, which it applied when it acquired new media properties in subsequent years, particularly ABC. Instead of forcing its unions to strike, Capital Cities preferred to diminish their effectiveness with a variety of techniques recommended by "union busting" consultants. The most effective technique that Capital Cities and other companies learned was the use of careful surveillance and the removal of militant union members before labor troubles reach a crisis stage. As the number of employees within Capital Cities has decreased, so have its labor problems. Nonetheless, its executives at the *Times-Leader* later disclosed to Keil that "bringing Wackenhut into Wilkes-Barre was 'a public relations disaster.'"[96]

In the early 1990s, Wackenhut was again in the news when reports circulated that it had conspired with the Reagan Justice Department to sell case-management software allegedly stolen from the Inslaw Corporation. Inslaw's software, *PROMIS*, was designed to permit cooperation by U.S. intelligence with security agencies all over the world. Harvesting profits from this secret deal involved laundering monies through the Bank of Credit and Commerce International (BCCI)—apparently a regular CIA practice during William Casey's reign as director of intelligence. Wackenhut was mentioned in one newspaper report as being a "[private] security firm, with alleged intelligence links" that had conducted arms research for Casey's CIA with the Cabazon Indians in Indio, California.[97]

Later the CBS news magazine "60 Minutes" reported Wackenhut's illegal study of long-distance telephone records and its threats against a U.S. congressman who threatened to investigate charges of corporate misconduct on the Alaskan pipeline in 1992. Wackenhut investigators defended their actions by saying, "Our role is as finders of fact; and basically, we're soldiers."[98]

The *Times Leader* labor dispute had profound implications for labor throughout the United States. Capital Cities' aggressive stance against the Wilkes-Barre newspaper unions in 1978 was closely imitated following the Reagan administration's decision in 1981 to fire striking air-traffic controllers and substitute permanent replacement workers.

It should not be surprising that by the time the anti-labor Reagan White House had induced the networks to adopt more conservative on-air reporting and entertainment practices in return for protection from corporate takeover artists, Capital Cities was poised to lead the charge to achieve greater private control over what were formerly considered the publicly owned airwaves.

Capital Cities was, indeed, made up of "all the president's men."

Chapter Four

Capital Coup—The Takeover of ABC

The FCC ownership limits, originally enacted to prevent a U.S. media monopoly by a few wealthy corporations, had interfered with Capital Cities' desire for a "free market" of broadcasting since 1970. Yet, the same ownership rules that prevented Capital Cities from expanding its station line-up also helped Capital Cities (and its privileged competitors) to earn high profits in most U.S. media markets, due to the scarcity of available commercial broadcast frequencies and the high entry cost for would-be station operators. In Capital Cities' case, profit margins at its owned TV stations hit 57 percent in 1982—about one third higher than the industry average at the time. (As of 1990, Capital Cities/ABC's owned TV stations continued to earn 50 plus percent margins.)[1]

Unable to buy additional broadcast properties, the company instead chose to build the firm by buying up publishing and cable television systems. At the same time, through their strong bipartisan political ties, Capital Cities began to lobby behind-the-scenes for a change in broadcast ownership rules in the company's favor.

Capital Cities, through its close ties to the Nixon White House, was able to place one of its former vice-presidents, James Quello, on the FCC in 1973. Quello became a vigorous supporter of U.S. broadcasters and their fight to massively deregulate the industry to allow for greater profit-making. Capital Cities executives donated $120,000 to Richard Nixon's 1972 presidential re-election effort and Quello (a registered democrat) himself contributed $1,100.[2] Although citizen groups vigorously opposed the appointment during his first round of Senate confirmation hearings because of his close ties to the broadcasting industry and his alleged contempt for increased women's and minority representation at WJR in Detroit, Quello was confirmed as commissioner in 1974. (Later that year, Nixon was forced to resign as president to avoid impeachment for his Watergate crimes, some of which were financed with legal and illegal political contributions to Nixon's 1972 campaign. In return, supporters were often promised political favors and federal appointments by Nixon's staffers.) In 1980, when Quello's first term expired, it was rumored that the Carter administration would not appoint him to a second one, since Carter wanted to appoint a minority candidate instead. *Broadcasting* magazine later reported that Quello had "some support" in the White House and was allowed to stay on the FCC.

When Ronald Reagan mounted his presidential campaign in 1980, Quello became a loyal Reagan supporter. In return, Quello was reappointed to the FCC by the Reagan administration in 1981, and in 1984 was renominated for another seven-year term. He continued to lead support for Capital Cities' lobbying efforts to expand the FCC broadcast ownership limits so it could purchase a major U.S. network.[3]

ABC Becomes a "Dinosaur"

Although ABC had reached the federal limit on television station ownership in 1948, it did not begin to diversify into book and record publishing until after its unsuccessful 1968 merger attempt with ITT. ABC eventually acquired publishing companies that produced upwards of 100 books and magazines a month (*Modern Photography, High Fidelity, Stereo Quarterly*, and *LA Magazine* among them), as well as some 25 record titles a year. All this earned ABC up to $30 million in 1984.[4]

The network also acquired Word, Inc., one of the nation's largest religious book and music publishers, and produced some critically acclaimed and moderately profitable feature films, such as *The Flamingo Kid, Silkwood*, and *Prizzi's Honor*. In addition, it operated theme parks, such as "Weeki Wachee Springs" and "Silver Springs" in Florida, "ABC Marine World" in California, and co-financed with the Schubert organization the Broadway plays *Dreamgirls, Cats*, and *Amadeus. (Cats* alone earned ABC and its partners more than $100 million in the United States.)[5]

The network owned prime real estate in New York, California, and other parts of the country. Although its ABC Entertainment Center in Los Angeles later turned out to be a major financial failure, most of ABC's real estate interests continued to bring in vital cash flow when other diversification efforts failed. The financial failures in pay-per-view and cable broadcasting, such as the ill-fated "Telefirst" premium movie delivery service and the "Satellite News Channel" (later sold to Ted Turner's

Cable News Network), lost more than $110 million between 1982 and 1984.[6]

Despite ABC's significant losses trying to diversify its corporate profit-making, it was regularly protected by the FCC-approved three-network oligopoly until Ronald Reagan took office in 1981. With a limited number of outlets for national advertising available, ABC (along with CBS and NBC) was able to take advantage of the virtually 100 percent rise in national television advertising expenditures that occurred between 1975 and 1979. The network's corporate profits rose from $29 million to $83 million (before taxes) during this four-year period. In 1979, ABC earned a gross income of $1.3 billion, and pre-tax profits of $186 million. It was the highest revenue year in the history of the company.[7]

Although ABC was the first U.S. network to break the $1 billion mark in revenues, its ratio of profits to revenues was nonetheless unacceptable to the network's major investor groups and creditors. The losses that ABC suffered in its various corporate subsidiaries continued to undermine Wall Street's confidence in its top management. With an increasing federal deficit and a widening trade imbalance, "free-market" economists pushed for higher corporate profits to bolster the U.S. competitive position in global markets. As a result of the high-profit potential of U.S. information and cultural products around the world, the networks became a prime target for Wall Street speculators, even though there had never been a successful takeover in U.S. broadcasting history.[8] At the same time, the networks came under heavy attack from those who believed that the media had become too influential in U.S. political affairs. Through the 1970s and 1980s, both conservative and liberal business elites moved forward with major broadcast regulatory and deregulatory efforts in an attempt to reduce the power of the networks. The Trilateral Commission's 1975 warning about a "crisis of democracy" seemed to guide the Carter administration's attempts to bring the networks more in line with U.S. international policy moves. (The administration drew heavily on the Commission's members, appointing no fewer than 25 of them to top posts.)[9]

The Carter administration barred ABC, CBS, and NBC from owning their own primetime entertainment programs until 1990—in effect, continuing the Nixon FCC's adoption of the prime time access rule in 1970. Had the Carter Administration not limited network program ownership through the financial-syndication rule-making of 1978, a takeover of any of the networks by a smaller company like Capital Cities during the 1980s would have been quite unlikely; for billions of dollars in profits (and the almost certain rise in value of U.S. network stocks) would accrue from the U.S. networks' ownership and control of worldwide production and distribution of programming. Beginning in 1981, the Reagan administration continued to apply political-economic pressure on the U.S. networks through its repeated attempts to privatize the U.S. airwaves.

The launching of new cable satellite-delivered networks—such as CNN, WTBS, and HBO—added to the networks' uncertain financial future at the end of the 1970s. Despite new labor-saving digital electronic advances that allowed television production to be done faster and more cheaply by these new competitors, the networks continued to depend on the FCC's rules that essentially protected the audience delivery capability of the three network oligopoly. ABC, CBS, and NBC adopted an attitude of indifference toward the new sources of competition that in time would threaten their audience reach into nearly every U.S. household, such as independent local stations, videocassette recorders, and satellite-delivered and cable television. Since the U.S. broadcasting policy also gave the U.S. networks the power to dominate the commercial market for national television advertising, the U.S. networks were almost guaranteed regular increases in revenues and profits.[10]

Unfit to Lead?

In the summer of 1979, ABC became mired in other problems that reflected poorly on its top management team. That year, the network lost much of its investor support after news broke of a major scandal involving its largest primetime Hollywood program supplier, Spelling-Goldberg Productions. Huntington Williams, in his revealing 1989 exposé on the Capital Cities/ABC merger, *Beyond Control: ABC and the Fate of the Networks*, describes the affair in detail.

Following investigations by the Securities and Exchange Commission and the Los Angeles District Attorney's office, ABC president Elton Rule and top officials of Spelling-Goldberg reportedly faced felony charges of grand theft and embezzlement for allegedly conspiring to defraud co-creators Robert Wagner and Natalie Wood of their contractually guaranteed profits from the ABC series, "Charlie's Angels."[11] Even though the SEC and the Los Angeles D.A.'s office later decided not to bring the case before a grand jury because they lacked sufficient evidence to prove the allegations, rumors of a possible criminal conspiracy continued to surround ABC and Spelling-Goldberg in Hollywood, Washington, and on Wall Street. An internal 1979 ABC investigation undertaken by an independent counsel also found that ABC had been innocent of any wrong-doing but reportedly criticized Rule and Spelling's mutual, overlapping business interests.[12]

To limit corporate damage, Goldenson and the ABC board of directors quietly barred Rule from ever participating in the network's programming again. The female attorney from ABC who had first discovered the network's role in the scandal was fired. Later, she reached a $975,000 out-of-court settlement with ABC.[13]

As a result of the scandal, many of Rule's former programming responsibilities were handed over to Frederick Pierce, ABC's head of research in 1979, even though he lacked Ivy League credentials and sufficient knowledge of Wall Street. After his promotion, Pierce met with the insurance companies, pension and trust fund leaders, and professional money-managers who controlled the majority of the company's stock, and naively cited ABC's need to boost revenues instead of profits. His business philosophy, though in tune with that of Goldenson and the rest of network leadership at the time, was questioned by some Wall Street analysts. Pierce did not address ABC's need to slash costs, to reverse ABC's declining profit margins and stock value.[14]

With ABC's patriarch Leonard Goldenson nearing 80 years of age, the prospect of having Fred Pierce named the future CEO of ABC began to unsettle several of ABC's largest institutional investors and creditors—all of who "controlled more than 80 percent of the company's stock."[15]

The End Is Near

Following Ronald Reagan's presidential victory in November 1980, profit margins—not revenues—became the only measure by which Wall Street judged the managerial competency of corporate executives. In ABC's case, large revenue streams and low profit margins were viewed on Wall Street and in the Reagan administration as an indication that its managers were not prepared to compete in a globally, market-driven U.S. broadcasting industry. Talk began to circulate that ABC was vulnerable to takeover.

In 1981, Leonard Goldenson was warned by outside management consultants that ABC might be acquired by a more capital rich corporate conglomerate in the next few years. He soon retained Joseph Flom, one of a handful of Wall Street attorneys regarded as an expert in corporate takeovers.[17] Later that year, Goldenson resisted another takeover attempt from tennis partner and fellow synagogue member Laurence Tisch.[18] Tisch had purchased a 6.5 percent stake in ABC (about 1.8 million shares), but later Goldenson was able to persuade Tisch not to take over ABC.[19]

In 1981, a $1 million internal ABC management report found that the ratings-to-profit ratio was poor and "indirectly called into question Pierce's management skills." In 1982, Goldenson scolded Hollywood producers about the spiraling rise in television production costs, and warned his audience of West Coast "movers and shakers" that bankers, investors, and the public would not support them in the future.[20]

Also that year, Reagan's FCC chairman, Mark Fowler, began making frequent public comments that most, if not all, of the New Deal-inspired FCC broadcast rules and regulations—originally passed in 1934 to protect the public from self-serving, monopolistic media corporations—violated broadcasters' first amendment rights.[21] Seizing upon the deregulatory actions begun by the Nixon administration and continued by the Ford and Carter administrations, the FCC wanted to facilitate the working of a so-called free broadcasting market. This would allow those awarded broadcast licenses freedom from government interference. They could pursue maximum profits without regard for the political, economic, or social consequences of such a profits-at-any-expense philosophy. Fowler and James Quello became the broadcast industry's strongest FCC allies in the Republican-led movement to free broadcasters from the onerous public-interest provisions of the 1934 Communications Act.

Not surprisingly, Capital Cities Communications, with its strong loyalty to the Republican free-market business philosophy, was in an advantageous position to capitalize on the Reagan plan to privatize the airwaves. Capital Cities, by then the largest and most powerful owner in ABC's 200-plus affiliated television station group, had already learned that the network was vulnerable to a corporate takeover.

By 1983, less than 2 percent of ABC's stock was controlled by its top management. With most of its investments in the form of stock, and its future in the hands of investors, creditors, and banks, a severe 1982 recession had forced ABC into a frenzied round of cost-cutting. It moved to become more efficient and prevent an unwanted corporate takeover.[22]

A Not-So-Free Market

Capital Cities was aided in its bid to move up in U.S. media ownership when Reagan interfered in the FCC's efforts to repeal the 1978 financial-syndication rules. If Fowler had been able to eliminate the "fin-syn" rules in 1983 and thus help boost the networks' profit-making prospects, it is highly probable that they would have been able to purchase one or more of the major Hollywood studios by 1986. By reaping the added cash flow benefits from the U.S. and foreign television syndication profits of a major Hollywood studio, the networks would have gained tremendous economic power to buy up other communication companies.

According to Leonard Goldenson, Reagan stepped in on MCA's (Music Corporation of America) behalf to keep Fowler from eliminating those rules. MCA had been Reagan's Hollywood acting agent and long-time political benefactor. He encountered widespread resistance from Mark Fowler and other FCC commissioners, who were firmly committed to helping the broadcast industry boost profits in every possible manner, even by a massive change of the existing rules. When Reagan's own FCC chair refused to cooperate in helping MCA, the Reagan White House moved to muster congressional support for MCA and the other "endangered" Hollywood studios.[23]

In 1962, Justice Department prosecutors alleged that MCA had helped Reagan to become the corporate spokesperson for General Electric as his reward for having sold out the Screen Actors Guild in 1952 by signing the monopolistic MCA-SAG waiver. Reagan was "seriously considered" as a co-conspirator in the Kennedy Justice Department's civil suit against MCA for its conspiracy to restrain trade in motion picture and network television production. However, the case was dropped when MCA later agreed to give up its talent agency business.[24]

By acting to protect Hollywood's interests, and indirectly the interests of Capital Cities, Reagan greatly fueled takeover speculation about the broadcast networks. Facing new competition from independent stations and cable, the three big networks—ABC, CBS, and NBC—could no longer dominate television viewing as they once did; nor could they control the supply of national network-advertising time to sponsors. By barring the networks from owning Hollywood studios, Reagan helped to ensure their fall by cutting off a potential gold mine of program syndication profits.

Indeed, a few months after Reagan's "fin-syn" intervention with the FCC, Leonard Goldenson was invited to lunch by the well-known New York investment banker, Felix Rohatyn of Lazard Freres. Rohatyn reportedly told Goldenson that Lew Wasserman, the CEO of MCA, wanted to buy ABC. Although the networks were at the time barred by the "fin-syn" rules from participating in the ownership of a movie studio, Goldenson stated later that:

> Since [Wasserman] got his pal Ronald Reagan to keep the Financial-Syndication Rules in effect, then he could also get him to scrap the rules when it served Wasserman's interests.[25]

Wasserman, of course, was Reagan's former Hollywood agent, the same man who convinced him to sign the SAG-MCA waiver in 1952.

The New Right

ABC became more vulnerable to a takeover when Reagan's New Right coalition began to attack what it claimed was the dangerous and irresponsible "liberalism" of the three big networks. Led by Casey and others in the administration, the New Right public relations offensive against the networks in 1983 seemed to be a reconfigured model of the earlier Nixon administration attacks on the media. This offensive dates back to Nixon vice-president Spiro T. Agnew's November 1969 primetime television address, in which he questioned the patriotism and so-called liberal bias of the networks. (In 1973, Agnew pleaded *nolo contendre* to felony charges of income tax evasion, bribery, and extortion arising from his service as the governor of Maryland prior to becoming Nixon's running mate in 1968. He was later forced to resign as vice-president.)

The New Right's 1983 attacks came from Right-wing groups such as Accuracy in Media, the John Birch Society, the Young Americans for Freedom, the Heritage Foundation, and other conservative-backed Washington think tanks. They literally picked up where the Nixon-Agnew administration and Senator Joseph McCarthy had left off in earlier decades resuming the witch-hunts that targeted U.S. liberals and radicals.

Considering the historic conservatism of the network leaders and the center-to-right framing of their programming over the years, the New Right's claims about the danger of overly liberal networks amounted to little more than disinformation. When the New Right went after ABC, probably the most politically conservative of all the networks for 40 years, this became especially apparent.

In November 1983, when ABC was about to broadcast, "The Day After," a fictional made-for-TV movie about the probable effects of nuclear war on a midwestern city, New Right pressure groups, with direct support from the Reagan White House, mounted a public relations offensive against "The Day After". This was the sort of programming that many Reagan conservatives considered "as a rallying point for opponents of Administration nuclear arms policies." They argued that "The Day After" was just one more example of the networks' "liberal bias."[26]

Conservative pressure became so strong that ABC even considered not broadcasting the program until one of its top Hollywood entertainment chiefs, Brandon Stoddard, threatened to resign in protest. In addition to being critically acclaimed, "The Day After" later drew more than 100 million viewers, thanks, in large part, to the wide publicity that conservative groups were able to generate before the film was broadcast.

Immediately after the broadcast, ABC aired a special version of its news discussion program "Viewpoint" (hosted at the time by ABC "Nightline" host Ted Koppel). The aim was to avoid an FCC fairness doctrine complaint by conservative groups. In this program, Reagan advisors, such as George Shultz and Henry Kissinger, were invited to promote the political view that the country could end the nuclear arms race against the Soviet Union if Pentagon expenditures were kept high enough. A few months later, at ABC's annual stockholders' meeting, Goldenson again bowed to the Reagan-instigated New Right opposition and announced that ABC would develop and broadcast the made-for-TV mini-series, "Amerika," to balance the so-called liberal perspective of "The Day After."[27] "Amerika," broadcast by ABC in 1987, was the fictional account of a Soviet takeover of the U.S. It glorified war and touted U.S. superiority over the Soviet Union.

Conservative forces continued to assault the other networks as well. In December 1984, three men in North Carolina, with the avid support of New Right Senator Jesse Helms (R-N.C.), filed papers with the Securities and Exchange Commission to establish "Fairness in Media." This was an effort to organize public opposition to CBS's "liberal" bias through the purchase and control of stock. Helms later sent letters on behalf of CBS to conservative voters throughout the country urging them to buy CBS stock in an effort to be "Dan Rather's boss." "Fairness in Media" followed a path similar to the one organized in 1965 by the ultra-conservative billionaire H. L. Hunt. He had been involved in an unsuccessful plan to buy up CBS stock in order to force the network to adopt a more conservative news policy.[28]

Yet, as later explained by Peter Boyer, author of *Who Killed CBS? The Undoing of America's Number One News Network,* CBS was far from a "liberal" network:

> The idea of CBS News as an organ of the left was a caricature
> of the grossest sort.... CBS News was about as left-wing as
> the Cedar Falls chapter of the American Legion.[29]

Helms's group was eventually defeated by CBS officials through a combination of legal maneuvers and public posturing.

As the New Right's pressure on liberals escalated in 1983, the Reagan FCC continued to deregulate the broadcasting industry, pushing it in an even more conservative direction. By removing market controls on broadcasters, the administration was ensuring that only the wealthy and influential would be represented in media decisionmaking. The FCC's decision to raise the station-ownership limits was directly emblematic of this.

After failing to repeal the "fin-syn" rules in 1983, Reagan FCC chairman Fowler announced in the spring of 1984 that he intended to repeal the "7-7-7" broadcasting ownership rules. The announcement triggered a trading frenzy in broadcast stocks on Wall Street, as investment banks prepared for a buying spree of broadcast properties and an even greater concentration of ownership within the industry. The "7-7-7" rules had, since the late 1940s, effectively limited most corporate mergers in U.S. broadcasting.

The FCC's repeal of the "7-7-7" ruling would mean that broadcast licenses could be traded like any other commodity. This change would offer the wealthiest corporations the chance to buy up as many licenses as they could afford. Initially, network leaders believed that the decision to expand "7-7-7" would provide their organizations with the most effective means to deflect takeover offers from more capitalized corporations. Not surprisingly, in May 1984, following Fowler's announcement, Goldenson asked his top aides for possible takeover scenarios involving ABC and other suitable corporate partners. Capital Cities reportedly was one of the corporations that Goldenson wanted information on.[30]

If Reagan had lost his 1984 presidential re-election campaign, Fowler's decision to raise the "7-7-7" limits may not have been approved by an incoming Democratic administration in the White House.[31] Consequently, ABC and most of the U.S. broadcast industry came to view a 1984 Reagan re-election victory as central to their continued dominance in U.S. broadcasting.

But ABC faced other problems. In June 1984, Cicely Coleman, a former top-level corporate aide, filed sexual harassment charges against James Abernathy, ABC's vice-president in charge of Wall Street relations. Coleman complained to the company's personnel officer that Abernathy had forced her to trade sexual favors for advancement into its corporate hierarchy. When ABC's corporate counsel learned of Coleman's harassment allegations, despite its corporate policy promising confidentiality and protection for any employee who came forward with such complaints, he apparently organized an executive campaign to force Coleman to quit her job. Coleman hired Mark Lane, a Washington attorney, who had written one of the first books to criticize the Warren Commission's investigation of the 1963 assassination of John F. Kennedy, *Rush to Judgement*. Lane had long pointed to the complicity of the broadcast networks in supporting U.S. power interests, domestically and internationally. After ABC fired Coleman for allegedly taking an "unauthorized business trip," Lane sued the network on her behalf in federal court for damages eventually totaling $15 million after finding that a pattern of sexual harassment of women existed at ABC.[32] Coleman eventually settled the case out of court with ABC, but her suit seemed to change ABC's reputation further.

A few months after Coleman filed suit against ABC, James Abernathy, the man Cicely Coleman accused of sexual harassment, was also accused by his secretary of plotting to topple ABC with the portfolio manager of its largest institutional investor, Boston-based State Street Research and Management. Within a matter of days, Abernathy was summoned back to New York from a family vacation and fired.[33] Abernathy's sudden termination sent additional signals to Wall Street that ABC's top leaders were in apparent revolt against Goldenson and Pierce, and might be receptive to a corporate *coup d'etat* by outside parties if the price was right.

Also contributing to the loss of confidence in ABC on Wall Street and in Washington during 1984-85 were reports of company-wide employee substance abuse. "FBI agents and private investigators" reportedly checked ABC's inter-office mail pouches for alleged drug shipments sent between New York and Los Angeles offices by ABC employees. There were also reports that catering employees at 1330 Avenue of the Americas, the site of the network's New York corporate offices, were distributing cocaine during morning and afternoon coffee breaks. ABC's vice-president of personnel, the vice-president in charge of sports sales, and several other executives suspected of engaging in illegal drug use, on and off the job, later resigned or were disciplined.[34]

Wall Street Moves

In the August 13, 1984 issue of *Forbes*, one of the most widely read magazines in the U.S. financial and business community, an in-depth article recounted ABC's many financial problems. According to Fred Pierce, speaking in an interview for Leonard Goldenson's autobiography, the contents of the report were so detailed and accurate that some ABC officials began to suspect that a top-level "mole" was deliberately leaking damaging information to the press in an effort to undermine the company's ABC's top leadership.[35] The article openly questioned the future of ABC with Pierce as Goldenson's heir apparent.

A week later, the August 20 issue of *New York Magazine* reported that ABC's board of directors were rising up against Pierce. In his defense, Pierce said that the *Forbes* and *New York* magazine articles were instigated by someone "who had designs on the company."[36]

Around the time that the *Forbes* and *New York Magazine* articles appeared, First Boston Company, one of the most powerful investment banks in the United States, recommended purchase of ABC stock since it appeared, among institutional investors, to be an excellent takeover candidate. Announcing that ABC's assets were undervalued in relation to its stock price, the First Boston report drove up the price.[37]

ABC's negative press treatment was in sharp contrast to the treatment Capital Cities received the previous year. In 1983, two major articles on Capital Cities appeared in *Financial World* and *Business Week* that helped to reinforce conventional Wall Street wisdom that Capital Cities was the darling of investors and creditors. Both articles described the high profit margins enjoyed by Capital Cities' investors. The corporation seemed to be the most prepared to prosper in the so-called free-market broadcasting environment encouraged by the Reagan administration.[38]

By September 1984, anonymous reports had begun to appear in the *Wall Street Journal* that Capital Cities Communications was on the verge of organizing a takeover of ABC. Although both companies denied it at the time, it was later revealed that Warren Buffett, one of the most respected Wall Street investors and financial sages, was quietly buying up large chunks of ABC's stock through his holding company, Berkshire Hathaway. His purchases continued to fuel reports that Capital Cities was about to purchase ABC, especially since Warren Buffett was a large investor in Capital Cities and held a seat on its board of directors.[39]

Following the reports in the *Wall Street Journal*, other predatory corporations began circling ABC. All were unsuccessful, however. Goldenson first turned away the Bass brothers from Texas, who together owned 25 percent of the Disney Studios. Subsequently, Goldenson rejected "friendly" takeover offers from Gannett, Coca-Cola, Pepsico, and Gulf & Western (the corporate parent of Paramount Studios).

In December 1984, Goldenson was told by the top analysts on Wall Street that ABC would continue to be a takeover target, due to its undervalued assets, low stock price, and a pro-monopoly administration in the White House. ABC began to look for a suitable marriage partner who would be willing to pay a high price for ABC's outstanding shares. Ironically, all of this takeover talk about ABC came at a time when it had just exceeded the $2 billion revenue mark for the first time in its 40-year corporate history.[40]

Making Its Peace

By October 1984, the FCC had managed to work out compromises with the Democratic leadership in Congress to amend the "7-7-7" ownership rule. Instead of permitting each broadcast owner to acquire an unlimited number of stations, which was the Reagan administration's original intention, Democratic congressional pressure forced the FCC to limit broadcast owners to acquiring up to 12 television stations, and then only if the combined reach of such stations did not exceed 25 percent of the potential U.S. television audience. Similar rules were also instituted for radio properties.

Although these ownership changes were not scheduled to go into effect until February 1985, advance word of the FCC's compromise was allegedly "leaked" to Capital Cities by Commissioner James Quello. Shortly before Christmas 1984, armed with the knowledge that the FCC and Congress were close to reaching a compromise on the "7-7-7" rule, Murphy approached Goldenson with an offer to buy ABC.[41] Instead of accepting Murphy's first offer, Goldenson, like any experienced attorney, went searching for additional negotiating leverage. He says in his book that he went immediately to Frank Cary, a member of the network's board of directors and a former CEO of IBM, to investigate the possibility of an ABC-IBM merger. Apparently, IBM, not wanting to enter a bidding war with Capital Cities, stated it had no interest in acquiring the network as a subsidiary.[42] Even if Goldenson had been successful in gathering support from IBM, Murphy would have probably found out about it. Murphy was elected to the IBM board of directors in January 1987.

During this time, ABC faced strong political pressure to sell the company from neo-conservatives who continued to attack ABC and the other broadcast networks' "liberal" bias. In November 1984, just before Murphy approached Goldenson with his first offer to buy ABC, CIA Director Casey had asked the FCC to revoke all of ABC's TV and radio licenses in retaliation for an ABC News report that suggested the CIA had assassinated a U.S. citizen in Hawaii. Although Casey's charge seemed to be more of a threat, it was the first time in the history of the CIA that the agency had attacked the patriotism and news coverage of a U.S. network in such a way. (In Casey's defense, the ABC report was based on questionable evidence.) In February 1985, when the FCC failed to move against ABC for its news coverage of the CIA, Casey again asked the FCC to apply Fairness Doctrine penalties to ABC.[43]

Casey's attacks, whether serious or not, did seem to have had a stabilizing price on ABC's stock—just at the time when takeover speculation should have pushed the price higher. Casey's public actions to discredit ABC certainly did not enhance the public view of ABC's leadership. On February 7, 1985, when Murphy called Goldenson with his second offer to buy the network—one week after the FCC had announced the new federal broadcast ownership regulations—Goldenson accepted Capital Cities' offer and began negotiations with Murphy to arrange a "fair" price.[44]

Despite its stated intention to buy ABC or a similar network, Capital Cities did not have the necessary capital funds to purchase the network and then defend it from takeover by other well-financed corporate raiders. Capital Cities turned to Warren Buffett, who guaranteed $517 million from his Berkshire Hathaway holding company. In a top-secret deal, known only by a handful of ABC and Capital Cities executives before it was announced publicly, Buffett received 18 percent of the newly combined corporation, Capital Cities/ABC. In return for his investment (made up of pension funds, insurance company investments, and other assorted financial interests), he also received a seat on the new Capital Cities/ABC board of directors and agreed to surrender his stock voting rights to Murphy and Burke, (the future chairman and president of the new corporate entity) which was to be called Capital Cities/ABC, Incorporated. At the time, Buffett stated that he had implicit trust in Murphy and Burke, and that Capital Cities had "the best management team in corporate America."[45]

Initial reaction to the Capital Cities takeover of ABC was favorable. *Barron's*, for example, reported that Wall Street analysts were saying that the merger was great for the shareholders of both companies.[46] The business trade magazine *Financial World* described ABC's limited options at the time. Not content to see only ABC toppled, FCC chairman Fowler reportedly told Turner Broadcasting officials the day after the Capital Cities/ABC merger was announced, that the commission would expedite any takeover attempt of a major network—not only ABC, but CBS and NBC as well.[47]

But it was Warren Buffett's participation in the Capital Cities takeover of ABC that made the deal possible, since Capital Cities' revenues in 1984 were only a fourth of those of ABC. Buffett's role as a financial partner was described glowingly by all the leading financial and business trade journals of the day. Very little public questioning arose as to whether such a giant global media merger would encourage or discourage critical citizen review of power in society, however.

After much haggling, Murphy and Goldenson agreed that Capital Cities would pay ABC stockholders $118 per share cash for the purchase. ($121 per share with warrants that ABC shareholders could use to buy Capital Cities stock at $250 per share over the next two and a half years,

Capital Cities closed at $215 per share at the time of the merger announcement.) This put the total value of the deal at $3.5 billion—about 17 times higher than ABC's 1984 earnings. Capital Cities insisted on including an escape clause that would permit it to end the merger if ABC's 1985 profits fell by more than 25 percent from the previous year, or if the FCC refused to expand the limits of broadcast ownership in 1986, as promised. Capital Cities in turn agreed to a provision granting almost $32.5 million dollars more to induce about 100 ABC executives to release their restricted shares of company stock. Had Capital Cities not done this, it is conceivable that these executives could have mounted a credible challenge to the merger by exercising their veto power as stockholders over a sizable block of stock. While they probably could not have stopped a takeover, they could have made it costly for Capital Cities to buy them out at a higher price later on.[48]

Perhaps the most crucial part of the Capital Cities/ABC purchase, however, was resolving the issue of who would control the combined corporate entity. It had been reported that Murphy wanted to pay cash (instead of leveraging the ABC purchase with Capital Cities stock) so that Capital Cities would be able to resist a potential threat from corporate raiders, and to exert full management authority over ABC, which he and the rest of the Capital Cities leadership had perceived as "bloated, wasteful, and poorly run."

As the final details of the deal were worked out, First Boston Company reportedly charged ABC $6 million for its help in arranging the Capital Cities takeover and pronounced the merger "fair."[49]

The 900-Pound Gorilla

Buffett's publishing holdings gave the Capital Cities/ABC entity almost instant credibility on Wall Street and in Washington. It was Buffett's suggestion that he become Capital Cities' "nine-hundred pound gorilla," the one who would protect the new firm from an unwanted takeover by more capitalized conglomerates. Buffett's description of himself as "protector" was repeatedly cited in newspaper and magazine accounts of the behind-the-scenes negotiations that led to the merger.

Known for his aversion to hostile takeovers and his reluctance to invest in companies he did not have absolute faith in, Buffett became Capital Cities' knight on Wall Street. Based on his numerous financial connections with other media corporations and his multi-billionaire status by the time of the Capital Cities/ABC takeover, he was already one of the most influential media executives in the country, if not the world. By providing what amounted to protection from other predatory corporate raiders, Buffett emerged as the one of the most influential U.S. investors in the post-war era.

He had been involved in newspaper publishing from an early age—first as a paper boy, later as a writer and editor, and then as a major U.S. media investor. In December 1973, Buffett acquired a 13 percent stake in the *Washington Post* and was awarded a seat on its board of directors. He also became a close family friend and financial advisor to *Post* editor Katharine Graham. After the Capital Cities/ABC merger, in order to comply with FCC media cross-ownership restrictions, he resigned his seat on the *Washington Post* board, preferring to retain his seat on the new Capital Cities/ABC board.

At the time of the ABC merger with Capital Cities, Buffett also owned more than one million shares of Affiliated Publications, the publisher of the *Boston Globe*. In 1977, he had acquired 100 percent of the *Buffalo Evening News*. Before that, in 1969, he had purchased Omaha's Sun Papers group. Under his stewardship, the *Sun* received the coveted Pulitzer Prize for its exposé of Omaha's Boys Town orphanage. The rest of Buffett's holdings were owned through Berkshire Hathaway, his $2 billion conglomerate.[50]

In addition to his newspaper holdings, Buffett owned 36 percent of GEICO (insurance), 9 percent of the Ogilvy & Mather advertising agency, 15 percent of the Interpublic Group (advertising agencies), 4 percent of Time, Inc., 5 percent of Media General Financial Services, 8 percent of General Foods, .5 percent of Exxon, and 17 percent of Handy Harman Precious Metals. The Buffett personal fortune was estimated at $650 million in 1985, when each share of his Berkshire Hathaway stock sold for $1,800.[51] In 1993, Berkshire Hathaway stock held by major institutional investors reached an all time high of $17,500 per share, the most expensive stock available on the New York Stock Exchange.[52]

The son of a four-time Republican congressional representative and holder of an MBA from Columbia, Buffett first began investing in the stock market in 1956 (at age 25). He became famous for researching his own stock selections.[53]

He retains no public relations advisors and handles his own publicity by often publishing articles and commentaries in leading financial and mainstream-news publications under his own byline. Running his world-wide investment firm from a modest suite of offices in Omaha, Nebraska, Buffett's small staff of seven assistants has become legendary—and so has his ability to gain preferential treatment on Wall Street.

Because of his considerable financial connections and media hold-ings, Buffett is a leading member of the small group of billionaire investors who oversee the U.S. media monopoly. CBS CEO Laurence Tisch once called Buffett "the greatest investor of this generation." Before the Capital Cities/ABC merger, Buffett had invited Tisch, Murphy, and a select group of other leading business executives and investors on biennial business junkets to Aspen, Colorado, or to England to discuss possible future trends in U.S. media stocks and investments.[54]

A "Friendly" Merger?

The first indication that the rash of 1980s media mergers may not all have been in the public interest came in a speech made by former ABC chairman, Leonard Goldenson, on April 7, 1986. A little over three months after Capital Cities/ABC, Inc., had become a new U.S. corporation, Goldenson spoke before 1,000 business executives in New York and declared that the rush of Reagan-inspired corporate mergers had created "a bottomless ocean of debt" and had "mortgaged the future."[55] As the pro-industry *Broadcasting* magazine reported at the time, "It [was] pos-sibly the nearest any senior member of the Fifth Estate [had] come to openly criticizing the mergers and acquisition frenzy of communications companies." One week later, in the April 14 issue of *Television/Radio Age*, Goldenson wrote an op-ed column, most of which came from his New York speech. He again pointed out that the increased national debt arising from U.S. media mergers would eventually be paid with citizen tax dollars.[56]

Goldenson again qualified his remarks, saying that ABC had only merged with Capital Cities to avoid being bought out by "unfriendly" corporate raiders. But the use of the word *friendly* to describe the merger must be carefully monitored with regard to who is telling the story, how much the person may have personally profited from the takeover, and where he or she might fit into the new corporation's campaign to paint a positive picture of the arrangement.

Several new books and articles discuss the considerable pressure that was placed on Goldenson to sell ABC following the Reagan presidential victory in 1980. In his autobiography *Beating the Odds: The Untold Story behind the Rise of ABC*, for example, he devotes an entire chapter entitled "Sharks" to the many offers—both "friendly" and "unfriendly"—that ABC received from larger corporations once the Reagan administration had announced its intention to radically deregulate media channels in 1981.[57] Goldenson states that by October 1984 he felt personally betrayed:

> Several of Wall Street's deeper pockets were interested in taking control of ABC...The consensus was that the pressures on ABC would continue. The company was in play, and the stakes were very high.[58]

Since his influence on Wall Street had declined, Goldenson could not reasonably continue to defend ABC from an unwanted takeover, especially since the Reagan administration and Wall Street had already determined that the sale of the network would be in the "public" interest. The Washington and Wall Street "consensus" that ABC was poorly run only added to the pressure on Goldenson to sell the company.

Frederick Pierce, the former president of ABC, has since alleged that someone from the highest level of ABC management began leaking confidential, financial information to the New York financial press in August 1984—just before rumors of a Capital Cities' merger with ABC began to appear in the New York press. This allegation is interesting in that this was the first time, since the Capital Cities/ABC merger, that a former ABC official had publicly implied that there appeared to be a deliberate effort made to topple ABC in 1984-85. Since it was learned that Casey had not placed his nearly 34,000 shares of Capital Cities stock into a blind trust and had made millions on the 1985 ABC takeover, Pierce's allegation has only appeared "on the record" in Goldenson's 1991 autobiography. Goldenson chose not to publish through either Capital Cities' or ABC's publishing companies. This decision may indicate that he wanted to finally set the record straight—to make clear that the Capital Cities/ABC merger may not have been "friendly" as FCC officials, Congress, or U.S. citizens had been led to believe in 1985-1986.[59] (Pierce "resigned" from Capital Cities/ABC in January 1986—six days after the merger became official, and retained a seat on its board until 1989. Leonard Goldenson became a member of the board and was given the largely ceremonial post of chairing the Capital Cities/ABC executive committee, which he continues to hold in 1993.)

There are those, (certainly a small number) of course, who have suggested that the long-time government and private intelligence connections of Capital Cities' top executives may reveal added significance to the extraordinary takeover of ABC, a company four times larger than Capital Cities.

In 1987, *L.A. WEEKLY,* an alternative weekly newspaper, published a lengthy article by investigative reporter Andy Boehm that described Capital Cities' close ties to U.S. intelligence agencies, just as Casey's role in the Iran arms-for-hostage affair was beginning to be publicized. The *L.A. WEEKLY* article, entitled "The Seizing of the American Broadcasting Company," suggested that William Casey, as Reagan's CIA director, may have capitalized on his extensive OSS and CIA intelligence connections to drive down the price of ABC stock, thereby adding to the considerable pressure already placed on the network to accept a "friendly" merger offer from Capital Cities. More alarming, however, was Boehm's suggestion that the takeover might have been part of a wider Reagan-Bush-Casey effort to make the network less of a national forum for discourse that might be critical of U.S. government or corporate decisionmaking.[60]

Casey had much to gain politically from a Capital Cities takeover of ABC, in addition to the obvious windfall profits that he would realize from the Wall Street speculation represented by his 34,000 shares of Capital Cities stock. Indeed, there may have been several reasons why he might have wanted the deal to go through:

(1) "Intimidation of journalists" to not broadcast negative stories on the CIA.

(2) "Infiltration of ABC News" in order to supply "cover" for espionage purposes and to misdirect network investigative news-gathering away from certain agency-restricted news areas.

(3) "Personal and corporate gain" for Casey and others as the result of forced price reductions of network stocks (through agency connections) to "bargain rates" to guarantee a better price.[61]

(4) Protection for politically conservative U.S. media cartels that would seek to expand a global monopoly over information and cultural products, as well as U.S. dominance in geopolitical-economic affairs.

All of these scenarios seem plausible considering Casey's close, long-term ties to Capital Cities during its meteoric rise, as well as his 40-year history as a member of the elite U.S. intelligence community. Although his refusal to place his nearly 70,000 shares of Capital Cities stock into a blind trust while serving as CIA director was first reported in 1985 by New York's *Newsday*, very few other mainstream U.S. media organizations devoted sustained attention to Casey's possible use of CIA intelligence-research assets to personally profit on the Capital Cities coup against ABC.

None of the more ominous connections between Capital Cities, Resorts International, and the earlier Mary Carter Paint Company, have been talked about in a public forum before or after the merger of Capital Cities and ABC was first announced in 1985.

Indeed, the numerous ties of Capital Cities' early founders to U.S. intelligence agencies remain troubling, nevertheless, and should have raised numerous questions about concentrated media ownership during the Capital Cities/ABC merger hearings before the FCC in 1985 or during the subsequent congressional hearings in 1987 and 1989 on the growing U.S. media monopoly. Such links between U.S. broadcasters and intelligence, espionage, and propaganda agencies, for example, would be especially crucial to the success of propaganda campaigns waged against U.S. citizens[62] "to support" potentially unpopular government or corporate decisions, such as U.S. military intervention abroad or the creation of more powerful trusts in the corporate sector.

While all of this may seem outrageous to some, it is entirely within the realm of possibility today, given the evidence that has come to light following the Watergate and Iran-Contra scandals, as well as during the Senate Hearings on Intelligence in 1975-1976 and the House hearings in 1978 on the assassination of John F. Kennedy. The seizure of key nodes of the U.S. media system to support potentially unpopular government/corporate/military decisionmaking by an unaccountable "shadow government" would be quite necessary. To maintain the "necessary illusion of democracy" and the "manufacture of consent," which authors Edward S. Herman and Noam Chomsky have described, "thought control" in democratic societies becomes absolutely essential.[63]

During the Iran-Contra hearings, the Reagan administration made private intelligence-gathering and so-called covert "black bag" operations a viable option in order to hide illegal government decisionmaking from congressional and citizen scrutiny. Many agents at the CIA have apparently objected to using private sector companies to conduct agency business covertly. The operations of "private spooks" and covert political action became a central issue in the Iran-Contra affair, as it had in the Watergate scandal during the Nixon administration.[64]

Capital Cities seemed an excellent candidate to carry out Casey's wish that U.S. media companies provide propaganda or operational cover for domestic/foreign agency covert actions.[65] Besides Casey's large ownership stake, all of Capital Cities' leaders had shown their willingness to support political figures like Richard Nixon, Allen Dulles, Spiro Agnew, Ronald Reagan, and numerous others who, throughout their careers, showed their disdain for democracy by subverting the U.S. Constitution while serving in public office. These influential power brokers provided Capital Cities with every possible regulatory waiver and corporate tax-break possible, enabling it to become the most favored broadcaster in the United States by 1985 when it took over ABC.

Enormous pressure was placed on ABC to sell out to Capital Cities so as to stop an unwanted takeover from more capitalized and powerful transnational corporations. When a corporation is forced to merge with another to avoid a buyout by yet another one, the use of the word *friendly* to describe what amounts to paying for protection seems misleading. Considering the statements from former ABC officials, it seems highly doubtful that Goldenson would have sold ABC to Capital Cities willingly, a company whose officials had contempt for his preference of running ABC like a Hollywood studio instead of a Wall Street investment bank, had ABC been able to muster a credible challenge to Capital Cities' $3.5 billion offer.

In merging with Capital Cities, Goldenson, however, was also acting out of self-interest, since few companies of Capital Cities' size would have been willing to pay ABC 's stockholders $118 per share in cash at a time when the stock price was mired in the $60 range. Had he not accepted Murphy's offer (they were said to be good friends), it is more than likely that ABC would have been the target of a hostile corporate raider who could have paid far less for ABC simply by slowly acquiring its shares on the open market.[66]

In retrospect, the Capital Cities takeover of ABC appears to be more than simply a friendly merger. One of the most significant media developments in U.S. history, the Capital Cities/ABC merger has never been scrutinized by the vast majority of citizens in the United States—mainly because the mainstream media simply accepted it (and other U.S. media mergers) as a sign of the times, and, quite inevitable.

While no laws were broken in the Capital Cities/ABC takeover, the widespread lack of citizen knowledge about the history of the two companies, and of the possibility their past ties to either U.S. intelligence or organized crime figures is yet another sign that the U.S. media system has rarely, if ever, served democracy.

Even though we seldom admit it, our perception of the world is largely shaped and guided by the media. It is also true that those who have access to, or control of, those media through personal or corporate wealth have considerably more power than those who do not. Our constitutional right to listen to others and to be heard by enough of our neighbors to make a difference is, in large measure, subject to the desires of those who control the U.S. media. If we do not know who owns Capital Cities/ABC or the other networks, or how those companies were created, how can we possibly trust that they will provide us with information and cultural products that protect democracy when it may not be in their corporate profit interests to do so?

Media ownership is power. Those who lack access to the media cannot become full partners with those who do—not now, not ever.

In Chapter Five, I will show how Capital Cities/ABC continues today to concentrate its holdings within its U.S.-based media monopoly, and how it still supports political candidates who in turn support its dominance of worldwide production and distribution of U.S. news, information, and entertainment.

Chapter Five

Capital Cities/ABC, Inc.: Leading the U.S. Media Cartel

By 1993, Capital Cities/ABC had become the unofficial "spokes-corporation" for the U.S. media cartel. Along with other U.S.-owned communications superpowers such as CBS, NBC, and Time-Warner, Capital Cities continued to fortify its position within the global media market. Despite regular reports of negative corporate earnings and a sour U.S. economy, the company's stock traded in the $640 per share range, one of the highest levels at which it had ever traded.[1]

Because of its favored status on Wall Street and in Washington, Capital Cities/ABC, Inc. will likely continue to play a major role, if not a leading one, in establishing the rules by which global media production and distribution will be governed in the years to come. It will certainly be among the five or six super-communications conglomerates that analysts have predicted will emerge by the year 2000, if recent global media merger activity continues unchecked by citizens or government.

In this Chapter, I will describe how Capital Cities/ABC, Inc., has moved to dominate every market in which it has operated since 1986, both domestically and internationally. The company's prime endeavor has been to argue extensively in Washington before the FCC, the Justice Department, and the federal courts, for even wider broadcast deregulation which would allow it (and its U.S. media cartel partners) to grow even larger. The inevitable result will be a media system that sells, and rarely criticizes, the government or the corporate structure that protects its continued existence.

I will also discuss the range of Capital Cities/ABC's operations in radio, television, and publishing in the period 1986-1993 to show how this corporation downsizes and disciplines its labor force, lobbies for anti-democratic regulatory waivers, and silences potential critics through the courts.

Capital Cities/ABC is not a "bad" corporation. It is only playing by the rules of the advertiser-supported media system. The name of the game for those who seek to form business monopolies and cartels is expanding profits and thereby reserving power and privilege for a few.

The Capital Cities Workplace

Almost as soon as news of the Capital Cities/ABC merger was announced in March 1985, many top ABC executives began to cut back on corporate expenditures, hoping to make a good impression on their new bosses from Capital Cities. On a lower level, most of the network's rank-and-file union employees braced for the attacks that were almost certain to come from a notoriously anti-union company like Capital Cities. Among those not in a union, or in the nebulous area of ABC's middle management where there were no seniority lists to guide layoffs and firings, morale plummeted. After the takeover, Capital Cities instituted a series of layoffs and firings throughout ABC that forced all pre-merger employees to assess their future. By April 1987, about 1,850 employees had been laid off, many in the twilight of their careers and with many years of service to the old ABC.[2] These staff cuts and payroll reductions, amounting to some $100 million, were justified by the Capital Cities mandate to make ABC more cost conscious. The actual number of employees released by the new company, however, continues to be highly classified information. Capital Cities' officials generally restrict release of the exact number of laid off or fired employees to protect the company's image when charges are raised that it is only concerned about profits.

During the first few years following the merger, the most areas exempt from the new company's massive personnel reductions were the sales departments.[3] Employees in service or creative areas, who could not demonstrate their profit-making value to the organization in a quantifiable way, were relegated to secondary roles within the Capital Cities bottom-line management culture. Those who could not directly save the company money were considered expendable—a drain on network profits—despite public relations calls for teamwork from Capital Cities' leaders.[4] As merger talk continued to circulate at CBS and NBC, the broadcasting industry seemed to prepare for the trickle-down effects of the widespread cost-cutting that Wall Street and the Reagan administration had said was necessary if U.S. corporations were to compete in a tighter global market-place. Directly related to this blind reliance on market forces was the devastating effect such cutbacks had on labor. Reagan deregulation helped to turn the 1980s into the decade of the freelance worker. Paid by the day or assignment, and without any benefits, freelancers are always more compliant and less inclined to support union militancy. This result was not out of character with the aim of most of the pro-business decisionmaking of the Reaganites. Although the Nixon, Ford, and Carter administrations did their fair share of government deregulation of U.S. industries, Reagan went far beyond these earlier efforts to limit government interference in U.S. businesses.

Even at local stations not affiliated with the networks, employees at every level felt the effects of job layoffs, union harassment and intimidation, union busting, pay freezes, forced overtime, cuts in fringe benefits (including medical insurance) and pension plans, and declining amounts of locally originated programming.

Cleaning Up

Six days after the Capital Cities/ABC merger became effective in January 1986, Murphy and Burke appointed John Sias, who in 1984 had been responsible for earning 48 percent of Capital Cities' total profits and 63 percent of total revenues at its Fairchild publishing subsidiary in 1984.[5]

As the number-three man in the new company, Sias soon became the ruthless role model for many of ABC's former managers intent on gaining more power in Capital Cities/ABC. He quickly earned a reputation for being the epitome of the "hatchet man," the cold-hearted "bean counter" who cut costs and bodies from the payroll without concern for social consequences. To offset his Simon Legree-like image, Sias used the same style he had developed while running Fairchild Publications. He immediately went after every division of the former ABC to personally convince employees of the need to economize, follow orders, and pursue profit-making in an almost totalitarian manner.

Known as a practical joker who sometimes squirted employees with a water pistol or called meetings to order with a bull horn, Sias, despite his buffoonery, did not succeed in softening his fearsome reputation as a company man who would ruthlessly carry out the orders of his superiors.[6]

His obedience and loyalty to Capital Cities was so strong that he reportedly had refused to tell his wife of his imminent promotion to the number-three management position within Capital Cities/ABC for fear that a premature news leak might hurt the company's image.[7]

Capital Cities early on announced its centralized plan to stop employee drug use—on and off the job. Drug testing for all new hires at Capital Cities' subsidiaries was proposed, a policy based on the argument that illegal drug use impaired productivity and efficiency, and contributed to higher medical insurance costs. To underscore the seriousness of the policy, management threatened to bring in drug-sniffing police dogs to search (what it said were) some of the worst drug-use locations.[8]

Dan Burke, the president of Capital Cities/ABC, appeared on a panel discussion held by the American Society of Newspaper Editors. He reported that most companies had not faced up to the "potential seriousness of the usage of drugs in the workplace," but that Capital Cities had. Because this corporate policy seemed to mesh well with the Reagan-Bush "war on drugs" going on at the time, few questioned the legitimacy of Capital Cities' violation of an employee's right to privacy. In 1987, Capital Cities became one of the first U.S. corporations to require all prospective employees to submit to mandatory drug testing.[9]

To further support the government's war on drugs, Capital Cities/ABC later "donated" $34 million on advertising time and space to the Partnership for a Drug-Free America (PDFA). This nonprofit partnership uses popular strategies in advertising to reduce demand for illegal drugs. It's basically a consortium of media owners and advertisers, run by James Burke (brother of Dan Burke). In 1992, the PDFA accepted $5.4 million in contributions from legal-drug manufacturers and both alcohol and tobacco companies. This prompted some critics to suggest that the partnership was being used, indirectly of course, to channel America's addictions to legal drugs of choice.[10]

Besides drugs, the new management also attacked workplace sexual harassment, which had earlier resulted in ABC paying out over $1 million in out-of-court settlements and legal costs for victims of former ABC managers' sexual harassment. In-house training films, produced and shown to all employees and managers, explained how to recognize and report sexual harassment by ABC managers. Portions of these films were even shown on the "ABC Evening News" to reinforce the public relations message to audiences that Capital Cities/ABC was "cleaning up" the old network.[11]

Though it seemed an admirable corporate endeavor at the time, ABC's public campaign against sexual harassment had more practical effects. With such propaganda in place, juries and judges might be less inclined to award former ABC employees high damages for any proven sexual harassment that might occur in the future.

Despite Capital Cities' public commitment to equal opportunity hiring, only nine women and one African-American male joined the 150 white males who attended the 1986 executive-management retreat in Phoenix.[12] In fact, neither Capital Cities, nor the former ABC, ever had a woman or person of color on its board of directors until Anne Dibble Jordan joined the Capital Cities/ABC board of directors in 1988. To this day, none of the new company's executive officers is a woman or a person of color.

Controlling the Working Class

One of the leading factors that has helped to make union workers more accepting of widespread cutbacks and more authoritarian management practices has been management's effectiveness in keeping broadcast unemployment high. From 1986 to 1993, Capital Cities/ABC and its other partners in the U.S. broadcast cartel have routinely worked together to hold labor costs down and push for even greater management control over the workplace.

If the overall number of union workers is lowered, there is less possibility that a union work-stoppage will threaten corporate profits. Through a diligent campaign of rank-and-file intimidation and harassment during noncontract-renewal periods, Capital Cities/ABC took the lead in reducing the bargaining power of its nonunion and union workers. With the continuing introduction of automated work practices, early retirement buyouts and layoffs, and widespread staff transformation, a ready pool of experienced, but out of work, broadcast workers has been created and used by management to force the entire U.S. broadcasting workforce to become more productive and less able to demand a fuller share of corporate profits.

The unfortunate results of the 1987 strike by the National Association of Broadcast Employees and Technicians (NABET) against NBC, the CBS-International Brotherhood of Electrical Workers

(IBEW) contract negotiations, and the continued failure of the broadcast trade unions to organize the cable industry have contributed to the decline of all broadcast unionism.

In June 1987, about 2,800 technicians, writers, and producers went on strike against NBC in the largest U.S. broadcast union work-stoppage since the 1977 NABET strike at ABC. NBC found that it could stay on the air with replacement management and non-union workers despite a one-third drop in its workforce. With its new corporate parent General Electric, NBC resorted to the kind of patriarchal and unfair labor negotiating practices that GE itself had stopped using years before as a result of "legal challenges and sophisticated resistance tactics" by GE's other unions. For all intents and purposes, NBC "locked out" its workers by forcing NABET to accept a final contract offer that it knew union workers would not accept.

After 17 weeks off the job, NABET employees returned to work without having received even one concession. The strikers ended the protest essentially to save the union local and their jobs. The network stayed on the air with an unskilled workforce, further underscoring how technology, and the increased cost-saving and efficiency it often brings, serve top management rather the union rank-and-file. The major issue in the strike arose from NBC's desire to hire freelance employees so that it could eliminate in-house union positions.[13]

Also in 1987, the IBEW negotiated with CBS. The contract offer was far worse than what NBC-GE had offered the NABET workers. The proposal attacked the IBEW's hard-won seniority work rules, which provided CBS employees with a "last hired, first fired" safeguard that also protected older workers' rights to higher pay and more generous vacation and pension benefits. The CBS and NBC attacks on IBEW and NABET, respectively, reflected the continuing cartel-like employment practices at the U.S. broadcast networks.[14]

In 1989, Capital Cities/ABC threatened to implement a new contract offer that had not been ratified by the union. In negotiating with its largest employee union, then representing 2,150 employees (including camerapersons, technicians, and some newswriters), Capital Cities/ABC offered what seemed to be a generous 21 percent increase in salary over four years. But in return, the company demanded major concessions in the form of lost job jurisdiction and tougher work rules, promising to eliminate nearly 400 NABET jobs if the union did not sign the company's "final offer."[15] NABET eventually gave in and agreed to the demands. Since 1989, NABET and Capital Cities/ABC have had relatively few visible problems, since the company has been able to force the union into giving up more and more control over its once tough seniority rules and ceasing its objections to the hiring of freelance workers. Most of the company's success in defeating its unions—as is the case with the other networks—has come from its increasing oligopolistic control over most employment opportunities in broadcasting, cable telecasting, and publishing, and the widespread introduction of labor-saving technology.

As the broadcast unions have been forced into becoming more cooperative, some network employees have undertaken their own civil suits against Capital Cities/ABC to protest racial discrimination and instances of wrongful discharge following management intimidation of workers. In 1992, a federal judge ruled that Capital Cities/ABC had been guilty of "flagrant misconduct," and declared that two NABET graphic artists from ABC's Washington news bureau had won their race discrimination case against their employer by default. More specifically, the judge found that Capital Cities/ABC managers had sent "a management spy" to ABC-NABET grievance meetings in Washington, and that its high-powered corporate law firm (Wilmer, Cutler & Pickering) "had taken substantial and inappropriate actions" to conceal evidence and mislead the court. According to one legal expert, who found the court's decision "remarkable" and "unusual," Capital Cities/ABC had lost the case before it went to trial because the federal judge had found overwhelming evidence that it had not only conspired against its workers, but had then engaged in a "cover-up" to deceive the court.[16]

Top Management Rewards

Despite routine 40 to 50 percent annual profit margins that Capital Cities/ABC enjoys from its locally owned-and-operated broadcast stations, not everyone in the company shares in the wealth and property enjoyed by top management. Citing ABC's and NBC's high union labor costs, such as the NABET average base salary of $50,000 plus (not including overtime or other penalty pay) and program fees, the networks regularly call for further cutbacks.

Yet, the wide disparity between the pay structure of those at the very top and those at the bottom of Capital Cities' employee hierarchy reveals that the networks are not as badly off as they often say they are. The top five executives at Capital Cities/ABC, Inc., all earned handsome salaries, even in a recessionary year like 1991:

Thomas S. Murphy, Chair:	$834,349
Daniel B. Burke, Pres., CEO/COO:	$960,742
John B. Sias, Exec.VP/Pres. ABC:	$833,770
Michael P. Mallardi, Sr. VP/Pres.,	
Broadcast Group:	$726,056
Ronald J. Doerfler, Sr. VP/CFO:	$816,332 [17]

However, these figures do not indicate the executives' total compensation. They also receive incentive bonuses and stock awards that are provided by Capital Cities under the company's Supplemental Pension Plan, Publishing Plan, or employee retirement plan. The above salaries also do not include bonuses provided under the Incentive Compensation Plan or the 1991 Supplementary Compensation Agreements with Murphy, Burke, and Sias. Under the Incentive Compensation Plan and Supplementary Compensation Agreements, the following awards were made:

Murphy:	$2,999,254
Burke:	$2,972,569
Sias:	$2,945,884
Mallardi:	$3,406,970
Doerfler:	$2,839,142 [18]

Finally, executive compensation was also boosted in 1991 by the substantial stock holdings of all five top executive officers in Capital Cities/ABC stocks. By the end of 1992, Thomas Murphy owned a *minimum* of 123,283 shares with an approximate value of $61,641,500; Daniel Burke owned a minimum of 62,571 shares with a market value of approximately $31,285,500; John Sias owned a minimum of 20,242 shares, worth $10,121,000; Michael Mallardi owned a minimum of 14,218 shares, worth $7,109,000; and Ronald Doerfler owned a minimum of 22,177 shares, worth $11,088,500.[19]

Capital Cities/ABC publishes both an Annual Report and a Form 10-K—two documents required by all U.S. companies whose stock is traded publicly. But the Securities and Exchange Commission does not require that these documents provide complete details as to how much the network's top executives earn. Rather, total compensation figures must be estimated from the above documents and from the oblique language in the Capital Cities/ABC, Inc., document Notice of Annual Meeting of Shareholders, which is distributed only to company stockholders—just prior to the annual stockholders meeting. The average citizen does not generally gain access to this supposedly public information unless they are stockholders or know someone who is.

Pressure to Perform

The unrelenting pressure that Capital Cities/ABC places on its managers and employees to make high profits has resulted in scandal and, in some cases, litigation. In 1987, John Severino, the station manager of KABC-TV, the company-owned-and-operated television station in Los Angeles, admitted that he had conspired with subordinates to fraudulently boost the ratings of its local news broadcasts in May 1987. KABC-TV's media analyst, a 13-year veteran with ABC before the merger with Capital Cities, tried to report this to the public, but was subsequently fired and his investigative unit disbanded. Severino soon resigned. Officials of Capital Cities/ABC refused to comment on the matter.[20]

The pressure to boost the ratings on the "ABC Evening News" may have also led to fraudulent practices. Capital Cities/ABC earned the dubious distinction of becoming the first media conglomerate to fake news footage by dramatizing an allegation from anonymous sources at the FBI and State Department. In July 1989, news anchor Peter Jennings apologized to viewers for having aired faked footage of Felix Bloch, a former American diplomat suspected (but never formally accused) of accepting a briefcase from a KGB agent and spying for the Soviets. As ABC's Sam Donaldson later said, the news fake "could have led viewers into 'believing that they had actually seen the event' when really they had not." This deceptive practice eventually spread to all of the U.S. networks.[21]

In its publishing division, Capital Cities/ABC's often sensation-seeking news practices have led to the courts. The publisher, editor, managing editor, and a columnist of *The Wilkes-Barre Times-Leader* were indicted on felony wiretapping charges in 1991. *Times-Leader* columnist Steve Corbett conducted a telephone interview with a jailed dentist, who was later convicted of killing his wife; but Corbett did not inform the dentist that the conversation was being taped. Capital Cities' attorneys later charged that the case was "politically motivated" by the Luzerne County District Attorney's office. The *Times-Leader* became the site of a bitter labor struggle that affected the entire community after Capital Cities purchased it in 1978. Although eventually dismissed by the court, the case received national attention as an example of how newspapers had encouraged tabloid-style journalistic practices to boost circulation and corporate profits.[22]

The pressure to maintain Capital Cities/ABC's rating dominance can also be seen in network radio. During the 1991 Persian Gulf War, Unistar Radio, one of the largest competitors of the company's Satellite Music Network (SMN), charged that SMN was pirating for use its radio feeds from Turner Broadcasting's Cable News Network.[23]

But the most egregious display of Capital Cities/ABC's often sensasionalist local news practices came to light in Buffalo, New York. In February 1993, a New York appeals court in Rochester upheld a $15 million libel judgment against the company for questionable journalistic practices at WKBW-TV in 1982 (Capital Cities sold WKBW-TV after buying ABC in 1985).

That judgment against Capital Cities/ABC was believed to involve one of the highest awards ever upheld by an appeals court. In its 1991 ruling, the intermediate appeals court said that WKBW-TV had aired "groundless speculation and conjecture" by the FBI, and then acted with "actual malice" by trying to deny its own responsibility and blame its libelous coverage on its FBI sources.[24] In December 1993, the New York State Court of Appeals in Albany overturned the $15 million verdict against Capital Cities and ordered a new trial. Nineteen U.S. news organizations, such as NBC, CBS, Fox, and other U.S. media corporations filed a joint friend-of-the-court brief asking the Albany court to overturn the verdict against Capital Cities.[25]

Political Lobbying and Public Relations

From its earliest years, Capital Cities' has cultivated strong ties to federal regulators in order to gain advantages over its competitors and to boost profits. The period 1986-1993 was no exception, thanks to a Reagan-Bush pro-industry FCC.

Although the 1985 Capital Cities/ABC merger was the largest non-oil takeover in U.S. history at the time, Reagan's FCC chair Mark Fowler led one of the shortest FCC reviews of such a deal on record, especially considering the size of the merger. Instead of questioning how such a takeover might affect news practices or citizen-access to the airwaves, the FCC focused on how it would better serve the "public interest." The Commission did almost everything it could to encourage the Capital Cities/ABC merger, and others like it.

Because the combined assets of Capital Cities and ABC exceeded broadcast ownership limits, Capital Cities sold its stations in Houston, Dallas-Fort Worth, Buffalo, and Hartford-New Haven, as well as several of its radio stations and 54 cable systems throughout the United States. Most of the profits from these sell-offs went to paying off part of the debt incurred in the purchase of ABC.[26] Capital Cities/ABC was also successful in obtaining a key FCC waiver that allowed it to continue operating two highly valuable, television stations in New York and Philadelphia (on adjacent channels 7 and 6, respectively). The waiver concerning these stations, located in the first and fourth wealthiest U.S. broadcast markets, was to be worth millions to Capital Cities/ABC—not only in future profits, but also in added leverage and marketing power that was gained in the national program-syndication market. The company's Philadelphia station, WPVI-TV, was worth a minimum of $350 million in 1985 and, had the FCC not provided Capital Cities/ABC with the waiver, its sale would probably have represented the largest local television sale in history.[27]

The company was further helped in 1989 by the FCC decision to change the "one-to-a-market" rules, which had limited owners to one broadcast or publishing outlet per market. This decision made it possible for Capital Cities/ABC, for example, to retain its multiple ownership of properties in such lucrative broadcast and publishing markets as New York, Chicago, Los Angeles, Detroit, Washington, D.C., Dallas-Fort Worth, Atlanta, and Minneapolis.[28]

To fortify its U.S. power base, the company has not been shy about using the public airwaves to support its private Washington lobbying efforts to acquire even more media properties. In December 1989, at a time when decisions on crucial FCC regulatory waivers were pending, ABC's "20/20" broadcast a primetime report touting the past benefits of government deregulation in the telephone, airline, gas and oil, trucking, and other industries. "The competition of a free market held down costs better than government did, but the bad news drowned out the good news of deregulation," argued "20/20" consumer reporter John Stossel. All in all, "the total gain to the country is huge." Stossel compared U.S. government regulation before Reagan's 1980 election to the centralized planning of the former Soviet Union, but failed to mention the massive deregulation of the broadcast industry that had taken place from 1978 to 1989. He also neglected to disclose that the networks were waging an intense lobbying effort at the FCC to repeal the financial-syndication rules that promised to bring in billions in future revenue from the domestic and international syndication of off-network programs.[29]

Capital Cities and the FCC

Capital Cities' favored treatment from the Reagan-appointed FCC probably did not come without some strings. Ronald Reagan, Jr., had been hired as a special entertainment correspondent for ABC's info-tainment morning program, "Good Morning America" (GMA) in July 1985 during the time when the Capital Cities/ABC merger was in FCC review. (Reagan, Jr. had at the time minimal experience as a television reporter. His hiring may have played a role in persuading the FCC to provide Capital Cities/ABC with maximum regulatory waivers to allow it to retain its most profitable properties and thus be able both to finance the merger, and to continue enjoying its high profit margins. Reagan, Jr. continued in his GMA on-air capacity through July 1990, during which time Capital Cities/ABC received nearly every regulatory waiver it asked for from the FCC.[30]

In 1986, Capital Cities probably used its Reagan-Bush political connections to have another "one of its own" appointed to the FCC, Patricia Diaz-Dennis. The appointment of Dennis, a Reagan supporter and ABC's former West Coast vice-president for labor relations, helped ensure that the FCC would continue to protect Capital Cities' interests.[31] With the pro-broadcasting votes of Reagan FCC chair Mark Fowler and two of the other four commissioners having also been former vice-presidents of the company, Capital Cities gained majority control at the FCC almost overnight. Even though there were policy issues that divided the Commission at times between 1985 and 1992, the tenor of the rule-making that followed these appointments was nearly always pro-business. During the same period, Capital Cities also enjoyed close ties to the Bush administration through company president Dan Burke, a neighbor of the first family at its summer retreat in Kennebunkport, Maine.[32]

Although Dennis left the FCC in 1989 to become a corporate attorney for the long-distance carrier U.S. Sprint, one of her staff appointments, Robert Pepper, remained at the FCC to continue the Reagan deregulation of U.S. broadcasting. In 1992, Pepper headed the FCC's Office of Plans and Policy and authored a somewhat controversial report, *Broadcast Television in a Multichannel Marketplace,* which endorsed nearly all of the broadcast industry's pleadings for less regulation and more freedom to concentrate ownership.[33] Along with Pepper, FCC commissioner James Quello continued to lead Capital Cities' fight on the FCC through 1993. At the age of 79, he had become one of the longest-sitting commissioners in the history of the FCC. Well known around Washington, D.C. for his unwavering support of the right of U.S. broadcasters to self-regulate, Quello has also been a vigorous opponent of violence and sex on the airwaves, and says he listens to the Howard Stern radio program to make sure Stern does not violate the FCC rules on these matters.[34]

Since 1973, Quello has rarely deviated from supporting Capital Cities/ABC or corporate control in general over the media. During FCC hearings in the period 1990-93, Quello supported the broadcast industry's fight to remove the "lowest-unit charge" for political advertising, thus helping to ensure that broadcast stations make windfall profits and that only the wealthiest candidates can afford to advertise.[35] In 1992, three Capital Cities/ABC television stations in Los Angeles, Houston, and Fresno were accused in citizen complaints to the FCC that they had overcharged political candidates for airtime.[36]

Quello also publicly campaigned to remove the current radio and television ownership limits from current levels—12 television stations, 12 AM, and 12 FM radio stations—providing that no owner reaches more than 25 percent of the potential U.S. television or radio audience. He also supported changing the rules to allow corporate broadcasters to acquire up to 1 percent of all U.S. radio stations (approximately 100 at the time) and up to 24 television stations (but these owners would be limited to 35 percent of the television audiences).[37] Although these efforts stalled with the Clinton presidential victory in 1992, the decisions were still pending before the FCC.

Through Quello and the Bush FCC, Capital Cities was also successful in obtaining permission for the broadcast networks to own cable systems again. Under the rules adopted in 1992, they had the right to acquire cable systems that served up to (in total) 10 percent of the U.S. homes wired for cable or up to 50 percent of homes in a given market.[38] Quello also led the fight, on behalf of U.S. broadcasters, to force cable operators to pay broadcasting stations for the right to carry their over-the-air signals.

Finally, the networks gained their ultimate victory from the FCC when in April 1993 the Commission voted to eliminate the financial syndication rules. With Quello presiding as interim chair for the Clinton administration, the Commission gutted most of the rules that had remained as the principal barrier to the regulatory freedom to establish a broadcast cartel of five or six colossal communication corporations.[39] The April 5, 1993 issue of *Broadcasting* perhaps captured Quello's service to the broadcast industry best when it devoted its front cover to a picture of him. The accompanying caption read, "Quello's FCC Remakes the Industry."[40]

Capital Cities/ABC's influence on the FCC seemed to continue in 1993. Clinton administration aides began to circulate the name of Senate Communications Subcommittee senior counsel Toni Cook as a candidate to chair the FCC, but her name was removed from consideration a few months later. Cook would have been the first African-American and the first woman ever to head the FCC. Her mother, Ann Dibble Jordan, had served on the board of Capital Cities/ABC, Inc., since 1988. Her stepfather, Vernon Jordan, acted as Clinton transition director from 1992 to 1993.[41]

Losing Money?

Even with profits of nearly $1 billion a year, the leaders of Capital Cities/ABC still argue for more broadcast and cable deregulation so as to widen their control and improve their bottom-line. In 1989, ABC quietly held talks to purchase Time, Inc., while taking on little or no debt.[42]

By looking closer at profit-and-loss statements, one can see that many of the corporate media's proclamations about falling audience levels are merely a smoke screen. "Just under 80 percent of 1989 sales (which totaled $4.96 billion) and 86 percent of profits (1989 total: $922 million)"[43] came from broadcasting; the rest came from publishing. Corporate radio sales and profits (8 percent and 11 percent, respectively) were relatively small in comparison, but not in terms of Capital Cities/ABC's combined political influence or economic impact. Since Capital Cities (or any of the major networks) refuses to provide an exact breakdown on what each of its divisions earns, it is difficult to determine which are truly profitable, and, more importantly, which are not. Generally, those divisions that make substantial profits are not discussed by network executives, while those that earn small or no profits receive the most attention. The ABC television network, responsible for 62 percent of Capital Cities' revenues, produced only 20 percent of its broadcasting profits. Capital Cities/ABC's television network's profit margin was reportedly 7 percent.[44] Most media reports describing the U.S. network's "falling profits" seemed to focus only on those divisions making little to medium profit levels.

The real secret of the network's substantial profit margins, however, lies in its eight local television stations. ABC enjoyed 54 percent profit margins from its stations in New York, Los Angeles, Chicago, Philadelphia, San Francisco, Houston, Durham-Raleigh, and Fresno; while CBS and NBC earned 36 percent and 42 percent profit margins from their local stations, respectively.[45] With that kind of profit margin, protected by the FCC-legalized U.S. broadcast oligopoly, it is not hard to understand why the networks have continually argued for the removal of all federal limits on local station ownership.

It is a mistake to think that the networks were, or are, losing money to the extent they say they are. In 1989, the three major networks collectively earned over $1 billion in total profits on combined revenues (from broadcasting operations) of more than $10 billion.[46] Due to the large number of conflicting, and at times even misleading, financial reports that are produced by the networks to argue for less regulation, it is extremely difficult for the average person to distinguish what is true from what is not. Yet, all too often, these figures are used by federal regulators to determine whether or not to allow even greater levels of oligopoly.[47]

For instance, speculation begin to circulate in 1991 that Capital Cities/ABC was considering adding to its already highly profitable local television-station group. As it had looked into buying another station in Boston or Atlanta, CEO Daniel Burke announced to Wall Street analyst in 1992 that Capital Cities/ABC profits would not improve dramatically. At the same time, Burke revealed that Capital Cities/ABC was financially solvent enough to consider seriously a major acquisition, worth five to eight billion dollars.[48]

His comment also came on the heels of his asking for major reductions in overall network program costs from sports programming suppliers.[49] Yet, industry trade magazines reported that total programming costs at the network had not significantly risen from their levels in

1986-1991. In one article, *Broadcasting* magazine raised questions about the misleading manner in which network leaders like Burke were citing loss figures while asking for less regulation from Congress and the FCC. Although Burke tried to portray his network as squeezed by costs, the cost increases (adjusted for inflation) had amounted to just 1 percent per year.[50] Further complicating the picture, in 1990 when Capital Cities/ABC was leading all three networks in earnings in what amounted to a nearly $11 billion market, it had raised charges for air time instead of lowering its advertising rates.[51]

Still, while Capital Cities/ABC and the other networks were maintaining that they were losing money, all were attempting to buy up more media properties. On December 8, 1992, Burke told an investor's conference in New York that the company was scouting for acquisitions and had a cash and debt capacity of as much as $5–$8 billion. It was "something we desire devoutly," he said at the time.[52] Industry trade magazines speculated that ABC might be looking seriously at buying Paramount Studios for $8 million. Paramount was reportedly worth about $5 million in 1993.[53]

Two months later, in February 1993, Turner Broadcasting announced that it had held "high-level talks" with Capital Cities (and other media companies) to discuss several merger scenarios. Turner officials said they would like to pursue a merger with ABC, but that federal regulations would likely prevent a successful outcome since Turner was already capitalized to some extent by the Time-Warner media conglomerate. Time-Warner already owned nearly 20 percent of Turner Broadcasting. Earlier, in 1992, Capital Cities considered making major investment stakes in Cablevision (the third-largest U.S. cable operation), and other companies.[54]

In April 1993, Capital Cities/ABC announced that it would invest in one or more growing companies by putting up not capital but advertising time on its various media outlets, including the ABC Television Network, the owned stations, ESPN, and ABC Radio. In fact, Capital Cities/ABC had even moved to set up a subsidiary—Capital Cities Capital—to coordinate such investment activity in the future.

Such advertising-for-securities swapping would indirectly help to increase the demand for national advertising time by reducing the overall time available to most advertisers. At the same time, Capital Cities/ABC would literally be guaranteeing marketers a chance to succeed even without a huge advertising budget. In return, the network would often gain 15 to 25 percent equity stakes (worth $5 million to $20 million) in many of those companies needing to advertise in order to enter the highly competitive national marketing environment. As its cash surplus swelled, Wall Street speculated that Capital Cities/ABC was on the verge of purchasing King World for $2.2 billion in December 1993. King World is one of the most powerful program syndication companies in the U.S., and produces or distributes the following: "Wheel of Fortune," "Oprah Winfrey," "Jeopardy," "Inside Edition," "American Journal," and others. Such a merger would give Capital Cities/ABC virtual control over some of the most profitable syndicated programs in U.S. television industry.[55]

Interlocking Corporate Ties

Since the merger of Capital Cities and ABC and sweeping U.S. broadcast deregulation in the period 1981-1992, the cross-commercial ties between the network and other major U.S. media conglomerates and advertisers have continued to proliferate. These rapidly expanding, interlocking arrangements provide compelling evidence of the U.S. broadcast cartel's growing stranglehold over information and culture in this country.

In March 1992, ABC Productions (ABCP), the network's in-house production unit formed to capitalize on the newly liberalized FCC financial-syndication rules, moved to make seven pilots for the new entertainment season. ABCP produced "Class of '96" for the Fox network, two hour-long pilots for CBS, several pilots for NBC-TV, movies for HBO and ABC's partly owned cable network Lifetime, and, of course, several programs for the ABC television network.[56] This was the first of several such joint programming efforts among the supposedly fiercely competitive U.S. cable and broadcast networks.

In August 1991, ABCP sold the two-hour film "Fugitive Among Us" (starring Peter Strauss and Eric Roberts) for broadcast on CBS. It was the first production of ABC for another network. Later that year, Time-Warner's HBO said it would produce and premiere two half-hour comedy specials that were scheduled to air on ABC, and then on the Fox network. The two shows, to be jointly financed by ABC, Fox, and (Time Warner owned) HBO's production unit, were to premiere on the pay-cable channel in 1992, and then air as pilots for a weekly series on ABC and Fox. With Viacom's Nickelodeon channel, ABC agreed to develop the primetime series, "Hi Honey, I'm Home." Premiering on the network's schedule in July 1991, the series was then rebroadcast on Nickelodeon's "Nick at Nite" cable channel the following weekend.[57]

In yet another cross-sponsorship, Kodak, along with Johnson & Johnson and Pepsi-Cola Co., sponsored the "Sea World Mother Earth Celebration," a special that ran on ABC in May, then on its partly owned A&E cable network, and yet again on Nickelodeon. ABC also formed a programming partnership with Viacom's MTV network by contracting to air "MTV's 10th Anniversary." ABC licensed the show for two runs on its own network, after which the show would be scheduled for broadcast on MTV itself.[58]

Further exploiting the sales opportunities available to these two giant conglomerates, ABC joined with "E," the HBO-managed 24-hour entertainment news channel. A special called "Entertainment 91, The Top 20 of the Year" was produced by "E" and hosted by comedian Dennis Miller. Sears, one of the largest U.S. retailers and advertisers, reportedly asked ABC to broadcast the "E" special on the night of December 26 in order to promote its after-Christmas sales. A marketing spokesperson for "E" later commented on the mutual benefits of the partnership: "Sears gets the promotion it wants; ABC gets a special for free, and we get a fabulous showcase for the exposure we have been looking for." "E" repeated the special just two days after it appeared on ABC.[59]

Scoffing at potential criticism that the networks were acting like a programming and distributing cartel, Bob Iger, ABC's entertainment chief, said that the network was more concerned about the quality of programming than which production company made it, *Variety* reported. "Advertisers see this as a helpful trend," Iger said. "[This] is the way advertisers will be working throughout the 90s and into the next century."[60]

Proving Iger's point, Lifetime Television, ABC's partly owned cable channel, announced in 1993 a new programming venture with the multibillion-dollar drug and personal product marketers Bristol-Myers and Procter & Gamble. According to *Broadcasting*, Lifetime has been at the forefront in co-producing programs with national advertisers, literally turning over its air time to these sponsors for broadcasting their ideas and product pitches. While developing the Bristol-Myers show "Amazing Love Stories" for primetime, Lifetime hoped to repeat the success of its earlier Bristol-Myers co-production "The Days and Nights of Molly

Dodd." Bristol-Myers held a major financial interest in that program, which raised the controversial issue of product placement. "Various episodes showed Molly, in a drugstore or elsewhere, with Bristol-Myers products in the background." Lifetime President-CEO Doug McCormick defended the "program-commercial" practice: "It was only done when appropriate, and it was done with taste."[61]

One argument against such programming initiatives, of course, is that the advertiser becomes the leading arbiter of what is covered or not covered in a given program. In programs that are supposedly set up to advise, this can result, directly and indirectly, in offering viewers information that enhances the appeal of the sponsor's products. In answering this charge, Lifetime is not shy. "The bottom line is that the more programming that gets produced—however it gets produced—the better off the viewers are," says CEO McCormick.[62]

In April 1993, the ABC Television Network and *Reader's Digest* announced a partnership to produce a one-hour TV special for the fall of 1993, entitled "Reader's Digest: On Television." The network was to earn sales revenues from selling commercials (and then television rights), while *Reader's Digest* was to keep direct-mail sales revenues of videos of the program.[63]

Home Shopping

In an effort to further exploit the sales potential of what have become private corporate airwaves, ABC has also sought to cash in on the popularity of home-shopping programs, now a more than $30 billion-a-year business. In 1992, the network began developing and testing such a program: "NiteCap." Transactional programming could offer ABC numerous tie-ins to its other national sponsors. This could reinforce other sales and advertising efforts on the network's telecast channels.

Overseen by Phil Beuth, the vice-president who also oversees ABC's news and information program "Good Morning America," "Nite-Cap" was tested in 47 markets around the country beginning in October 1992. It aired right after ABC's "Nightline" interview program with Ted Koppel. The program was hosted by actress Rae Dawn Chong and Robin Leach ("Lifestyles of the Rich and Famous"). Leach offered this comment on his role in "NiteCap": "I'm now doing what many have accused me of doing throughout my career—being a carnival barker." The one-hour show included celebrity interviews and infomercials for an unusual array of products.[64] Its other attraction to ABC and its affiliates was that local stations carrying the program got 5 percent of the gross sales of each product sold in their respective viewing areas. The more stations on the network, the more ABC could charge its advertisers to cross-promote other products and services.

In January 1993, ABC put its widely criticized home-shopping program plans on hold due to low ratings and affiliate opposition. After spending two months evaluating the four-week test of "NiteCap," the network decided not to go forward with it. Both NBC and CBS were reported to be exploring similar transactional programming arrangements.[65]

While it pursued home-shopping programs of its own, Capital Cities/ABC continued to license merchandising products that are promoted and marketed through its daytime soap operas: "All My Children," "One Life to Live," "General Hospital," and "Loving." In a partnership with the QVC home-shopping network to sell its products, ABC sold $260,000 of "All My Children" merchandise in one hour. As a part of the joint sales effort, QVC shopping host Pat James DeMentrie made a cameo appearance in an episode of the program, and actress Susan Lucci, who played the character Erica Kane on this soap opera, made a guest appearance on QVC during which she spoke live via telephone to viewers watching at home.

Capital Cities/ABC executives have refused to comment on the amount of revenue raised by such merchandising deals at ABC.[66]

In the Sponsor's Interest

In 1990, the networks began integrating advertisers' logos and other forms of identification into their cross-promotions for various programs, but none involved "pitches" from the stars of a network series until Capital Cities/ABC took the lead in initiating them.

To help sponsors make their ads better than the programs, for example, ABC entered into an exclusive deal with the Nestle Beverage Company to promote Taster's Choice Instant Coffee. In a running series of special Taster's Choice commercials entitled "Sharon and Tony," a couple were brought closer and closer through their love of the company's instant coffee. ABC promised Nestle that it would promote the event on its extensive network of soap opera "900 number" promotions and in the magazine Capital Cities publishes for soap opera fans. Nestle was also set to promote the commercials that were to run on ABC with in-store displays, a *TV Guide* display advertisement, and an extensive public relations campaign. Asked about the promotion, *Advertising Age* said: "[It] vividly demonstrates how the pressure to land business in this recession has sparked new flexibility and creativity by both media and advertisers. Nothing is overlooked."[67]

Even the ABC's Wide World of Sports logo was sold by ABC to advertisers. On selling out its franchise to Energizer batteries for the amusing "Bunny" ads, ABC also arranged to have longtime Wide World host Jim McKay plug the batteries. "They came to us and licensed the footage," said an ABC spokesperson. "It's good for them, good for us and a good way to introduce people to Wide World."[68]

In a similar move, ABC Sports, through its own video subsidiary, signed a deal with CBS-Fox Video Sports to promote the men's fragrance Drakkar Noir, while promoting two of the newest home videotape releases made from past Wide World of Sports segments: "The Thrill of Victory" and "The Agony of Defeat." This tape promotion, the first such effort by ABC Sports, was timed for a 1992 Father's Day release. Like other of the network's cross-promotions, the deal was to be promoted by a $1.3 million television advertising campaign.[69]

This is only the beginning. Developing a cross-media package entitled "Cap Cities Electronic Minute," Capital Cities/ABC offered advertisers spots on all of its TV and radio networks and stations, and on the three cable networks in which ABC had a financial interest: ESPN, A&E, and Lifetime. Through this marketing arrangement, the network offered its clients "roadblocks," spots running as near as possible in time to each other on all of the media outlets so intended consumer targets could not easily escape the commercial messages. Packages were to be further keyed to target audiences' consumer interests. Beers, for example, would get more airtime on the heavily male-oriented ESPN rather than on Lifetime, which targets female viewers. These packages would be offered in a price range of $400,000 to $500,000. If this kind of marketing idea succeeded, ABC would expand it by offering clients similar commercial tie-ins to its specialized publications such as *Supermarket News*.[70]

One month later, in August 1992, ABC announced it was joining forces with J.C. Penney Co. and GTE to expand an in-store television network being tested in its national chain of mid-priced department stores. As part of the deal, an hour-long video show produced by ABC Sports aired in 1992 on TV sets placed in roughly half of J.C. Penney's 1,283 department stores. ABC Sports was reported to have offered their services to other retailers later.[71]

When Sport Is Not Competitive

In September 1990, the FTC brought charges against Capital Cities/ABC, contending that the network had illegally conspired "to restrict competition in the marketing of college football." According to the FTC, the ABC and ESPN $300 million rights agreement with the College Football Association (CFA) for 1991-95 "violated federal anti-trust laws and injured the millions of football fans who watched CFA games each week." The conspiracy created "higher rights fees, fewer games telecast, [and] lower overall viewership and resulted in game selection unresponsive to consumer preference," according to FTC regulators.[72]

However, in August 1991, Judge Raymond Timothy dismissed the complaint against ABC in federal court on the grounds that the FTC lacked jurisdiction over the CFA because of the association's nonprofit status. Even though ABC took the court's decision as an endorsement of its alleged monopolistic practices, the judge did not rule on any of the anti-trust issues in the agreement (which gave ABC and ESPN exclusive rights to all CFA members' games in 1991-95). Since the association has the largest number of participating schools, Capital Cities/ABC was thought to have a stranglehold over U.S. college football telecasting. The FTC charged that ABC (with pre-existing rights to Big Ten and Pac-Ten games) had acquired the CFA games so as to monopolize the national advertising market in college football. With no competition, it could raise advertising rates arbitrarily.[73]

To exploit profit-making on college football even further, ABC entered into an unprecedented partnership with Showtime Entertainment Television to offer regional football games on a pay-per-view (PPV) basis. From this partnership, named ABC-SET, each ABC affiliate would receive as always the appropriate weekly college football game for its particular market, and SET would offer viewers in the same market additional games from other regions of the country on a PPV basis.[74] The experiment was most important because it offered the networks a means to test consumer reaction to PPV telecasts that contained advertising messages. In other words, ABC-SET offered pay-per-view service with commercials and represented a potential dual revenue stream.

But the experiment raised questions regarding the future of the networks if they were allowed to own cable systems. With federal laws prohibiting their purchase of an unlimited number of local television stations, the networks could in time set up their own national distribution system by buying up cable systems and lobbying the FCC to drop cable ownership rules. If the networks owned cable systems, they could determine how much those systems would have to pay in return for access, and thus eliminate the battles over affiliate compensation (the money broadcast networks pay to local affiliates for carrying network comercials and programs) that have continued to trouble network executives.[75]

Cable-Video Enterprises—The U.S. and Beyond

Capital Cities/ABC is widening its global control over the mass media by opening up new markets and expanding into U.S. and foreign cable programming and ownership through its ever-expanding division, Video Enterprises. Part of the reason for the division's rapid growth is that even with the massive federal deregulation of broadcasting and cable television during the Reagan-Bush years, there are still more liberal rules regarding the cross-ownership of cable properties, and no U.S. rules or regulations governing the overseas purchase of foreign media.

Broadcast cartelization is most graphically illustrated by the corporate ties of Capital Cities/ABC's most profitable cable network, ESPN. Started by the Getty Oil Company in 1979 and acquired by its minority partner ABC in 1984, ESPN is today the second most profitable operation in the Capital Cities/ABC empire, after the group of local radio and television stations. With 61.4 million subscribers in the United States and 34 million in 75 other countries (as of April 1993), ESPN now tops CNN as the leader among U.S. cable channels, having earned an estimated $282 million in 1991. Wall Street analysts predicted that ESPN's pre-tax profits for 1992 would be $140 million, indicating 40 to 50 percent profit margins. If true (Capital Cities/ABC is not required by law to provide actual profit figures for each division), ESPN profits would represent over 20 percent of Capital Cities/ABC's corporate pre-tax total (1992: $685 million). ESPN has been more profitable than ABC Sports, ABC News, and even

ABC's entertainment division. Its workforce has no unions and includes a great number of freelance employees who work with no fringe benefits.

Capital Cities/ABC has created a second world sports channel, ESPN-2, which began operating in 1993. The company, one of the largest U.S. broadcasting and cable conglomerates even before the venture, is using ESPN-2 as a means to capture a greater share of the U.S. advertising market. ESPN-2 also serves to neutralize government regulation enacted to give broadcasters an additional means of revenue. In 1992 Congress, hoping to inject new life into broadcast television, gave telecasters the right to charge local cable systems for retransmitting their signals. Capital Cities/ABC and Hearst announced that cable systems could carry the programs of any ABC- or Hearst-owned station for free if they carried ESPN-2. ABC-TV's affiliated stations, which are not owned by ABC or Hearst, are not protected by this agreement, however, further indicating that huge media conglomerates will continue to have the power to avoid even the most well-intentioned FCC regulations that may impact their profit prospects.[76]

What is so ironic about all of this is that Capital Cities/ABC was the media conglomerate that appeared to put the most lobbying pressure on the FCC and Congress to allow broadcasters to charge local cable operators for carrying their signals, which those operators had been able to do without charge before 1992. Capital Cities' favorite FCC commissioner, James Quello, had become the most outspoken within the FCC in pushing for changes in the regulations that would make the cable industry compensate the broadcasting industry for carrying its signals and programming. Capital Cities/ABC's continued freedom to use all of its broadcasting, cable, and publishing properties to gain maximum profit advantage over its competitors (and, at the same time, dominate government regulatory proceedings), is yet another indication of how powerful a force it is.

ESPN has far more profit potential than does the ABC-TV network. For instance, like most other national cable networks, it brings in two streams of revenue: subscription fees from local cable franchises (through household fees) and advertising revenue from national sponsors. (Cable operators are also provided several minutes per hour of local advertising time in which they can sell advertising to community sponsors.) Some analysts believe that the current "over-the-air" television system will eventually be transformed from a set of local affiliated stations into a cable system. Besides the chance to make more money from cable subscription fees and advertising, there are fewer FCC regulations governing cable system programming than television broadcasting. With increasing cable and broadcast programming and distribution partnerships, it is more than likely that all of the cable industry will soon be controlled entirely by the same media conglomerates that presently dominate broadcasting. As of 1993, Capital Cities owned 80 percent of ESPN, and Hearst Broadcasting controlled the remaining 20 percent. While Hearst's minority stake is often mentioned by Capital Cities/ABC to show that it is not monopolizing the country's media marketplace, a closer look proves otherwise.

Hearst has two seats on the ESPN board of directors and owns six local television stations nationally, five of which are ABC affiliates. It owns more ABC affiliates than any other U.S. corporation, except Capital Cities/ABC itself. Besides ESPN, Hearst participates in the following, among others: a partnership with NBC and ABC in the ownership of the cable network; the Arts and Entertainment Network (A&E: 78 percent by Capital Cities and Hearst, the remaining 22 percent by NBC); a joint investment with Capital Cities/ABC and Viacom in Lifetime Television (Capital Cities/ABC and Hearst each own a 50 percent stake); a joint investment in the New England Newschannel with Cablevision, Inc. one of the country's largest Multiple System Operators (MSO); Hearst Entertainment Productions, which sells TV programs to Capital Cities/ABC as well as other broadcasting and cable distributors in the United States and abroad; Hearst Entertainment Distribution, Ellipse Programme (a joint venture with French media owners); newspaper syndication and merchandise licensing operations through its King Features Syndicate, Cowles Syndicate, and King Features Licensing; and First Data Bank electronic publishing services.[77] Because of these overlapping media partnerships in broadcasting, publishing, and video enterprises, Capital Cities/ABC and Hearst are in fact very closely allied.

As a result of their partnerships, ABC and Hearst continue to work together to ensure favorable government regulation through their ties to the FCC. The close links of ABC and Hearst continued to be reflected in Hearst's 1993 hiring of an important Capital Cities/ABC ally during the Bush administration, former FCC chairman Alfred Sikes. In his four years chairing the Commission, Sikes did a great deal to advance the interests of both Hearst and Capital Cities/ABC and other U.S. media corporations. In accepting the appointment, he followed the "revolving-door" tradition of other FCC chairpersons who, after leaving the FCC, accepted jobs with the same corporations that they had formerly regulated. Former Reagan FCC chairs who took this route include Dennis Patrick (president of Time Warner Telecommunications, which integrates new technologies with cable) and Mark Fowler (president of Bell Atlantic Personal, a cellular company seeking entry into Personal Communication System, the reported next generation of cellular communications). Although Hearst announced that Sikes would not be lobbying for the company, these appointments, nevertheless, ensured the continued domination of U.S. telecommunications frequencies by corporate interests.[78]

Besides the U.S. broadcasting industry, Capital Cities/ABC has moved to dominate the cable industry, the global media market for U.S. products, and also off-shore programming operations. In October 1989, for example, Capital Cities/ABC Video Enterprises president Herbert Granath explained ABC's plans to produce programming for European audiences, as well as continue to develop co-productions for the national ABC-TV network. "We hope there will be more participation by quality producers," Granath said. "There are opportunities on both sides of the Atlantic." [79]

The A&E network continues to maintain its ties with international co-producers, such as the BBC and production companies in Germany and Mexico.[80] In addition to launching regular program service to Latin America and Japan in 1991, Capital Cities/ABC—through its ESPN network—bought the United Kingdom-based W.H. Smith cable programming network for $110 million. ESPN already owned a 25 percent stake in the European Sports Network, one of the many W.H. Smith properties that has been providing sports programming to the United Kingdom, the Netherlands, France, Spain, and Sweden. In addition, Capital Cities/ABC became a 50 percent partner with France's Canal Plus and Compagnie Générale des Eaux.[81]

In 1993, the giant U.S. talk show program distributor Multimedia ("Donahue," "Sally Jesse Raphael," and the "Jerry Springer" talk shows), made multimillion dollar deals with many of the ABC-owned television stations. It also announced that it would begin exporting formats from some of its most successful tabloid interview shows to Spain, Germany, and France. And in addition, three 50-50 joint partnerships were announced with two production companies already co-owned with Capital Cities/ABC. They were to replicate successful U.S. talk shows and share in the foreign revenue. Although officials at Multimedia were not sure how European audiences would react to the often tabloid content of U.S.-style talk shows, Ethan Power, Multimedia's vice-president of international development, said, "some topics might not float well; we will have to see how far we can push the audience."[82]

Furthering expanding into Europe, Capital Cities/ABC bought a 10-20 percent interest (not required to be reported by U.S. law) in Germany-based Tele 5, a cable service that can be seen in some 12 million German households. This acquisition represented the first ownership stake by a U.S. network in the deregulated European broadcast industry.[83]

As part of its venture in home video production and distribution, Capital Cities/ABC announced that it was forming a new home video unit to gain a share of the $12 billion domestic home video market with programming and various ABC talent and franchises.[84]

There had been reported speculation that Capital Cities/ABC would one day merge with Paramount Communications. Paramount both distributes PPV programming through an agreement with Request TV, the largest U.S. PPV operator, and has substantial book publishing interests in its subsidiaries, Simon & Schuster, Prentice-Hall, Pocket Books, Macmillan, and others.

A Paramount and Capital Cities/ABC merger would further concentrate the ownership of the media conglomerates in the U.S. In light of the obvious television programming and distribution capability of the two companies and their subsidiaries, a Capital Cities/ABC-Paramount combination would become one of the most powerful global media corporations ever created. Paramount's properties include its motion picture studios and a substantial film library, the USA cable network, the Madison Square Garden arena, the New York Knicks basketball team, the New York Rangers hockey team, and TVN, a satellite sports service.[85] Capital Cities/ABC and Paramount, along with two Mexican media giants, made an unsuccessful joint bid for Mexico's two Mexican television channels, the daily *El Nacional* newspaper, and a Mexican movie theater chain in 1993.[86]

Paramount Communications and Viacom, Inc. (the latter is one of Capital Cities/ABC's programming and former cable partners in the Lifetime cable network) announced that they would merge in a $8.2 billion deal in September 1993.[87] Viacom had combined revenues of $6 billion in 1992. Later, QVC—the largest U.S. home shopping network—joined forces with TCI—the largest U.S. cable operator—to make a rival bid for Paramount. Viacom was ultimately successful in acquiring Paramount in February 1994.

However, this merger does not preclude a further merger with Capital Cities/ABC, Inc., in the years ahead. A takeover of Paramount Viacom International would represent the largest media merger of all time, and would require substantially more than the $14 billion in operating capital that was required to complete the merger of Time and Warner Communications in 1989. Based on its 1985 takeover of ABC, Capital Cities seems to be one of the few media corporations in the world that could manage to line up the investor and regulatory support to complete such a merger.

ABC News Bends Right

In 1989, Capital Cities/ABC, Inc., became the highest rated U.S. television news service since ABC and United Paramount Theater merged in 1953. As a result of that rating superiority, ABC News was expected to earn its parent conglomerate a reported profit of $50 million in 1990, according to *The Wall Street Journal*.[88]

With this newly found prosperity and its on-air claim to be the most watched U.S. news source, ABC News seems to have drifted more toward the right of the political spectrum since the merger. ABC anchor Peter Jennings revealed in a 1993 *TV Guide* interview that conservative viewpoints will get more air time on "ABC World News Tonight with Peter Jennings." Declaring that the program's "American Agenda" feature had had a liberal slant, Jennings said he wants to pay more attention to conservatives, "claiming that their ideas are 'more provocative and less predictable on some issues.'"[89]

Today, ABC News concentrates on being profitable and does not report, on a sustained basis, on issues that may "rock the boat" and directly interfere with its behind-the-scenes corporate lobbying or profit-making. While it likes to portray itself as a "watchdog on government power," Capital Cities/ABC, through ABC News, in many cases has become noticeably "advertiser friendly," in an effort to improve its bottom-line. It sold 80,000 copies of U.S. General H. Norman Schwarzkopf's press conference in which he described how the allied forces had won the Persian Gulf War. Introduced by Peter Jennings, ABC (and its distribution partner, MPI Home Video) advertised the tape as "Schwarzkopf: How the War Was Won" and subtitled it "The Briefing." [90] During the 1991 Persian Gulf crisis, *Washington Post* TV critic Tom Shales reported that (of the U.S. networks) ABC News was the "friendliest to and the least critical of the Bush administration and its policies." [91]

In 1987, reports reached the public that ABC News correspondent Barbara Walters had broken network policy by secretly passing two notes from international arms dealer-intermediary Manucher Ghorbanifar to President Reagan. Ghorbanifar was a central figure in the Iran-Contra arms-for-hostages swap. She broke ABC News policy when she did not tell her superiors of Ghorbanifar's request. ABC News later said publicly that Walters would not be disciplined for her covert diplomatic role in the affair. [92]

Given the history of links between U.S. intelligence and federal law enforcement and the networks, this incident, like others, raised questions as to how "independent" network news organizations are from internal and external political and marketing pressure to influence news-gathering and reporting. [93]

Meanwhile, however, ABC News' ties to other U.S. media conglomerates are becoming more and more visible. Following the highly embarrassing NBC News scandal involving faked news footage on its primetime magazine "Dateline" and on "NBC Nightly News" in 1992, ABC News President Roone Arledge met with GE chair Jack Welch to share advice on how to repair the journalistic reputation of NBC News and, indirectly, save the reputation for veracity of the U.S. networks as a group. [94]

Defending Capital Cities/ABC's other relationships with CBS and NBC by citing the need to cut costs, ABC News officials have continued to enter into journalistic agreements with the other networks' news organizations. For instance, ABC and *Time* magazine agreed to co-produce a series of TV news specials that were also to be the subject of major articles in the newsweekly. This deal grew out of a special hour-long 1980s retrospective ABC and *Time* magazine co-produced in 1989 and a special issue on gun control that was also the topic of a primetime ABC news special in January 1990. [95]

Through Capital Cities/ABC, U.S. public television has also become more fully integrated into national commercial broadcasting partnerships. Taking advantage of PBS's viewer support and elite image, ABC joined with it to rebroadcast the ABC News "Town Meeting" interview with Soviet leaders Mikhail S. Gorbachev and Boris N. Yeltsin in 1988. Earlier, PBS rebroadcast highlights from a "Town Meeting" in which "ABC Nightline" host Ted Koppel moderated a discussion on Israeli-Palestinian relations. PBS said it had received the program free of charge "as a public service" and stated that ABC had provided it. Since ABC also planned to sell a home video of this popular discussion at a later date, the PBS exposure was like additional money in the bank. Whether PBS would share in the revenues generated by the on-air sale of this home-videocassette was not reported.[96]

Capitalizing on Capital Cities' conservative Catholic ties, in April 1991, ABC News made U.S. network television history on the program "20/20" by broadcasting for the first time a public exorcism. The network was given permission for the telecast by conservative Cardinal John O'Connor of the New York Archdiocese because the "devil [was] real, his evil [was] spreading and exorcisms approved by the church [were] being used to rid some people of their demons." In December 1993, Fairness and Accuracy in Reporting (FAIR) charged that the executive producer of "20/20," Victor Neufeld "kept producers on his program from investigating or reporting on stories about the dangers of nuclear energy and other environmental hazards because his wife is a public relations executive with clients in the [U.S.] energy industry."[97]

News Competition?

Under pressure from Capital Cities/ABC to make profits, ABC News has become an equal competitor to the network's Entertainment, Sports, and other corporate operating subsidiaries. News has become a product, and therefore is only seen as a viable "public service" offering when it can make huge profits. To please sponsors and create a favorable climate in which to sell its products and services, ABC News, like the other network news providers, has sometimes become a virtual public relations (PR) arm, serving the profit objectives and conservative political interests of corporate America by using news-like reports and features supplied by outside public relations firms. And news is always more profitable when it is planned or provided free-of-charge by PR firms. Even when ABC cuts its worldwide staff massively, it continues to dominate U.S. news-gathering and profit-making. At the same time that ABC News announced a cut of nearly 10 percent in the ranks of its journalists in 1991, for example, it launched an overnight, anchored news program. At first the network wanted to charge its affiliates for this new service, but later changed the policy when its stations objected. Instead, it kept 60 percent of the advertising inventory and demanded that program affiliates broadcast a minimum of two hours of the program nightly.[98]

Such additional efforts to increase profit margins drove the networks even closer together than they were before the massive mergers in 1986-1987. For the 1990 and 1992 national elections, ABC, NBC, CBS, and CNN, as well as *The New York Times* and over 100 newspapers and local stations, formed a huge consortium to conduct exit-polling interviews. Each of the networks paid "an estimated $3 million" to participate; but newspapers and local stations paid considerably less. When academics pointed to the possibility that the elections could be influenced or manipulated through a centrally controlled source of election information, the head of the consortium, Warren J. Mitofsky (the former head of the CBS News elections unit) commented, "If the academics want to raise money to do other surveys, let them go out and raise the money for it."[99]

In a similar way, ABC has also exploited its central control over U.S. news-gathering by initiating pool arrangements to serve other networks and local stations—for profit, of course. In 1988, ABC Radio started the Washington Audio News Distribution Service (WAND). This affiliate distributed coverage of all major and minor news events in the Washington, D.C., area—including those at the White House, State Department, Pentagon, and congressional hearings and press conferences—to all of its subscribing radio news organizations. In 1991, some of these clients included Associated Press Radio, Mutual-NBC radio, the Voice of America, National Public Radio, Unistar Radio, the UPI radio network, the British Broadcasting Corporation (BBC), and the Canadian network, CBC.[100]

But this move toward centralized news coverage in Washington was embarrassing for many subscribing broadcasters of the ABC-owned WAND. During an interview with the *Washington Journalism Review*, the ABC News radio bureau chief refused to discuss "specific" clients because, he said, "broadcasters fear the image of going into a joint operation with their competition."[101] Apparently, WAND service also carried over into television news. The Washington bureaus of CBS, NBC, ABC, and CNN all agreed in 1991 to a one-month experiment to pool their coverage of President Bush's daily schedule, as well as press conferences and speeches with other major broadcast organizations in the capitol. While pool coverage was not a new development among the networks, previously the practice was limited to largely pre-planned news coverage of special events and presidential addresses or press conferences.[102]

In 1992, ABC announced plans to begin a news-wire service for its radio stations and affiliates carried via satellite, offering 24-hour a day service from Reuters America and Gannett News Media—the publisher of *USA Today*. ABC radio denied that it was taking on Associated Press as a news-wire competitor.[103]

Capitalizing on deregulation and reducing costs are also evident in the Capital Cities/ABC part-ownership of the PR Newswire, "a wire service specializing in business press releases." It transmits to some 600 news organizations in the U.S., including *The Wall Street Journal, The New York Times, Newsweek*, the *Washington Post, USA Today*, the three major networks, Associated Press, Reuters, and the Knight-Ridder Financial News. The company was established primarily "to promote corporate interests and influence public opinion," according to Martin A. Lee and Norman Solomon, authors of *Unreliable Sources: A Guide to Detecting Bias in News Media.*[104]

With pervasive network cutbacks in overseas news coverage, a growing market has developed for foreign reports and dispatches. World Television News (WTN) has become a major supplier of news from abroad for the U.S. networks. But ABC moved on this international supplier of news and information by purchasing an 80 percent share of WTN stock in 1989. In doing so, Capital Cities/ABC entered into a business partnership with Rupert Murdoch's (owner of the Fox network) Australia Nine Network, and the British news service International Television News (ITN).[105]

In addition to contracts with CNN and ABC, WTN has an additional 50 U.S. subscribers. Together with its larger competitor, Visnews, the London-based WTN has become a primary supplier of news footage from around the world. As of 1992, WTN and Visnews served clients in 84 countries worldwide. News material is generally not credited when it airs. It is hard to tell what is WTN or Visnews and what is not. Despite recent gains in the number of subscribers and outlets for both WTN and Visnews, "ABC, NBC, and CBS are reluctant to say how much footage from Visnews and WTN they broadcast."[106]

To further serve more corporate clients, WTN formed a new subsidiary, Transcontinental Television, designed to distribute press releases and public service announcements from corporations, government agencies, nonprofit organizations, and a number of public relations and advertising firms.[107] This video news-release activity has emerged as a major means of cutting costs in television news. And to further cut costs, ABC News also announced that it was embarking on the controversial practice of using corporate video news releases (VNR) to enhance its news coverage.[108]

It is likely that ABC will to continue to dominate worldwide news-gathering, considering its controlling interest in WTN and the startling fact that ABC News and BBC News have become news-gathering partners. As WTN's major competitor overseas, the BBC will now share crews and equipment and will collaborate on news programming.[109]

The growing dominance of ABC News has even made it possible to sell "old news" as "new news." In October 1991, the network announced that it had begun offering to advertising clients recycled "human interest stories" from ABC programs on the cable network The Discovery Channel. The new Discovery program, "Moments of Courage," repackaged one-to-five-year-old "20/20" segments that "featured examples of individual courage." This curious partnership duplicated a similar 1989 deal between ABC and A&E. It began with the series "The Eagle and the Bear," which also featured old news footage from ABC.[110]

Widening its reach even further into alternative news markets, ABC News went on the road in 1992 in a program partnership with the American Transportation Television Network (ATTN), a new truck-stop information service. The agreement gives the U.S. truck stops access to ABC's 11 daily news feeds. In return, ATTN agreed to supply ABC with news about the transportation industry. In other words, in return for exclusive access to audiences at ATTN-member truck-stops, which Capital Cities/ABC then sells to corporate sponsors, ABC News broadcasts ATTN-produced news releases on the transportation industry. This is an arrangement from which both ABC and ATTN profit.[111]

ABC Radio—More Monopoly

One of the most important sources of profit and influence remains Capital Cities/ABC's radio holdings. In addition to its roster of 14 owned-

and-operated major market AM and FM stations—in New York, Los Angeles, San Francisco, Detroit, Chicago, Washington, D.C., Fort Worth-Dallas, Atlanta, and Minneapolis—that collectively reach up to 25 percent of the potential U.S. radio audience, Capital Cities owns the ABC Radio Networks. Offering eight different program services, as well as an array of news and information programs, ABC Radio had approximately 3,200 affiliates in North America and the Caribbean area as of December 31, 1992.[112]

Capital Cities/ABC also has contractual agreements with other production companies for the lease of its offices, studios, and satellite-delivery system, to syndicated conservative national radio commentators such as Rush Limbaugh, Barry Farber, and others. Although these "outside" talk shows are not counted as part of ABC's program roster, they originated from the production facilities of Capital Cities/ABC. There is no FCC limit on the number of radio stations one U.S. network may have.

When all of the U.S. radio programs that ABC has a part in recording, producing, or distributing every day are added up, the radio empire of Capital Cities/ABC again comes into view. Out of the approximately 11,000 operating radio stations in the U.S. (as of 1993), Capital Cities/ABC touches over half of them in some way—by direct service or indirectly through partnership agreements that provide advertising representation, news services, studios, satellite time, offices, and other marketing help.

The power of this vast empire to dominate the U.S. radio industry cannot be underestimated. At a time when national sponsors are asking for more value from their advertising purchases, Capital Cities/ABC can offer group-sales packages that exploit its great media holdings. It can dominate the marketplace for national advertising, even if the sale of these packages means controlling its affiliated stations for the benefit of the network's own profit-making. Capital Cities/ABC's local radio affiliates, for instance, have charged that ABC Radio officials have marketed stations to national advertisers without their consent. ABC responded that it had the right to determine how its affiliates would be marketed to national advertisers.[113]

Yet, the profit-boosting benefits of corporate oligopoly do not translate into positive social results, such as more jobs. In 1992, ABC Radio Networks eliminated an undisclosed number of jobs and shifted others to the Dallas offices of the Satellite Music Network (SMN), which the network had purchased in 1990, yet denied that they were shifting operations to take advantage of Capital Cities/ABC's national radio empire.[114]

Although SMN offers low-cost programming services to stations in small and medium markets, it and the national satellite-radio company Transtar have been charged with contributing to a loss of local control by many radio stations in small communities. Because of the overlap of many of the ABC-SMN program and ABC news services in many radio markets, Capital Cities/ABC-originated programming can be heard on up to five or six local stations—and possibly more—thereby helping to maintain a virtual ABC monopoly in those areas.

In January 1992, ABC Radio Networks and its cable network subsidiary, ESPN, announced plans to launch a "jointly managed [U.S.] sports news radio network." The ESPN network was set to offer 16 weekend hours of original programming for radio, and would be marketed to advertisers and stations by ABC.[116]

Disney studios and ABC radio announced in 1992 a new 24-hour-a-day children's radio network for different age groups of children under twelve. The operation was to begin in spring 1993 and would implement numerous merchandising and advertising deals between Capital Cities/ABC and the Disney Studios.[117]

In 1993, ABC Radio Networks made a significant investment in European radio, mirroring the global outreach of ABC's other operating divisions. It purchased a minority stake (about 33 percent) in the London-based Satellite Media Services, Ltd. (SMS), a company that distributes radio programs and commercials. SMS is the only radio company that distributes its products by satellite to the whole of of England's commercial radio market. It is therefore positioned to dominate the entire United Kingdom radio market with ABC Radio as its partner.[118]

Capital Cities/ABC has even signed up the U.S. airlines with its "pay per listen" channels. ABC radio and In-Flight Phone Corporation have agreed to begin providing programming. Passengers on select flights can listen to ABC Radio programming, including news, sports, and music, as well as "pay-per-listen" programs.[119]

Limbaugh, Farber, and Harvey = Reagan Radio

In 1993, as U.S. talk radio became a bastion of centrist and right-wing commentators,[120] Capital Cities/ABC was doing its part to keep Reaganism alive by carrying an array of conservative radio commentators such as Rush Limbaugh, Barry Farber, and Paul Harvey. ABC Radio was also doing its part through its radio stations and networks, as well through occasional exclusive marketing and studio-leasing agreements with "outside" networks such as Limbaugh's "Excellence in Broadcasting" network (The "EIB" network) and Farber's "Daynet Radio Network," among others.

Rush Limbaugh owes his discovery and launch into national radio to Capital Cities/ABC. He was originally hired from a Sacramento AM radio station in 1988 by former ABC Radio Network President Edward McLaughlin. Limbaugh came to New York for a one-month "on-air" trial on Capital Cities/ABC's flagship radio station, WABC(AM), and later began to offer his daily three-hour program to local radio stations throughout the United States. For the first two years of his national radio broadcasting, ABC Radio handled all the marketing contracts for Limbaugh's advertising sponsorships. He is continuing to work out of WABC's offices and studios in New York.

Limbaugh, a vigorous supporter of Reagan's ultra-conservative vision of a totally privatized corporate America, reportedly came to McLaughlin's attention through industry contacts. The commentator's spirited, daily defense of Lt. Colonel Oliver North, William Casey, and the rest of the Reagan administration had begun to attract large conservative audiences in Sacramento during the Senate's 1987 Iran-contra Senate hearings. He has said that the "secret of his success" is to simply express his opinions, but not have guests, excluding liberal or progressive voices and points of view he considers "unworthy of attention." He blames all of America's problems on "big-spending Democrats, the lazy poor, and trouble-making minority rabble-rousers." As one of the most prominent, unabashed Reagan supporters on the national media stage, he usually delivers the same message: support corporations and the wealthy, cut taxes, make the military stronger, and boost the so-called free-market economy.[121]

It is important to note that "The Rush Limbaugh Program," and conservative programs like it that exclude other opinions, were developed following the sweeping broadcast deregulation zealously pursued by the Reagan and Bush administrations from 1981 through 1992. Limbaugh's program, for example, might be quite different had the Reagan FCC not thrown out the 1987 Fairness Doctrine requiring stations to provide a reasonable opportunity for the discussion of opposing views on controversial issues of public importance.[122]

As of January 1993, Limbaugh's show was being broadcast on over 500 radio stations across the country. He has more listeners than any other U.S. talk-show host (an estimated 12 million weekly). Although he frequently appeals to those excluded from government and corporate decisionmaking, in 1992 Limbaugh signed a new multi-year radio contract that EFM officials called one of the most lucrative in the history of radio.[123]

During the 1992 election year, Limbaugh supported the ultra-conservative Reagan-clone Pat Buchanan throughout the early Republican primaries, but then changed his position after it became clear that Buchanan would not win. Limbaugh was relentlessly courted by the Bush White House and, to win his support on the air, was even invited to spend the night at the White House in June 1992.[126] After Bush reportedly carried his bags for the overnight stay, Limbaugh devoted his programs to the Republican effort to re-elect Bush. He invited him onto the program as well as Vice-President Dan Quayle, and parroted Bush's promises that "the economy was poised for a dramatic recovery."[127] At the 1992 Republican convention, Limbaugh shared box seats with Barbara Bush, the president's wife. He did not provide Democratic or other candidates running for the presidency in 1992 any reasonable amount of equal time in the name of balance.

When Limbaugh's syndicated television show (produced by former Bush media advisor, Roger Ailes) debuted nationally in September 1992, it resembled a program-length commercial for the Bush campaign. Again, because of the Reagan-Bush efforts to weaken the 1987 Fairness Doctrine, Limbaugh was not required to offer any opposing viewpoints to his broadcast audiences. FAIR has reported that, during the last two months of the 1992 U.S. presidential campaign, many of Bush's Ailes-inspired campaign themes ended up as major topics on Limbaugh's radio and television programs. When asked to provide equal time for opposing viewpoints, he responded, "I am equal time."[128]

Furthermore, Limbaugh's television program is distributed nationally by another one of Capital Cities/ABC's major partners in overseas syndication, Multimedia. *EXTRA!*—FAIR's progressive U.S. media journal that regularly exposes the practices and the bias of corporate-based U.S. media—recently observed, "In the history of American television, it is hard to recall a similar instance in which a political partisan was allowed to sermonize day after day for his favored candidates and political party."[129] As of January 1993, Limbaugh's television show was carried on 206 stations and reached 98 percent of the country.[130] Late in 1993, Ailes was named president of the GE-NBC-owned CNBC Cable Network. Yet, he has continued to produce Limbaugh's television program.

Even though Democrat Bill Clinton was elected to the presidency in 1992, Limbaugh remains one of the most visible defenders of the Reagan-Bush years. Although he continues to portray himself as not a member of the mainstream media roster, nearly every one of his political, economic, and social beliefs and sermons reflects the positions of the majority of Wall Street investors and creditors, those who have considerable input into the direction of most U.S. media outlets.[131]

Another *de facto* ABC commentator doing his part to keep Reaganism alive is Barry Farber, who can be heard on the Daynet Radio Network, a company with contractual ties to Capital Cities/ABC. Like Limbaugh on his "independent" EIB network, Farber broadcasts from the ABC Radio Network's studio-office complex on Manhattan's west side. While Farber's program may be "editorially" independent of Capital Cities/ABC, he is aided and abetted by the conglomerate's media network of studios, satellites, and marketing connections. Thus he is able to spread throughout the United States his ultra-conservative program against liberals and progressives.

On one occasion, he told his listeners that the reactionary right-wing hate group, the John Birch Society (JBS), was quite "noble" in maintaining many of its positions throughout the Cold War era.[132] It urged resistance to racial integration in public schools in the 1950s, repudiation of peaceful co-existence between the Soviet Union and the U.S., and aggressive use of nuclear weapons against communist powers. JBS founder Robert Welch led a national drive to impeach Chief Justice Earl Warren for requiring school integration following the 1954 Supreme Court ruling *Brown vs. Board of Education.* Welch once said that the New Deal was a communist plot.

Another conservative commentator on the ABC network airwaves is Paul Harvey, who broadcasts daily from Chicago. According to the 1992

Capital Cities/ABC annual report, Harvey is "America's most prominent and popular radio commentator." Most frequently conservative in tone and respectful of U.S.-dominant institutions, Harvey has been broadcasting on ABC Radio for nearly 40 years. He emphasizes lighter and reassuring news stories that largely serve to support the myth of the "American dream where fairness and justice are available to all," and reliably denigrates those who criticize the U.S. political and economic status quo.[133]

Warren Buffett—The Most Important Director

Capital Cities could not have taken over ABC without the intervention of Warren Buffett and his Berkshire Hathaway holding company. During the seven years after the takeover, Buffett substantially increased his holdings and stature throughout the world financial community. At the time of the merger, he provided $517 million in capital to complete the historic $3.5 billion deal and in return received an ownership share in Capital Cities/ABC, valued at nearly $2 billion in 1990.[134] In 1993, Buffett was named the richest person in the U.S. by *Forbes* magazine.[135]

Buffett continues to work out of Omaha, Nebraska. From there, he projects a folksy, down-to-earth style in his business and personal affairs.[136] His knowledge of U.S. economic policy is considered by some on Wall Street to be more dependable than that of the Federal Reserve bankers. Buffett remains a Wall Street contrarian; he continues to follow his own code of financial ethics. In 1989, for example, he removed his California Savings and Loan Institution from a national savings and loan trade group because he favored the imposition of tougher sanctions against unethical ones from Congress.[137]

Buffett retains his status as the dean of Wall Street's friendly takeover artists and enjoys mostly favorable press coverage. Unlike Ivan Boesky, who was sent to federal prison for giving investment bankers confidential news of pending takeovers, Buffett reportedly deals only in takeovers where all the information is made public.[138] According to a profile done by *Fortune*, Buffett's rules for investment are very simple: "The first rule is not to lose. The second is not to forget the first."[139] He has continued to add to his holdings with spectacular deals to fend off hostile takeovers by U.S. Air, Salomon Brothers (an investment bank), Champion Paper, Gillette, American Express, and others.[140]

Buffett began to receive criticism in November 1990, however, because he had been able to obtain preferential stock deals that were not available to other investors. In the opinion of some financial experts, he has been able to buy controlling stock interests in many corporations for far less than it would have cost to get them on the open market. In the process, Buffett has assumed control of many U.S. corporations and a good deal of influence on the economy.[141]

Nevertheless, he continues to be the darling of the investment industry and its small group of major institutional investors. As of December 1993, shares in his holding company, Berkshire Hathaway, were selling at $17,500 each. His reputation was so revered by Washington and Wall Street that he was called in to serve as the interim chairman of Salomon Brothers when it faced criminal fines and sanctions arising from its violation of rules governing bids for U.S. Treasury bonds in 1991. It is widely acknowledged that Buffett's intervention saved the firm and its reputation from serious damage and censure from Wall Street and Washington regulators. It is also true that Buffett had much to gain from protecting Salomon's corporate reputation—*The New York Times* reported that Buffett owned 14 percent of the company's equity, valued at $700 million in 1991.[142]

Buffett is a close friend and financial advisor to *Washington Post* publisher Katharine Graham and CBS CEO Laurence Tisch. Until the takeover of ABC, Buffett held a seat on the *Post*'s board, but chose to give it up following the deal. Through Berkshire Hathaway, he continues to own a sizable chunk of *Time* and 15 percent of The *Washington Post* organization, which owns *Newsweek*. The *Post* now owns 54 of the cable systems that belonged to Capital Cities prior to the takeover of ABC.[143]

All of these interlocking corporate ties make Capital Cities/ABC one of the most influential media institutions in the history of the United States, in terms of its extraordinary power to shape public opinion.

Yet, as formidable as this may seem, there are ways to turn back the tide of overwhelming corporate control of popular expression in our society. I will discuss some of them in the next, and last, chapter.

Chapter Six

Making Media More Democratic

A theme of this book is that monopolistic control over media information and cultural production by an elite cadre of political or business insiders subverts democracy. When economic and political clout most determines who gets access to the media, power no longer rests with the people. When only few control the media—especially the most popular means of public expression in society—representative democracy becomes an illusion.[1]

As the gatekeeper of "truth" in our media-driven society, corporate media conglomerates have the extraordinary power to marginalize dissident voices and discredit political opponents who may threaten their bottom line, even in a relatively minor way. In helping to "manufacture consent," concentrated media ownership continues to provide elite business interests with an awesome state propaganda apparatus for citizen thought control. Corporate media systems, even when they promise profits, prosperity, and freedom have remained steadfast in their opposition to citizen control of media.

The Democratic Illusion

The history of elite management of ABC and Capital Cities is not the exception, but the rule in U.S. broadcasting. Very few broadcast stations have ever been controlled by those who could be considered common or average working people. In nearly all U.S. cities, the most powerful radio and TV stations have almost always been entrusted to the more "privileged" corporate citizens of the community—except during the early 1920's when for-profit broadcasting was largely viewed with suspicion in the United States.

A quick glance through the names of the current board of directors of Capital Cities/ABC, Inc., reveals that media board membership is based on having access to capital, political influence, and often "undisclosed" ties to the firm's top management. Not surprisingly, the board of Capital Cities/ABC is a carbon copy of the elite boards of directors and the executive leadership of CBS, NBC, and the other media conglomerates that continue to dominate media production and distribution in the U.S., and increasingly around the world.

The interlocking directorates and business agreements among Capital Cities/ABC and its partners in the global U.S.-dominated media cartel span across entertainment, sports, news programming, and nearly every other form of programming. Since the Capital Cities/ABC merger, ABC, for example, has formed program partnerships with the BBC, Time-Warner, *Reader's Digest*, Gannett, Paramount, Columbia, NBC, CBS, and Fox, among others, and has shared profits with almost every one of the parent corporations that now make up this exclusive corporate fraternity.

But again, this is nothing new. U.S. media monopoly and cartelization, the mark of elite ownership and control, have long been at work to prop up U.S. power throughout the world. It would be incorrect to think that the U.S.-based media cartel was not already monopolistic and inherently anti-democratic before the Reagan-Bush administrations took over in 1981.

Corporate manipulation, greed, and criminal misconduct did not start in the Reagan-Bush years; these evils are as old as U.S. monopoly capitalism. Over the last hundred years of industrial growth, private corporate monopolies have been regularly defended by government and business leaders as the most efficient means by which the country could ensure economic growth. Yet, the myth of serving the public interest through the private sector has more often served as a pretext to protect corporate interest, convenience, and necessity.

During the Reagan-Bush administrations, the FCC excused broadcasters from adhering to most rules and regulations protecting the public interest, "made it impossible for citizen groups to challenge renewal of station licenses, lifted limits on the number of stations that a single corporation could acquire," and gave broadcast owners permission to create giant monopolies.[2]

In return, these media superpowers—almost all of which were later linked in marketing and business projects extensively documented in my earlier chapters—nearly always supported the Reagan-Bush foreign and domestic policies. With billions of dollars in future profits on the line, they provided positive reports on the social effects of deregulation, as well as on the need for government to provide corporations with unprecedented freedom to make windfall profits at the public's expense.

The Reagan and Bush administrations also did much to encourage the U.S.-dominated media cartel's evolution as a government and corporate propaganda instrument, limit domestic and foreign political dissent, ensure corporate control over the U.S. political economy, and maintain U.S. imperialist power abroad. The media monopoly of 1992 consisted of 20 communications conglomerates. In 1983, more than 50 such conglomerates existed.[3]

Over the last several chapters, I have concentrated on the *before*, *during*, and *after* of the 1985 Capital Cities/ABC merger. By focusing on this new conglomerate, often the unofficial "spokescorporation" for the U.S. media cartel, I have attempted to show how this corporation (and others like it) continues to dominate every media market it operates in, and how it routinely seeks to downplay the "power by a few" nature of its management structure from citizens.

That drive for profits and power can be clearly seen in the extraordinary 1985 Capital Cities takeover of ABC. Those companies' longstanding cooperation with the highest levels of U.S. political power was never fully investigated or revealed to the citizenry by Congress, the FCC, or the Justice Department. When the media system did not report to the majority of the citizenry about the inside corporate history and elite business ownership of both Capital Cities and ABC before the takeover, that was not the result of conspiracy or cabal. Rather, the lack of candor reflected the shared interests of corporate elites who acted to protect their firm's power, privileges, and profits.

The current corporate control of the media cannot be reduced until government is forced, through political action, to somehow shift the balance of media power in favor of common people. The average citizen has very little knowledge of decisionmaking at the networks. Media executives and their corporations, more than ever before in the history of U.S. broadcasting, are able to hide behind their first amendment rights in order to prevent greater citizen participation in their affairs.

So, What's a Better System?

It is not enough to suggest that our media system needs to be transformed. We must also focus some attention on the political and economic inequities and injustices inherent within our limited democratic society. Media structure and practice reflect the nature of the society in which they exist.

James Curran, a British communication theorist who has written extensively about making access to media more politically, economically, and socially fair, notes this in his book, *Bending Reality:* "The media accurately reflect and represent the prevailing structure and mode of power. It is in politics and the state, not in the media, that power is skewed."[4]

Given the increasing separation of U.S. society along class lines and the continued reliance on the so-called free market system, it is unlikely that an advertiser-supported local or national media system could ever serve all citizens. Clearly, those who lack power in society also lack economic resources; and corporate-dominated media companies will tend to use their political, economic, and social clout to prevent a fairer and more just distribution of media resources. An exclusively privately-owned media will always seek to protect private profits and privilege.

It seems illogical to believe that a media system based on the so-called free enterprise system (actually a euphemism for "the use of privately or publicly owned property for private profit"[5]) could ever benefit the general public—those who do not already have a high level of disposable income or political-economic power—let alone empower them to make media more egalitarian, representative, or democratic.

Instead of the current U.S. media system, which typically favors only those with access to power, I would like to see a more democratic one, in which:

1) the individual becomes an active partner in, and not a mere object of, communication,
2) the variety of messages exchanged increases, and
3) the extent and quality of social representation or participation in communication are augmented.[6]

I define "democratic media" here in the way that the late Sean MacBride did. During the late 1970s, he chaired a distinguished international communications commission dedicated to developing and guaranteeing "freedom and the free flow of information" through the auspices of UNESCO (United Nations Educational, Scientific, and Cultural Organization).

According to MacBride, the real hope for greater social democratization must come from efforts to integrate communication power horizon-
tally across the class, racial and ethnic, and gender divisions that exist
within a society or nation. A democratic media system must be based on
reciprocity; it is democratic only if it allows the nation's citizenry to be
heard and seen with equal force and visibility.[7]

More important, however, is the principle that democratic media
must have the freedom to communicate radical and unpopular ideas and
opinions without fear of retribution by sponsors or the government. As
the 20th-century novelist and political activist, George Orwell, once said,
"[True] liberty...means allowing people freely to say things you do not
want to hear."[8]

Ralph Nader, the U.S. consumer advocate, has been particularly
eloquent and persuasive in his campaign for a more democratic, equal,
and critically based U.S. media system. He argues that we need a new
"tool box for democracy" so that, in our respective roles as voters,
consumers, taxpayers, workers, and shareholders, we can become more
politically and economically aware as citizens:

> [We need to get] valid information in a timely fashion, be able
> to communicate to one another as citizens, and be able to
> mobilize to get action to recover our government, to have
> government of, by, and for the people instead of, by and for
> GM, DuPont, and Union Carbide ...Now we don't have
> television that is programmed for the people...We own the
> public airwaves, why should the tenants, the radio and TV
> stations, control it 24 hours a day? Give us a break.[9]

Indeed, anyone committed to making the U.S. television system
more democratic should keep in mind that the current U.S. media system,
which is network-dominated and advertising-subsidized, first emerged
not through consensus, but through conflict.[10]

Even though network for-profit, commercial broadcasting was once
thought by some to conflict with the needs of a democratic society (by
conservatives as well as progressives), the "public interest" appeals of
corporate broadcasters won for them a communication system that stimu-
lates economic growth at the expense of more representative, diverse
media.[11] Seeking to counter U.S. corporate media, Nader and his colleagues at the Center for Responsive Law developed a plan and model

statute for the Audience Network—a non-profit corporation that would each day program 60 minutes of prime-time or commercial radio and television stations on citizens' issues. The Audience Network would be paid for by private funds from members ($10 annually) and would also act as a broker with non-profit groups that wish to make and air their own programs. The programming would run the gamut from culture to politics, and from entertainment to scientific topics. Nader's Audience Network was a step in the direction for a more democratic and citizen based media.[12]

What You Can Do

Any attempt to make our media system more representative of the diverse interests and ideas of all of the citizenry must begin in our own local communities, at the grassroots level.

One idea would be to form a local media council in your local community, school, library, or religious group. Such a council should include representatives of all segments of the population: teachers, librarians, students, and parents; groups concerned with women, children, senior citizens, and gay and lesbian issues; people of color; church-based organizations; educational, health, environmental, legal, and other professional associations; local consumer groups and agencies; and any others who may already be committed to broadening the freedom and diversity of media communication in a local community. These community councils could also align themselves with journalists, artists, writers, actors, directors, and other workers seeking more creative expression and freedom.

A media council would demand more time for community issues and concerns than is presently being offered by the local newspapers, cable systems, and radio or television stations that are supposed to be "serving" the community. Organized and coordinated letter-writing to the owners and managers of local and national media outlets, as well as their advertisers, can often be quite effective in bringing change.

In 1992, for example, Ralph Nader tried to convince Congress to force local cable companies to allow local, independent, and democratically controlled consumer action groups to insert messages into the residents' monthly bills. These notices could have described the goals of the consumer groups and allowed them to solicit funds and members. Such subscriber-consumer groups could have then monitored the policies and practices of their local cable company, and represented consumer interests in regulatory and legislative proceedings and with the cable companies directly.[13]

Citing a highly successful model, the Citizen Utility Board (CUB), which has represented taxpayers in several states, Nader and other national consumer advocates contend that monopolistic public agencies could be forced to listen to citizen calls for more diversity. "The most successful CUB (in Illinois) has 170,000 members and its advocacy has saved the state's consumers some $2 billion over the past several years. Other CUBs exist in Wisconsin, Oregon, and San Diego." This public interest type of innovation, for example, could have been used nationwide to pressure local cable operators to include more political, economic, and social alternative programming on their local, supposedly "public" access channels. At Nader's urging, Rep. Edward Markey (D-Mass) added provisions to set up citizen cable councils as part of a 1992 legislative effort to re-regulate the U.S. cable industry. Markey's and Nader's efforts, however, were thwarted by a major political lobbying effort by the U.S. cable industry. The Senate later passed a much more watered down cable re-regulation bill in 1992 that continued to protect corporate profit-making over consumer rights.[14]

To support more efforts such as Nader's plan for a more citizen-directed media, your local media council could also organize a community letter writing campaign to your own elected and appointed representatives in Congress, the White House, the FCC, and the Justice Department. Tell these officials that your community finds concentration of ownership in the media, public or private, to be unacceptable and undemocratic. Tell your elected representatives to demand that Congress, the FCC, and the FTC pass tougher legislation, and federal rules requiring broadcasters and cable systems to do annual community ascertainment of the needs and concerns of the local community and become more representative of the diversity of the audiences they serve. Force commercial broadcasters and cable operators to offer more educational, and socially progressive programming.

Organize public demonstrations of all local media to call attention to the excessive commercialization of media that drives out controversy or presents alternative viewpoints from being aired in broadcasts and cable programming. Such demonstrations and boycotts could be organized around specific themes such as calling for fewer commercials and less violence on children's television, the inclusion of more alternative views and opinions in your local newspaper, or more coverage of local political-economic issues on your local cable system.

Your local media council could benefit democracy by organizing community support to force local cable operators to offer public access programming that is truly an alternative to what is now offered on broadcast radio and television. Thanks to a heavy round of cable deregulation in the 1980s by the Reagan-Bush FCC, cable companies were empowered to make windfall profits by raising rates, and were released from most of their public-access obligations. In most U.S. cities, local cable public-access has become another extension of the huckster-driven marketplace. In many communities, local cable operators self-censor public-access in order to keep their cable systems free of controversy and potential local citizen or sponsor opposition. As a result, in many communities, local cable operators do not provide any kind of meaningful public-access service to the local community that they serve. In some cities, citizens who want to use the public-access facilities of their local cable operator must pay to be trained to use the equipment; a double charge since most are already cable customers.

There are, however, several national alternative cable services, for example, that could be used to bring some balance to local cable access. Nearly all of them are routinely barred from many local-access cable systems because they are regarded as too political or controversial. Paper Tiger, Deep Dish TV, and Homegrown TV, for example, are available to local cable system operators free-of-charge via satellite or by videotape shipment to participating cable systems. Operating at a much lower budget than premium cable services like TNT, Discovery, TNN, A&E, that charge cable operators a fee based on the size of their subscriber base, many cable companies have been able to bar access to these alternative services by claiming that they lack the production values or other technical requirements of so-called "quality" public-access programming.

Paper Tiger, Deep Dish TV, and other national alternative services are directly critical of corporate control over the national and local U.S media system. These programs offer stories on the corporate control of the economy, racism, alternative energy, or any other topics that are not routinely covered on mainstream media outlets.[15] While these alternative program services may not always be up to the standards of broadcast technical quality, they are intensely rooted in the local community and maintain a sense of global consciousness that is quite different from what one would see on ABC, CBS, NBC, or Fox.

And there are other models that can be used to widen the diversity of local cable-access channels in local communities. You could request that your local cable company add the nationally syndicated, alternative, Pacifica radio service to your system via satellite link-up. Your cable system could combine audio from Pacifica with a video community bulletin board that would give every resident of your community a chance to present, free of charge, current events, news, and information in your community. Due to continued deregulation and commercialization of cable channels, community bulletin boards, once available in most local cable systems, have been eliminated.

Pacifica, a progressive alternative broadcasting service, began as an outgrowth of Pacifica's five stations across the country in Berkeley, New York, Washington, D.C., Los Angeles, and Houston. Originally set up to be oppositional to the mainstream media, the Pacifica stations comprise the largest source of progressive alternative daily news in the country. Pacifica is non-commercial, non-governmental, and funded almost solely by its listeners. Pacifica's flagship station, KPFA(FM) in Berkeley, for example, regularly provides program topics that are traditionally excluded from the mainstream media: feminism, ecology, homosexuality, racial equality, tenants, and immigrants' rights reform, unionism, anti-war and anti-imperialist foreign policy initiatives, anti-nuclear movements, and other concerns.[16]

But, above all, always demand more local programming on the issues that affect your community for that is where democratic action really begins.

Media Literacy

In your local public library, school, or religious group, your media-literacy council could help to organize media-literacy and awareness workshops where critical media-reading, viewing, and listening skills could be taught to every member of your local community. Teaching media literacy is already required in the public schools of Australia, Canada, and Great Britain, and others are following in this direction. Children, at an early age, should receive advice and training in critical viewing of newspapers and broadcasts, how to exercise independent judgement, and learn to draw their own conclusions from various media portrayals.[17]

Media literacy must be elevated to the same level of importance as the ability to read and write. In a democracy such as ours, where nearly 80 percent of citizens receive most of their news and information from television, one must know the structural limitations of the media system in order to become better informed and capable of making rational voting choices. Media literacy would also include knowledge of the social, economic, and political characteristics of the media as they are currently organized. This knowledge would also include historical grounding into how the U.S. media industries developed, as well as a thorough exposure to the various scholarly research on how media affects society, the individual, and our collective culture.

For instance, at the School for Experimental Education in Etobrioke, Ontario, Canada, Media Arts students study minute portions of U.S. network shows to look at their underlying values, messages, and assumptions about power; students look at not only what is represented, but also at what is not communicated. Camera angles and editing techniques are discussed while students also are instructed as to the "signified" parts of the story line, and the implied assumptions about power, politics, economics, and social position reflected in many U.S. network programs.[18]

Besides teaching the fundamentals of media literacy in newspapers, magazines, television, motion pictures, recording, radio, and other mass media in every school in the U.S., every grade school, middle school, junior and senior high school should be equipped with closed-circuit audio/video systems, studio facilities, graphics capability, and the electronic hardware and software necessary to allow students to produce their own media products.[19]

Every school could require students to master media skills by producing community newspapers and local cable-access programs, and developing media products that reflect their interests and concerns. In the same way that students are now required to demonstrate mastery in reading, writing, and mathematics, so would a basic level of media literacy be required of everyone.[20]

What Government Must Do

As much as I would like to propose that the entire U.S. commercial system of broadcasting be transformed so that corporate advertisers do not dictate program content, I will try to be realistic. The current U.S. media system is a product of the political and economic system through which it developed, and that system needs radical transformation.

The U.S. media, or government policy, cannot be divorced from the social, political, economic, and technological roots from which it develops. Media will only become "more for the people," and representative of all U.S. socio-economic groups when considerable effort is expended by citizens at the local, regional, and national level to transform the U.S. system we have now. Media will always reflect the inequities of power within the political-economic system and also the level of democratic representation in the society at large; one cannot be divorced from the other. Any citizen attempts to make media more representative and fair in its representation of social reality must be within the context of moving our political-economic system toward one that is less discriminatory against those who lack capital.

Eventually, I believe that the majority of U.S. broadcast and cable media channels should be placed under citizen control through non-profit, public foundations. While total expropriation by government may seem to offer hope to those who currently do not have access to the media, a completely public-owned media would most likely continue to be dominated by elite interests, such as in the case of the British Broadcasting Corporation, or the publicly owned media systems of totalitarian countries. Instead, the U.S. media system should offer a decentralized service to its citizens, with a mixture of public and private levels of service. All media, however, would have to remain, by law, under the control of the average citizen — through direct representation and meaningful involvement in media decisionmaking.

Since monopoly capitalism continues to shape economic, political, and social life in the United States and the world, at least for the near future, I propose a media plan that will reduce corporate control with tough federal regulation measures to protect the public against corporate monopoly, trust-building, and domination of the media agenda for commercial profit. The larger issues of citizen empowerment and wider participation by all socio-economic classes in government and corporate decisionmaking might be open to serious public discussion once media comes more under the control of average citizens.

"Corporatizing" Public Broadcasting

Erik Barnouw — perhaps the most eloquent and respected U.S. broadcast historian — points out in his *The Image Empire* that had the U.S. federal government authorized sufficient funding for public broadcasting in the 1950s, a truly alternative U.S. public media system could have provided a realistic countervailing force to the corporate media system of today.[21] In 1993, as conservative political groups continue to force U.S. public broadcasting to become "market driven," in other words, less capable of opposing dominant U.S. power interests, attacks on public broadcasting's funding have forced it to become an agent for social control, just like commercial mass media.

Even though Japan, Britain, Germany, France, and other capitalist democracies have adequately financed non-commercial systems of broadcasting as a "check and balance" to their commercial systems, the U.S. has failed to do so. There was often political opposition from political insiders who had a direct, vested interest in seeing that commercial broadcasting remain the dominant U.S. media system. In New York, for example, when the State Regents proposed a system of state-supported public educational stations for New York city and other locations in the 1950s, Governor Thomas Dewey vetoed it.[22] Dewey, besides being politically opposed to the public financing of broadcasting, may have also been acting out of self-interest. In 1954, you will remember, Dewey and several other influential investors established what later became Capital Cities/ABC by buying their first *commercial* radio and television station in Albany, New York. The Regents proposal might have increased viewers for public broadcasting, and siphoned viewers, ratings, and profits from commercial broadcasting.

Like the battle over corporate takeover of commercial broadcasting, the battle over how to pay for a legitimate, democratic public broadcasting system is also an old one. The late Walter Lippmann, author of *Public Opinion* and a columnist for *The New York Herald-Tribune*, said in the 1930s that commercial broadcasters everywhere, even in the U.S., should be required to pay a rental or royalty to use the public airwaves for their own profit maximization. Such monies, said Lippmann, could be used to fund a public system of broadcasting that would serve as a balance to corporate media.[23]

Building on Lippmann's and others' notion of royalty for commercial broadcasters, the Ford Foundation in the 1950s suggested that the U.S. government place a royalty on domestic commercial-satellite revenue to fund a public U.S. broadcasting system.[24] The U.S. space program, for example, has been almost totally funded through tax dollars since the end of World War II and has helped to spur the development of satellite-delivered networks, digital electronics, robotic technology, computers, and other labor-saving devices that have allowed U.S. commercial broadcasters to automate operations, extend their programming range, and increase profits at the taxpayer's expense.

Today, public broadcasting continues to be dominated by elite interests and in no way can be considered representative of the U.S voting population. In 1992, out of the 1,500 non-commercial radio stations in the U.S., for instance, only 39 were owned by African-Americans and 13 were owned by Hispanic groups.[25]

Long thought of as a "check and balance" to commercial broadcasting, a closer look at "public" broadcasting in the U.S. shows that it caters to the corporate interest through sponsors and benefactors who have decisionmaking power over programming.

During the Reagan-Bush trickle-down economic period and the openly avowed political intimidation of any progressive or alternative media systems in the U.S., public television became almost fully coopted by commercial interests. In addition to dramatically shrinking public funds for PBS programming, Reagan-Bush literally pushed public television into the arms of corporate sponsors looking to reach educated and wealthy audiences for their advertising and lobbying messages.

For example, oil companies were underwriting, in full- or part-time, 72 percent of primetime PBS television by 1981. In 1983, corporate contributions to National Public Radio totaled $2.7 million, rising to $10.6 million by 1988. Corporate donors gave $70 million for PBS programs in 1989, with 20 firms paying more than $1 million each for the privilege of being a PBS corporate sponsor.[26]

As Jeff Chester, co-director of the Center for Media Education puts it, "Almost the entire primetime of PBS is geared to be nothing more than commercials for the Fortune 500." In this kind of "for profit" environment,

PBS producers have also begun to tailor their programs to attract corporate sponsors.[27]

Critics of the PBS commercial policy have charged that although its programming guidelines are supposed to prevent conflicts of interest between funding organizations and corporations, there is often self-censorship on the part of producers knowing that if they disrespect or do not please their sponsors' companies, they will lose their funding. Almost always, this kind of self-censorship is not disclosed to the audience. "This seems to me more dangerous than the most blatant or deceptive advertising on commercial TV," says Jill Savitt, research coordinator for the Center for the Study of Commercialism in Washington, "because when something is on PBS and a company underwrites it, that company gets the trusted authority of PBS, a sort of innocence by association," says Savitt. "People expect the program to be fair and accurate because it is shown on PBS."[28]

During the Reagan Era, the CPB executive board, which allocates funding for programming proposals that are suggested by local PBS stations, was packed with conservative ideologues who drastically reduced funding for projects outside of the mainstream media interest. Within this conservatizing of PBS, independent film and video makers who in previous years may have been able to challenge the political and economic status quo through PBS programs, now have little opportunity to present their programs on PBS. Along with the Reagan mandate to force the Corporation for Public Broadcasting into a more conservative direction, PBS corporate sponsors have also supported the "team player" approach with respect to the kinds of programs they are likely to fund on the PBS schedule.

This conservative bias is particularly evident on regularly scheduled PBS news and discussion programs. As Martin Lee and Norman Solomon point out in their 1990 book, *Unreliable Sources: A Guide to Detecting Bias in News Media*, PBS's "The MacNeil/Lehrer News Hour" has become a carbon copy of network news shows. So consistent in its center to right slant, a Conservative Political Action Conference Poll called it "the most balanced network news show."[29]

But the most visible evidence of PBS's respectful stance toward corporate sponsors is its right-wing line-up of talk shows. With William Buckley's "Firing Line," "The McLaughlin Group," and "One on One," "Nightly Business Report," "Wall Street Week," "Adam Smith's Money

World," and others, PBS continues to serve corporate America. The PBS regular program schedule is almost totally dedicated to center to right-wing view.

During 1991-92, several PBS programs increasingly came under attack from Lawrence Jarvik of the ultra-conservative Heritage Foundation, Republican Senators, Jesse Helms and Robert Dole, and other conservative groups who accused PBS of being "unfair" and "unobjective." Senators Dole and Helms even tried to limit funding for programs such as Bill Moyers' "World of Ideas" documentary series such as "Eyes on the Prize," "Making Sense of the Sixties," and "Frontline," because of their alleged "liberal" bias. Yet, "Frontline" supporters argue that these attacks have been initiated as a political retaliation against program themes criticizing Republican government/corporate policies.[30]

The conservative fight to control PBS continues in 1993. In April, Senator Robert Dole threatened to withhold funding from the Corporation for Public Broadcasting until "broadcasters agreed to an amendment putting the corporation in charge of insuring 'strict adherence to objectivity and balance in all programs...of a controversial nature.'"[31]

Dole and his conservative colleagues continued their attacks against PBS, specifically citing its "left-wing ideology" in documentaries like "Frontline." In its defense, CPB began a plan to "monitor" public broadcasting for political content by allocating $796,000 to insure "balance and objectivity" in controversial programming. As one NPR producer described the "objectivity" plan on the op-ed page of *The New York Times*:

> The plan converts the corporation [CPB] established as a political heat shield to protect public radio and television from intrusion by Government censors, into a conduit for the political whims of Congress. It places the corporation in an improper regulatory and editorial role and blurs the line between Government financing and editorial freedom.[32]

The above statement adds further credence to the charge that attacks on CPB's "liberal bias" have continued against other CPB recipients.

In 1993, Dole also went after the Pacifica Foundation to deny it CPB funds after Pacifica's Los Angeles station, KPFK(FM), broadcast a program on Afro-centrism that Dole called "hate-radio." Pacifica has charged Dole with using political pressure to censor Pacifica's well-known, oppositional, progressive political programming.

C-SPAN—Funded by a "For-Profit" Cable Industry

In the debate on public television, C-SPAN is often cited by many as a great example of public-spirited television that enhances critical thinking. C-SPAN, providing regular coverage of congressional hearings, symposia, call-in discussion programs from Washington, D.C., as well as politically themed programs from around the world on C-SPAN, C-SPAN-II, and its radio network, is solely funded by the U.S. cable television industry, through subscriber contributions from its local system operators across America.

With a budget that has grown from $400,000 per year to more than $18 million per year from 1979 to 1993, the public relations benefit of C-SPAN to national cable industry lobbying efforts should not be underestimated. During the years that C-SPAN has seen its greatest growth, the cable industry received sweeping deregulation changes that allowed U.S. corporate cable operators to make millions of dollars in profits. When Congress moved to pass the Cable Act of 1992 for price-gouging by U.S. cable operators (that began as soon as the Reagan-Bush FCC moved to deregulate the U.S. cable television industry), the presence of C-SPAN became a vital public relations weapon in the U.S. cable industry's lobbying arsenal against Congress.

C-SPAN, as important as it is as a national resource for U.S. democratic participation and citizen political awareness, has also faced criticism for not being more critical of the U.S. cable industry. As Jeff Chester, co-director of the Center for Media Education says:

> [C-SPAN] does a terrible job at covering cable issues and rarely does it have any guests on the call-in or interview shows who are critical of the cable industry. It's been a PR bonanza for the cable industry, but its avoidance of issues critical of the industry has been shameful.[33]

Perhaps the reason why C-SPAN has become so popular since it began in 1979, has more to do with the fact that most U.S. citizens want to become more politically active and aware. Yet, C-SPAN remains totally funded by U.S. cable operators. C-SPAN's board of directors is similarly made up of U.S. cable industry executives.[34] The presence of a non-profit C-SPAN remains, nonetheless, an ideal upon which the U.S. corporate media system can base its transformation.

Paying for an Alternative System

Since the beginning of commercial U.S. radio broadcasting in the 1920s, the advertiser-supported media system has been defended by broadcasters as a "free" system, without cost or obligation to the vast audiences who consume its imagery and messages. In return for a mass audience, broadcasters sell advertisements to sponsors who market their products and services. The revenues that come from these advertising sales are then used by broadcasters and other media to fund the entertainment programming as well as the implied public service obligations of news and informational programming. To characterize such broadcasting as "free" is grossly misleading.

To conclude then, that the broadcast system in the United States is shaped primarily for its base of national advertisers/sponsors should, at this point, be more than evident. Broadcast media today, because of economic constraints, must serve wide audiences in order to thrive financially in the government-protected oligopolistic media marketplace. It seems more than reasonable to suggest that those who derive the most profit from the so-called public airwaves — the corporate powers that advertise and own media — should bear the brunt of financing a meaningful, alternative citizen free-speech media system in the U.S.

At present, media owners are permitted to use what are essentially public airwaves and cable channels to serve private corporate interests. As a collective political and economic power of immense magnitude, these corporations are under little obligation to provide direct remuneration to the government, on behalf of the people, for this exclusive right to operate within a government-protected monopoly.

Broadcasters pay no fee (as of 1993) for the airwaves they use — either at the time of a station purchase, upon its sale, or on an annual basis — based on the revenues the broadcasters are allowed to make at the public's expense. Cable operators, while they must pay a small percentage of their revenues to the local municipality that protects their monopolistic status, also have similar freedom to make huge profits at the public expense. On the surface, the fee schedule might seem a reasonable price to pay due to the high cost of operating a broadcast media facility with advanced technology. At least it does to the industry-dominated FCC.

However, when one considers that, in addition to not being obligated to pay a significant portion of revenues back to the public, all media operators are also eligible to claim huge federal and state tax-deductions on programming costs as well as the interest on the debt to buy even more media properties, one realizes that the U.S. media monopoly that we currently have is a heavily subsidized public trust. Indeed, 100 percent of its profits go toward expanding private corporate empires that presently are under no obligation to fully disclose their finances or worldwide operations. Yet, to solely charge media operators for the right to use the airwaves and media channels without exacting some equal measure of financial responsibility from those who also profit from this system — sponsors and advertisers — seems grossly unfair.

The concept of charging media operators to use the airwaves is not a new one. The idea of placing a tax on advertisers, those who also shape and guide the vast majority of media fare, is. Because of the tremendous profits that can be made from unlimited expansion in media and media advertising services, it seems only right to place a price on this highly profitable economic activity, since it also helps to drive out alternatives in political and economic decisionmaking. In a business where profit margins can range as high as 50 percent and as low as 20 percent, almost all of which is guaranteed by government-protected monopolies based on advertising revenues, some of these corporate profits could provide the necessary capital to begin a realistic and independent alternative media system. If one considers that all advertisers and media operators simply pass the costs of operation onto the public to be paid in the form of high product and service costs, it is not unreasonable to ask that more of these costs be shared by those directly profiting from the U.S. advertiser-supported media system.

In 1965, Dave Berkman, a Communications professor at the City University of New York, suggested a plan by which commercial broadcasters would be freed of all FCC program restrictions in return for a ten percent usage fee that would be based on the annual net profits from each broadcast facility. At the time, Berkman estimated that this fee would have amounted to about $40 million per year which could be used to fund an alternative media system in the U.S.[35] When the Johnson administration later created the Corporation for Public Broadcasting in 1967, as a means to maintain social control of the U.S. population then rising up in opposition to the Vietnam war, a meager $4.5 million (for the first year) was provided, far under what would provide adequate service.[36]

Despite the Carnegie Commission's urging for a tax on television receivers to pay for a national U.S. Corporation for Public Broadcasting in 1967, industry pressure from television manufacturers stopped the broadcaster's tax from becoming a reality. Taxing the broadcast spectrum continued to be talked about by public broadcasters, but not in a major way, ironically, until the "trickle-down" economic Reagan administration came to power in 1981. Acting to "free" broadcasters from statutory regulation, Reagan FCC chairperson Mark Fowler suggested the idea of a spectrum tax as a "fee" in return for the massive deregulation broadcasters had long wanted in 1982. Fowler was promoting a reconstituted version of Berkman's 1965 plan, in which Fowler specifically tried to use the tax as part of quid pro quo to encourage Congress to codify broadcast deregulation and to fund public radio and television.(The Fowler broadcast tax would have applied to all who use the electromagnetic spectrum, not just broadcasters.)[37]

In 1991, with the mounting federal budget deficit approaching crisis levels, Congress suggested a spectrum fee to fund FCC operations, while the Bush administration looked into the possibility of charging broadcasters to use the airwaves as a way to reduce the federal deficit. But the all-powerful broadcast lobby group, the National Association of Broadcasters (NAB) again managed to persuade Congress and the White House that this was not in the corporate interest. That same year, Lawrence Grossman, a former president of PBS and NBC News and then a fellow at Columbia University's Freedom Forum, said that all commercial stations should pay a 1 percent or 2 percent spectrum tax to help finance public broadcasting. Grossman also suggested that some cable channels on every cable system should be kept open for public use.[38]

In 1988, the revenues from the top 100 media companies— newspaper chains, network and local radio and television broadcasters, cable operators, movie studios, and others—reached $66.1 billion.[39] In 1990 and 1991, total national advertising expenditures by corporate sponsors in the U.S. hovered in the area of an estimated $120 billion.[40] Considering the fact that most of these monies are used to fund privately owned media systems (operating on the public airwaves and municipally approved cable channels) that greatly benefit from corporate tax deductions on interest and investment as well as other government subsidized research and development, it seems only reasonable to suggest that a small portion of annual media revenues should finance a public and alternative U.S. media system.

For instance, just 1 percent of all 1990-1991 monies earned, or spent, on U.S. advertising or U.S. media conglomerates that produce information and cultural products would generate an annual fund of an approximate $1.2 billion that could be used to establish and maintain a viable alternative media in the United States. Two percent would gather a total of $2.4 billion. These figures would represent an approximate fivefold increase in the funding of a genuine alternative media system for the U.S. over what is presently provided by federal tax dollars to non-commercial media through the Corporation for Public Broadcasting. Most of this money would grow through direct viewer sponsorship as well as other substantial corporate funding.

Perhaps a more realistic figure for alternative media, though, might be 5 or 6 percent of total media revenues and advertising to offset the already overwhelming advantage of commercial media in the U.S. This higher percentage would generate an annual fund of approximately $10 to $12 billion to fund alternative media programming services, stations, and cable channels, as well as several national and regional alternative print-publications that could reinvigorate national, regional, and local political and economic dialogue.

One of the arguments against taxing those who use the airwaves is that consumers would eventually pay higher costs for products and services, since advertising costs are always passed onto consumers. Considering that "hidden" costs are already paid by consumers for the expenses of producers, slightly higher costs might be worth a more democratic and politically equal public media system. The social consequences arising from 70 years of so-called free broadcast media has already weakened democratic participation by average citizens.

But adopting such an advertising tax to pay for public media will not come without a fight. In March 1993, the District of Columbia proposed a 6 percent tax "on all advertising sold or imported into the city" through "circulation, viewership or listenership" as part of Mayor Sharon Pratt-Kelly's plan to raise $50 million to cover a $500 million gap in the city's $3.4 billion budget. While no part of Mayor Kelly's taxation of advertising was earmarked to fund alternative media, tremendous opposition to the plan by advertising and media companies again illustrated how much power corporations have to decide who will pay the social costs of unlimited media proliferation.

The Association of National Advertisers (ANA), the lobby group representing all of the transnational corporate advertisers, led the fight against the D.C. advertising tax. Dan Jaffe, a spokesperson for ANA, called it, "a regulatory nightmare." From the perspective of funding almost bankrupt urban economies by corporations who have little obligation to return any public service to the communities in which they operate with total freedom, often shaping the political, economic, and social fabric of such communities, the D.C. tax on advertising is interesting indeed.[41] Three states, Hawaii, New Mexico, and Washington State, all have some form of advertising taxes to pay for public services.[42]

The measure failed, however, when many media businesses threatened to leave Washington, D.C. if it were enacted. Yet, despite the defeat of Pratt-Kelly's plan, an interesting question remains. Should those who profit from the public exposure to propaganda pay some social costs for the exclusion of alternative dialogue within the commercial system of media structure and usage?

Toward a More Democratic Media

Deregulation of the broadcast media has, like so many of the Reagan-Bush corporate-favoring decisionmaking, contributed to a greater separation between social classes. It has also increased the political-economic division between those who are information-rich, and those who are information-poor.

There is less diversity of program choices today than there was before the FCC began to deregulate the U.S. broadcast sector in the late 1970s, yet corporate profits and stock prices are at all time highs. Also true is that many more major metropolitan newspapers are inter-locked via corporate connections to other segments of electronic media ownership. The result is a national and local press that has become a lapdog to government and corporate power.

In order to raise citizen awareness of the tremendous concentration of ownership within the media industries, I would call for substantially more federal oversight of media corporations and their parent companies by the FCC, FTC, and the Commerce and Justice Departments than what exists today. A logical first step would be to reform the federal regulatory structure that now oversees U.S. media structure and practice.

Currently, the Federal Communications Commission, like other federal regulatory bodies, is primarily dominated by ex-officials of media companies, all of whom have been appointed on the basis of political, economic, or social ties to the upper echelon of corporate America. Although the commission is mandated by law to include a balanced representation from both the Democratic and Republican parties, the vast majority of past FCC commissioners have far more links to power than the average citizen. These ties are often the only reason why one is placed on the FCC, or other federal regulatory agencies.

During the Reagan years, the number of FCC commissioners was reduced from seven to five after political squabbling between the Reagan administration and the Senate over Reagan appointments to the FCC. I recommend that the FCC be restored to seven commissioners to encourage more dialogue and debate, and I propose that all federal regulatory bodies be opened to the electoral process. At a minimum, there should be rules that limit terms of commissioners, as well as stricter regulations limiting the shuttling of ex-commissioners between government and the industries they are regulating.

Federal disclosure laws to force media conglomerates to reveal all profit and loss statements to all foreign and domestic subsidiaries should be required. These laws would provide regular, independent, accounting oversight of all financial records and interests by federal authorities. Each year, all media corporations would be required by law to make public the following: a list of all confiscations, expropriations, or litigation by other foreign and domestic companies; a list of the largest shareholders in each country where the media company does business along with corresponding data on all top corporate executives and board members and their holdings in other media firms; a list of all joint ventures between the media corporation and any foreign governments and a list of all cooperative corporate efforts within government, military, and or intelligence agencies dating to the inception of the firm. In the age of super-global conglomerates that have subsidiaries in many nations, such information would help citizens and public interest groups determine the extent of corporate control or cooptation, as well as who is in charge.

In addition, I would call for new federal ownership limits reducing the number of broadcast stations, cable systems, newspaper and publishing houses that one corporation could own. Specifically, government should ensure that no corporation, or groups of corporations, be allowed to monopolize both the global production and distribution of media programming. To encourage greater diversity of media ownership, there should be more tax incentives for minority-owned businesses. Congress should bring back the Fairness Doctrine, which the FCC threw out in 1987, requiring all broadcasters and cable operators to present a balanced presentation of controversial public issues. In addition, lowest-unit rules for political advertising should be reinstituted so that the wealthiest and most influential candidates will not be the only ones who can afford to run for public office.

I would also recommend the establishment of a democratic alternative media system to serve as a counterbalance to government-corporate control over the media. There should be a national radio and television network created, which would be dedicated to encouraging free speech and to developing alternative broadcasts on the arts, politics, and economics.

The networks I am proposing would be funded through user taxes on national and local advertising revenues, the sale of every U.S. broadcast station or cable systems and a yearly user tax on all broadcasters, cable systems, and newspapers that are also owned by U.S. media conglomerates.

These free-speech networks would be funded by Congress (through the CPB), but would be separated administratively from PBS to encourage more diversity. No CPB-funded station would be able to accept any corporate sponsorship monies. In order to keep political and economic interference in the operation and programming decisions of these networks to a minimum, I would urge that their governing body, as well as their entire staff, be required by law to closely reflect the racial, ethnic, gender, and age diversity of the audiences they serve.

To further reduce political interference from government and corporate insiders, I would argue that free-speech media should include interest groups that do not have means to media through their annual billion dollar purchases: members of labor unions, groups of various ethnicities, colors and sexual orientation; feminist groups; teachers; working-class Americans; journalists from the alternative media; and others individuals from underrepresented voter blocs.

Ideally, local community media boards would elect the national and regional governing boards for free-speech radio and television from the general population, who would then hire their necessary staffs at the national level from a pool of professional journalists, educators, and others. There would be a stipulation that would guarantee that a majority of local and national governing board members (as well as the employees of these alternative networks) would not be dominated by elite, socio-economic classes of citizens. Guidelines could be instituted that would ensure that a majority of voting members of local media councils would accurately reflect the socio-economic, racial, and gender representation of their constituent areas.

The free speech networks of power I propose would be staffed by educators, artists, and professional journalists, who would be experienced in video and film production. Programs would be produced directly by these networks, and would include even greater diversity and more voices. These networks would hire independent production companies. I am sure that with the initiation of such a truly public-service network structure, there would be many network and local producers, anchors, reporters, and technicians from U.S. commercial broadcasting who would be interested in working on free speech radio and television projects that might include news and information documentaries of various kinds; multinational discussion programs; educational programming on science, arts, and culture; alternative political and economic programs; media criticism; local and regional town halls on issues of community interest; among other topics.

Free speech radio and television would broadcast on designated satellites and production facilities distributed throughout the U.S. and the world. In addition, federal law would require that these networks be available in every broadcast and cable network in the U.S. In markets where there are currently no spaces for new channel assignments, local arrangements would be made to add service to all metropolitan cable systems until a suitable broadcast facility could be assigned or mandated by law.

Simply offering such new service in every market throughout the United States is the beginning. In addition, each commercial broadcast and cable facility would be required by law to air up to 30 percent of free speech radio and television programs each year, with no fewer than 10 percent of these programs to be aired in the local station's primetime viewing periods each year. Considering that each free speech network would be on the air a maximum of 168 hours per week (24 hours, 7 days per week), 8,736 hours of free speech programming would be available to present alternative views each year.

During election periods, all political candidates on local, regional, and national ballots would be offered advertising time on the free-speech networks. Commercial broadcast stations could use a portion of their mandated requirement to air these ads. In 1992, political spending for ads reached an all-time high, candidates spent an estimated total of at least $300 million on political advertising at the national and local levels.[43] With the removal of lowest-unit political rules by the FCC, these figures promise to rise even higher in future years, which will further penalize those candidates who cannot pay for media access. Those political candidates who lack sufficient capital resources, have been excluded from reaching potential voters with their advertising messages.

A more equitable media system would necessarily include a strong educational component. Federal media taxes would be used to finance local cultural centers, and centers for media empowerment in every U.S. town and city. These cultural places staffed by media professionals and others would serve as meeting centers for the local media councils I mentioned earlier. By setting up these "media shops" by themselves, or in combination with the facilities of the local library or public school system, each community would have a ready-made group to help it argue for more balanced and representative local media coverage through the public access facilities of their local cable system and broadcast radio and television stations.

Through the community cultural center, these local boards would provide media advice and expertise to members of the community, and be equipped with the technology to access archival footage and program logs from all broadcasters and cable operators (both commercial and noncommercial) for scholars, journalists, and citizens through a nationwide computer hook-up. Such research resources could be shared by local, regional, and national citizen-access groups to plan joint media productions, and coordinate opposition to any media program on the air, as a democratic check and balance. These community media centers would also assist in the organization of national, regional, and local town meetings via electronic connection on issues of public importance.

Ideally, each community would be responsible for hiring and electing its own local governing board for these media centers as it would its political representatives or members of the local school board. In addition to providing for geographical representation of media board officers, professional staff would be hired at each center. Affirmative action would ensure the hiring of women and minorities.

As George Orwell wrote in his novel *1984*, "Who controls the present controls the past; who controls the past controls the future."[44]

Media ownership equals power, and always has. When the majority of the U.S. citizenry do not share in the ownership, control, and power of mass media, "democracy" and "freedom" become illusions, disguising corporate tyranny and totalitarianism. Our greatest power to change this undemocratic, corporate-dominated media system will continue to lie not in the past or future, but in the present.

Notes to Chapters

Introduction

1. Ken Auletta, *Three Blind Mice: How the Three Networks Lost Their Way* (New York: Random House, 1991), 387.

2. William Greider, *Who Will Tell the People: The Betrayal of Democracy* (New York: Simon & Schuster, 1992), 331.

3. Joseph E. Persico, *Casey: From the OSS to the CIA* (New York: Viking, 1990), 575.

4. "Casey's Stake in Capital Cities," *The New York Times*, 27 March 1985, D-6.

5. Persico, *Casey*, 337.

6. Ibid., 337-342.

7. Andy Boehm, "The Seizing of the American Broadcasting Company," *L.A. WEEKLY*, 20-26 February, 1987, 14; "Licensing Payola Charged to F.C.C.," *The New York Times*, 21 June 1960, 23; Peter Kihss, "Inquiry on Hagerty Urged by Schwartz," *The New York Times*, 9 February 1959, 1.

8. Carl Bernstein, "The CIA and the Media," *Rolling Stone*, 20 October 1977, 5.

9. Jim Hougan, *Spooks: The Haunting of America: The Private Use of Secret Agents* (New York: William Morrow, 1978), 381; Boehm, "Seizing," 14; Howard Kohn, "The Hughes-Nixon-Lansky Connection: The Secret Alliances of the CIA from World War II to Watergate," *Rolling Stone*, 20 May 1976, 40; Gigi Mahon, *The Company That Bought the Boardwalk: A Reporter's Story of How Resorts International Came to Atlantic City* (New York: Random House, 1980), 11-13, 42.

10. Hougan quoted in Boehm, "Seizing," 14.

11. Noam Chomsky, *Necessary Illusions: Thought Control in Democratic Societies* (Boston: South End Press, 1989), 2, 3, 5.

12. Ben H. Bagdikian, *The Media Monopoly*, 4th ed. (Boston: Beacon Press, 1992), ix.

13. Edward S. Herman and Noam Chomsky, *Manufacturing Consent: The Political Economy of Mass Media* (New York: Pantheon, 1988), xiii.

14. Herbert I. Schiller, *Information and the Crisis Economy* (Norwood, N.J.: Ablex, 1984), 61.

15. Chomsky, *Necessary Illusions*, 29

Chapter One

1. Nicholas M. Horrock, "C.I.A. Ties to Journalists," *The New York Times*, 28 January 1976, A-10.
2. Nicholas M. Horrock, "C.I.A. Panel Finds Plainly Unlawful Acts That Improperly Invaded American Rights," *The New York Times*, 11 June 1975, A-1; John M. Crewdson, "Intelligence Panel Finds F.B.I. and Other Agencies Violated Citizen's Rights," *The New York Times*, 29 April 1976, A-1.
3. "100 Leading National Advertisers," *Advertising Age*, 12 May 1975; As a result of the 1980s corporate trust-building, General Foods was later acquired by a much larger tobacco and foods transnational conglomerate, Philip Morris Companies. In 1991, Philip Morris was the second largest U.S. advertiser, with annual ad spending that topped $2 billion. See also "100 Leading National Advertisers," *Advertising Age*, 23 September 1992.
4. This figure is a rough estimation based on total employee cuts reported in *Three Blind Mice*. The U. S. networks, like most corporations, are under no legal obligation to release exact figures on workers who have lost their jobs as a result of the massive restructuring caused by corporate mergers. See Ken Auletta, *Three Blind Mice: How the TV Networks Lost Their Way* (New York: Random House, 1991).
5. K. Tarasov and V. Zubenco, *The CIA in Latin America* (Moscow: Progress Publishers, 1984), 96-97.
6. Nathaniel C. Nash, "Chilean Officers Testify in Human Rights Cases," *The New York Times*, 8 July 1993, A-10.
7. Armand Mattelart, *Multinational Corporations and the Control of Culture* (Sussex: Harvester Press, 1979), 239-241.
8. Jonathan Kozol, *Illiterate America* (Garden City: Doubleday, 1985).
9. Auletta, *Three Blind Mice*, 465.
10. Ibid., 466.
11. Sterling Seagrave, *The Marcos Dynasty* (New York: Fawcett Columbine, 1988), 195-96.
12. Jack Anderson, "Filipino Agents Hunt Foes in U.S.," *Washington Post*, 11 August 1979, B-11.
13. Don Junas, "The Marcos Network and Murder," *Covert Action Information Bulletin*, Summer 1990, 45.
14. "Marcos Convicted of Graft," *The New York Times*, 24 September 1993, A-7.
15. Michael Morgan, Justin Lewis, and Sut Jhally, "More Viewing, Less Knowledge," in *Triumph of the Image: The Media's War in the Persian Gulf, A Global Perspective*, Hamid Mowlana, George Gerbner, and Herbert I. Schiller, eds. (Boulder: Westview Press, 1992), 216.

Chapter Two

1. Todd Gitlin, "Invaders from ABC: A Study in the Pathology of Network Television," *Mother Jones*, January 1987, 34; Nancy E. Bernhard, "Ready,

Willing, Able: Network Television News and the Federal Government, 1948-1953," in *Ruthless Criticism: New Perspectives in U.S. Communication History*, William S. Solomon and Robert W. McChesney, eds. (Minneapolis: University of Minnesota Press, 1993), 291-312.

2. Erik Barnouw, *A Tower in Babel: A History of Broadcasting in the United States, Vol. I-to 1933* (New York: Oxford University Press, 1966) , 59; Robert W. McChesney, "The Battle for America's Ears and Minds: The Debate Over the Control and Structure of American Radio Broadcasting, 1930-1935" (Ph.D. diss., University of Washington, 1989), 23-27.

3. Robert W. McChesney, *Telecommunications, Mass Media and Democracy: the Battle for Control of U.S. Broadcasting, 1928-1935* (New York: Oxford University Press, 1993), 12-18.

4. The "Blue" network was also nicknamed the "Brown" network because of its policy to accept laxative commercials that the other U. S. networks would not. See Leonard H. Goldenson with Marvin J. Wolf, *Beating the Odds: The Untold Story Behind the Rise of ABC* (New York: Scribner's and Sons, 1991), 140.

5. Sterling Quinlan, *Inside ABC: American Broadcasting Company's Rise to Power* (New York: Hastings House, 1979), 20; Goldenson, *Beating the Odds,* 96-97, 140.

6. "The Many Corporate Faces of ABC," *Broadcasting,* 6 December 1965, 28.

7. In 1941, there was widespread concern in Washington and on Wall Street about the growing power of the radio networks to shape and mold public opinion. However, the debate about whether to limit their expansion was not one that most Americans shared in. See Erik Barnouw, *The Golden Web: The History of U.S. Broadcasting, Vol. II, 1933-1953* (New York: Oxford University Press, 1968), 168-71.

8. Then two months later, Noble allowed Henry Booth Luce's Time, Inc., to purchase a 12.5 percent stake in his network for $500,000. Advertising executive Charles J. La Roche also acquired a 12.5 percent stake for the same amount. Later, both sold their shares back to Noble. See "Corporate Faces of ABC," *Broadcasting,* 28.

9. With no money to pay sales clerks, Noble became one of the first U. S. businessmen to use children as salespersons on a commission basis. During World War I, due to a sugar shortage, Noble made Life Savers smaller, and yet still managed to raise prices because of the high demand for the candy. See Goldenson, *Beating the Odds,* 97.

10. Quinlan, *Inside ABC,* 9.

11. Ibid., 19.

12. ABC's first network television program was "On the Corner," starring Harry Morgan, and was sponsored by the Admiral Radio Corporation. See "Corporate Faces of ABC," *Broadcasting,* 28.

13. Annenberg's family was mentioned in connection with U. S. organized crime figures on more than one occasion. See Anthony Summers, *Official*

and Confidential: The Secret Life of J. Edgar Hoover (New York: G.P. Putnam, 1993), 227.

14. Annenberg until that time owned WFIL-TV, Philadelphia; WFBG-TV, Altoona, Pa.; WLYH-TV, Lancaster-Lebanon, Pa.; WNBF-TV, Binghamton, N. Y.; WNHC-TV, New Haven Conn.; and KFRE-TV, Fresno, Calif. He also founded the Annenberg Schools of Communications at the University of Pennsylvania and the University of Southern California and contributed to the communications program at Temple University. See also Les Brown, *The New York Times: Encyclopedia of Television* (New York: Times Books, 1978), 18.

15. Goldenson, *Beating the Odds*, 99-100, 104; There were reports that Noble had first attempted to sell ABC to CBS, rather than to Paramount Theatres. (ABC's biggest competitors, CBS and NBC, had almost 60 affiliates and nearly 100 percent coverage of American television homes at the time. DuMont, the third largest TV network, had slightly more coverage than ABC).

16. Ibid., 102-103.

17. The DuMont Network eventually went dark in 1955, leaving just three national television networks—ABC, NBC, and CBS—to battle for U. S. audiences over the next thirty years. In 1985, remnants of the DuMont network were reorganized into the Fox network by the Australian media tycoon, Rupert Murdoch. See Quinlan, *Inside ABC,* 47; and Huntington Williams, *Beyond Control: ABC and the Fate of the Networks* (New York: Atheneum, 1989), 234.

18. Goldenson, *Beating the Odds*, 103-107.

19. In 1948, the Supreme Court ruled that the Hollywood studios could no longer own their own theaters. This ruling later led to the Justice Department sale of the Hollywood studios' worldwide theater chains. See Williams, *Beyond Control,* 36-38.

20. Quinlan, *Inside ABC*, 46-47; Goldenson, *Beating the Odds*, 114-15.

21. At the time of the forced Paramount divestiture of its studio holdings, it had 1500 theaters in the United States, 350 in Canada, 14 in England, two in France, and several more in South America. See Quinlan, *Inside ABC,* 11. At the time of the AB-PT merger, ABC had 355 radio affiliates, 14 primary TV affiliates, assets of $29 million, 1,991 employees, and 1,689,017 shares outstanding. UPT had assets of $141 million, 708 theaters in 37 states, some 20,000 employees, and about four million shares outstanding. In terms of AB-PT's competition, it was quite a different story. CBS had 74 affiliates and NBC had 71, but ABC had just 14. See Quinlan, *Inside ABC,* 47.

22. Goldenson, *Beating the Odds*, 108.

23. The technological difference between "primary" and "secondary" affiliate status is useful in revealing how far behind competitively ABC stood in relation to CBS and NBC. The term "primary" came into use to describe stations that receive programs live. These "secondary" stations are also called "DB," or delayed broadcast, stations because they received programs on film or tape. See Goldenson, *Beating the Odds,* 116.

24. Ibid., 122-23.

25. Ibid., 123-24.

26. Herbert I. Schiller, *The Mind Managers* (Boston: Beacon Press, 1973), 97. In 1960, when Disney wanted to move to NBC, AB-PT sold back its 35 percent interest in Disneyland for $7.5 million in cash and the profits from the company's merchandising and food concessions for five more years. The move was instigated by RCA to promote the sale of color television sets that it was then manufacturing. See Goldenson, *Beating the Odds*, 125.

27. Ibid., 62, 124; See also Ariel Dorfman and Armand Mattelart, *How to Read Donald Duck: Imperialist Ideology in the Disney Comic*, trans. David Kunzle (New York: International General, 1971), 42-46; and Richard Schickel, *The Disney Version: The Life, Times, Art and Commerce of Walt Disney* (New York: Simon and Schuster, 1968), 249-56.

28. Goldenson, *Beating the Odds*, 124-25.

29. See also Sally Bedell Smith, *In All His Glory: The Life of William S. Paley* (New York: Simon and Schuster, 1990), 295-97.

30. In his autobiography, Goldenson admits that Geritol "was mostly vitamins, including iron. The very worst thing you could say about it was that it was like chicken soup—it couldn't hurt you." See Goldenson, *Beating the Odds*, 130.

31. Goldenson, *Beating the Odds*, 148-49.

32. Ibid., 100-101. At the time, Noble owned nearly 60 percent of ABC and constantly used his clout at his other companies to accelarate his profit-making. For example, he ordered that his giant Beech-Nut Foods corporation buy advertising time *only* on ABC, even though he already owned a controlling interest in the network and personally profited each time a Beech-Nut advertisement was broadcast (all of which were tax deductible). Noble wanted to exploit every chance for profits at ABC.

33. Ibid., 153-61.

34. Ibid., 163-64.

35. Ibid., 167.

36. Goldenson, *Beating the Odds*, 214.

37. ABC owned a controlling interest of 51 percent in Cadena Centroamericana. It also owned portions of each individual station in the network, except for the Managua, Nicaragua affiliate, where it feared government expropriation. See Goldenson, *Beating the Odds*, 217; Quinlan, *Inside ABC*, 239-40.

38. Paley was asked by Nelson Rockefeller, then under-secretary for inter-American affairs at the State Department, to guage the extent of Nazi infiltration in South America as he tried to open up new streams of revenue for CBS abroad. See Smith, *In All His Glory*, 201, 305; Carl Bernstein, "The CIA and the Media," *Rolling Stone*, 20 October 1977, 55.

39. Goldenson, *Beating the Odds*, 218-19.

40. Ibid., 219-20.

41. Ibid., 220-21.

42. Ibid., 222-27.

43. Quinlan, *Inside ABC*, 240.
44. Quinlan, *Inside ABC*, 240; Goldenson, *Beating the Odds*, 231-32.
45. In 1957, because he considered himself a bona-fide news person, Daly objected to ABC's hiring of Mike Wallace to do the controversial weekly interview program, "Night Beat." In 1968, Wallace became one of CBS's star correspondents in *"60 Minutes."* Gil Fates, *What's My Line: TV's Most Famous Panel Show* (Englewood Cliffs, N. J. : Prentice-Hall, 1978), 32-33.
46. Lowell Thomas, later a founder of Capital Cities, was one of the leading narrators for Fox-Movietone newsreels in the 1930s and 1940s. These forerunners of today's television news broadcasts were shown in movie theaters between films, and so constituted a key source of national and international news for Americans, even though they more often presented government-corporate public relations reports and information. See Goldenson, *Beating the Odds,* 273.
47. Erik Barnouw, *The Sponsor: Notes on a Modern Potentate* (New York: Oxford University Press, 1978), 134.
48. Victor S. Navasky, *Naming Names* 2nd. ed. (New York: Vintage Books, 1991), 89.
49. Herman Klurfield, *Walter Winchell: His Life and His Times* (New York: Praeger, 1976), 178; and Anthony Summers, *Official and Confidential: The Secret Life of J. Edgar Hoover* (New York: G. P. Putnam, 1993), 84, 189.
50. The sponsor of "This Is Your FBI" was the Equitable Life Insurance Co. The advertising slogan was, "To your F.B.I., you look for national security... and to the Equitable Life society, for financial security. These two great institutions are dedicated to the protection of you,... your home, and your country." See also Richard Gid Powers, *G-Men: Hoover's F. B. I. in American Popular Culture* (Carbondale, Illinois: Southern Illinois Press, 1983), 222-23.
51. Noam Chomsky, *Necessary Illusions: Thought Control in Democratic Societies* (Boston: South End Press, 1989), 29.
52. Powers, *G-Men*, 243-44.
53. Herbert Mitgang, "Disney Link to the FBI and Hoover is Disclosed," *The New York Times,* 6 May 1993, B-1.
54. Richard Gid Powers, *Secrecy and Power: The Life of J. Edgar Hoover* (New York: The Free Press, 1987), 435-36. The sponsor of "The FBI" television program on ABC was the Ford Motor Corporation. "FBI" star Efrem Zimbalist, Jr., each week drove a Ford automobile on-camera as did all the actors. Ford's sponsorship of "The FBI" seemed to follow a pattern for Hoover. In 1939, he had worked closely with Harry Bennett, Henry Ford's right-hand man, to bust the unions in Ford's automobile maufacturing plants. The two were assisted by leaders of organized crime in "managing" Ford's union problems with a "private" militia. Summers, *Hoover*, 107-108.
55. Summers, *Hoover,* 186-88; 461-67.
56. The FBI's program partnership with ABC continued in the late 1980s and early 1990s, with the programs "Today's FBI" (whose marketing slogan was "Fighting today's crime with tomorrow's weapons,") and "The FBI: Untold

Stories." The FBI and ABC also produced a weekly program for the ABC radio network for many years. Powers, *Secrecy and Power*, 435-36 and 461-67; Powers, *G-Men*, 245, 255-59.

57. Goldenson, *Beating the Odds*, 276.

58. Ibid., 281-82

59. Ibid., 281.

60. Ibid., 283.

61. John M. Crewdson, "TV Newsman Spied on Russians in U.N.," *The New York Times*, 22 January 1976, 1; and John M. Crewdson, "Pose as Journalists Laid to 11 in C. I. A.," *The New York Times*, 23 January 1976, 1.

62. Carl Bernstein, "The CIA and the Media," *Rolling Stone*, 20 October 1977, 55.

63. Quinlan, *Inside ABC*, 88-89.

64. Goldenson, *Beating the Odds*, 252-54; "ABC's $370-Million Merger Expected to Brighten its Future," *Broadcasting*, 13 December 1965, 33; "Will ABC Have Biggest Bankroll?", *Broadcasting*, 6 December 1965, 27.

65. It was a plan that was almost identical to the reactionary one backed 20 years later by extreme right-wing Senator Jesse Helms to take over CBS. Media Unlimited (an extremist front organization for conservative action) devised a plan whereby a large number of people would purchase relatively small amounts of CBS stock (to avoid FCC disclosure laws), and then turn over their proxies to Hunt, who would put pressure on CBS for its "liberal" bias. See "Who Bought those 100,000 CBS shares?" *Broadcasting*, 26 July 1965, 80.

66. Goldenson, *Beating the Odds*, 254.

67. Since the amount of stock held by one entity would then have no bearing on total votes cast, Simon was prevented from exercising his stock rights to take over the company. See Goldenson, *Beating the Odds*, 256-57.

68. Quinlan, *Inside ABC*, 92-93; and Goldenson, *Beating the Odds*, 258. ITT actually began in 1882 as Postal Telegraph, a private company offered as an alternative to the oligopoly of Western Union and American Telephone and Telegraph. In 1920, Postal Telegraph became International Telephone and Telegraph, following the establishment of RCA. In 1959, ITT found itself mired in financial troubles, and hired Harold Geneen to turn the worldwide conglomerate around. He eventually bought more than 350 companies for ITT, building it into one of the most powerful corporations the world. See also Barnouw, The Sponsor, 10-12, 177-78.

69. "ABC-ITT Merger Filed at FCC," *Broadcasting*, 4 April 1966, 66; Quinlan, *Inside ABC*, 92.

70. "Sands in the Gears of ABC-ITT," *Broadcasting*, 7 November 1966, 27; "ABC's $370-Million Merger," *Broadcasting*, 33.

71. "Biggest Payroll," *Broadcasting*, 27.

72. Goldenson, *Beating the Odds*, 262; Armand Mattelart, *Multinational Corporations and the Control of Culture* (Sussex, England: Harvester Press, 1979), 239-240; Laurence Birns, ed., *The End of Chilean Democracy: IDOC*

Dossier on the Coup and Its Aftermath (New York: The Seabury Press, 1973), 159.

73. Goldenson, *Beating the Odds*, 263-64.

74. Quinlan, *Inside ABC*, 144.

75. Jim Hougan, *Spooks: The Haunting of America, the Private Use of Secret Agents (New York: Morrow, 1978), 239-43.*

76. Quinlan, *Inside ABC*, 151; Goldenson, *Beating the Odds*, 265-70.

77. Williams, *Beyond Control*, 54-55.

78. Quinlan, *Inside ABC*, 159.

79. Ibid., 237.

Chapter Three

1. L. J. Davis, "What's Happened to ABC Since It's Become Murph's Turf?" *Madison Avenue*, December 1986, 9.

2. Morris J. Gelman, "The Capital Man of Capital Cities," *Television Magazine*, March 1965, 43.

3. At the time, UHF was introduced by the FCC primarily to widen the national TV audience and stimulate competition among media operators. Most home TV receivers were not equipped to receive ultra-high frequency signals until the mid-1960s when a federal law was passed requiring all TV sets to be equipped for UHF reception. For most of the 1950s, UHF ownership was viewed as secondary, and inferior, to VHF ownership by viewers and advertisers alike. See Leonard H. Goldenson, *Beating the Odds: The Untold Story Behind the Rise of ABC* (New York: Charles Scribner's Sons, 1990), 165-66.

4. "The *Broadcasting* Magazine Hall of Fame: Class of 1992," *Broadcasting*, October 19, 1992, 3; and Gelman, "Capital Man," 43.

5. Lowell Thomas, *So Long Until Tomorrow: From Quaker Hill to Kathmandu* (New York: Morrow, 1977), 196-98.

6. It is important to point out that business-oriented Republican administrations were in office at the time of the original WROW-TV purchase, during the ABC takeover in 1985, and from 1969-72 when the company made most of its major broadcasting and publishing acquisitions. Most of the Capital Cities management groups have tended to support Republican policies of unfettered business expansion and less government regulation. See Huntington Williams, *Beyond Control: ABC and the Fate of the Networks* (New York: Atheneum, 1989), 217.

7. Thomas, *So Long Until Tomorrow*, 197-98.

8. Gelman, "Capital Man," 43.

9. Thomas, *So Long Until Tomorrow*, 200.

10. Ibid., 130-34.

11. Ibid.

12. See G. William Domhoff, *The Bohemian Grove and Other Retreats: A Study in Ruling-Class Cohesiveness* (New York: Harper & Row, 1974), 40, 83;

Lowell Thomas, *Good Evening Everybody: From Cripple Creek to Samarkand* (New York: Morrow, 1976), 112-14.

13. George Creel, a veteran journalist, became Wilson's official government propagandist. The Creel Commission, working through the Committee on Public Information, "sponsored 75,000 speakers, who gave 750,000 four-minute speeches in 5,000 American cities and towns." Wilson's government and supporters were pressed into launching a massive campaign to sway public opinion toward support of U.S. entry into the conflict, this war "to end all wars," and "to make the world safe for democracy." See also Howard Zinn, *A People's History of the United States* (New York: Harper Collins, 1980), 353-55; and Noam Chomsky, *Necessary Illusions: Thought Control in Democratic Societies* (Boston: South End Press, 1989), 29.

14. Thomas, *Good Evening Everybody,* 114.

15. Chomsky, *Necessary Illusions,* 29, 67.

16. Richard Jenkyns, "Just Deserts," review of *T. E. Lawrence: The Selected Letters,* Malcolm Brown ed., in *The New Republic,* 21 August 1989, 35.

17. Thomas, *Good Evening Everybody,* 107.

18. Ironically, Dewey, Casey, and other CIA-connected Capital Cities supporters/investors, while they were staunch anti-communists, were sometimes contemptuous of Hoover's FBI. Most of this stemmed from the fact that Hoover, in his constant pursuit of power, had opposed the formation of the CIA by the Truman administration in 1947. Instead, he wanted the FBI to follow the model of the KGB, the Soviet secret police, which had both foreign and domestic intelligence-gathering responsibilities. Although Hoover provided the Dewey campaign with secret FBI files for use against Republican opponents in the 1948 GOP nomination battle, he reportedly was threatened by the CIA. Anthony Summers, *Official and Confidential: The Secret Life of J. Edgar Hoover* (New York: G. P. Putnam, 1993), 154, 169-70, 197; Howard Kohn, "The Hughes-Nixon-Lansky Connection: The Secret Alliances of the CIA from World War II to Watergate," *Rolling Stone,* 20 May 1976, 40; and Burton Hersh, *The Old Boys: The American Elite and the Origins of the CIA* (New York: Charles Scribner's Sons, 1992), 21, 88-92, 231.

19. Andy Boehm, "The Seizing of the American Broadcasting Company," *L.A. WEEKLY,* 20-26 February 1987, 14.

20. Kohn, "Secret Alliances," 40.

21. Richard Norton Smith, *Thomas E. Dewey and His Times* (New York: Simon and Schuster, 1982), 303, 570-74; Kohn, "Secret Alliances," 40.

22. Boehm, "Seizing," 14; Kohn, "Secret Alliances," 40.

23. Boehm, "Seizing," 14.

24. Ibid.; Kohn, "Secret Alliances," 40; and Robert D. Morrow, *First Hand Knowledge: How I Participated in the CIA-Mafia Murder of President Kennedy* (New York; Shapolsky Publishers, 1993), 289-91; Gigi Mahon; *The Company That Bought the Boardwalk: A Reporter's Story of How*

Resorts International Came to Atlantic City (New York: Random House, 1980), 42-45.

25. Edward S. Herman, *Beyond Hypocrisy: Decoding the News in an Age of Propaganda* (Boston: South End Press, 1992), 159.

26. Kohn, "Hughes-Lansky-Nixon," 40.

27. Mahon, *Resorts*, 42-45; Morrow, *First Hand Knowledge*, 289-91.

28. Steve Swartz, "Resorts International Often Baffles Its Rivals in Gambling Business," *The Wall Street Journal*, 14 November 1985, 1.

29. Kohn, "Hughes-Nixon-Lansky," 40.

30. Al Delaugach, "Resorts Panel OKs Sweetened Trump Bid," *Los Angeles Times*, 2 February 1988, 2; "Will of Resorts' Late Chairman Gives Plenty to Friend, but Family Keeps Control of Stock (Heard on the Street)," *The Wall Street Journal*, 4 August 1986, 41; Frank Allen, "Pratt Hotel, in Move to Acquire Resorts, Bids for Crosby Estate's Controlling Stake," *The Wall Street Journal*, 29 July 1986, 57; Kohn, "Hughes-Nixon-Lansky," 40; Jim Hougan, *Spooks: The Haunting of America: The Private Use of Secret Agents* (New York: William Morrow, 1978), 80, 209, 223, 228, 229, 242, 381, 395, 399, 410; and Boehm, "Seizing," 14.

31. Davis, "Murph's Turf," 9; and Ken Auletta, *Three Blind Mice: How the TV Networks Lost Their Way* (New York: Random House, 1991), 34-35.

32. Reportedly, young Murphy's favorite course at Harvard was a course entitled, "Control." See also Stratford P. Sherman, "Capital Cities' Capital Coup," *Fortune*, 15 April 1985, 51.

33. Huntington Williams, *Beyond Control: ABC and the Fate of the Networks* (New York: Atheneum, 1989), 215.

34. Ibid. As an example of their early lean days, Murphy and Smith once painted only the three sides of the building that faced the street in order to save money (the fourth side faced the Hudson River).

35. Gelman, "Capital Man," 43.

36. Persico, *Casey*, 103-104.

37. Ibid.

38. Ibid., 337.

39. Martin Kondracke, "Tinker, Tinker, Tinker, Spy," *The New Republic*, 28 November 1983, 18; Frances Fitzgerald, "Death of a Salesman," *Rolling Stone*, 25 February 1987, 37.

40. Doyle McManus, "Shultz Attacks Casey as Secretive, Meddler: Says CIA Director Provided 'Faulty Intelligence' to Bolster His Policy Ideas, Including Arms Swap," *Los Angeles Times*, 24 July 1987, I-1.

41. Kondracke, "Tinker, Tinker," 18.

42. Ronald Brownstein and Nina Easton, *Reagan's Ruling Class: Portraits of the President's Top 100 Officials* (Washington, D. C.: The Washington Accountability Group, 1982), 616-19.

43. Kondracke, "Tinker, Tinker," 18.

44. Persico, *Casey*, 133-34.

45. Bob Woodward, *Veil: The Secret Wars of the CIA, 1981-1987* (New York: Simon and Schuster, 1987), 388-89.

46. Oliver L. North with William Novak, *Under Fire: An American Story* (New York: Harper Collins, 1991), 271-72.

47. Persico, *Casey*, 381-85; Gary Sick, *October Surprise: America's Hostages in Iran and the Election of Ronald Reagan* (New York: Times Books, 1992), 10-13.

48. Persico, *Casey*, 436.

49. Susan B. Trento, *The Power House: Robert Keith Gray and the Selling of Access and Influence in Washington* (New York: St. Martin's Press, 1992), 142.

50. Ibid..

51. Thomas, *So Long Until Tomorrow*, 200-201. Thomas credits Frank Smith with making this deal with the government of Israel; Also see Moshe Pearlman, *The Capture and Trial of Adolf Eichmann* (New York: Simon and Schuster, 1963), 90; Ken Auletta, *Three Blind Mice: How the TV Networks Lost Their Way* (New York: Random House, 1991), 37. (Ken Auletta's *Three Blind Mice* describes Cap Cities' Eichmann coverage, but offers no mention of Casey's role, as a long-time investor and corporate counsel, in helping to build Capital Cities.)

52. Thomas, *So Long Until Tomorrow*, 201.

53. Richard J. Barber, The American Corporation: Its Power, Its Money, Its Politics (New York: E. P. Dutton, 1970), 44-45.

54. Ralph J. Cordiner, *A Case Study of Management Control at General Electric* (New York: McGraw Hill, 1956), 49.

55. Ibid., 79

56. Ibid., 49.

57. William Greider, *Who Will Tell the People: the Betrayal of American Democracy* (New York: Simon and Schuster), 331-55.

58. Barber, *The American Corporation*, 90-91.

59. Sherman, "Capital Coup," 51.

60. Auletta, *Three Blind Mice*, 190.

61. Ibid., 192.

62. Sherman, "Capital Coup," 51.

63. Williams, *Beyond Control*, 216-17.

64. Auletta, *Three Blind Mice*, 192.

65. "Continuous Concern for Minorities Urged by Cap Cities' Chairman," *Broadcasting*, 14 October 1985, 31.

66. Sherman, "Capital Coup," 52; Davis, "Murph's Turf," 9.

67. Auletta, *Three Blind Mice*, 37-38.

68. Sherman, "Capital Coup," 51.

69. Auletta, *Three Blind Mice*, 35-36.

70. Thomas, *So Long Until Tomorrow*, 201-202; "Frank Smith, 56, Radio-TV Leader," *The New York Times*, 8 August 1966, 27.

71. "Why Cap Cities Is Sitting Pretty?" *Business Week*, 21 March 1983, 121; Sherman, "Capital Coup," 52.

72. "Sitting Pretty," 121.

73. Williams, *Beyond Control*, 216.

74. At that time, group owners could only own five VHF TV stations (seven, if they were UHF), seven AM stations, and seven FM stations. This was the law until the Reagan administration introduced extreme deregulation of the broadcast industry and permitted owners up to 12 TV stations (as long as their total audience aggregate did not exceed 25 percent of the national television audience), 12 AM stations and 12 FM stations (not to exceed 25 percent of the total U.S. radio audience).

75. Thomas J. Keil, *On Strike! Capital Cities and the Wilkes-Barre Newspaper Unions* (Tuscaloosa, Alabama: University of Alabama Press, 1988), 44-45.

76. Ann Stegemeyer, *Who's Who in Fashion* (New York: Fairchild Publications, 1990), 24-25.

77. Randall Rothenberger, "From Pauline Trigere, Dressing Down," *The New York Times*, 17 August 1988, D-1.

78. Keil, *On Strike!*, 45-46.

79. Auletta, *Three Blind Mice*, 35.

80. Keil, *On Strike!*, 46.

81. Ibid., 47.

82. "Cap Cities Sitting Pretty?" *Business Week*, 121.

83. Keil, *On Strike!*, 51.

84. Ibid., 51-52.

85. Ben H. Bagdikian, *The Media Monopoly* 4th ed. (Boston: Beacon Press, 1992), 3-5.

86. Keil, *On Strike!*, 65.

87. Ibid., 66-67.

88. Ibid., 78.

89. Ibid., 79-80; See also William W. Turner, *Hoover's FBI: The Men and the Myth* (Los Angeles: Sherbourne Press, 1970), 333.

90. Ibid., 112.

91. Keil, *On Strike!*, 86-87, 112-114.

92: Ibid., 154-64.

93. Ibid., 93.

94. Ibid., 88-89.

95. Keil (in *On Strike!*, 99) quotes Paul Domowitch, "People Are Falling for It—Hometown Bay's View," in *Violence in the Valley* (Wilkes-Barre, Pa.: Wilkes-Barre Publishing Co. 1978).

96. Ibid., 110.

97. Jack Colhoun, "Suicide Tied to October Surprise, Contragate, BCCI," *The Guardian*, 11 September 1992, 5; David Corn, "The Dark World of Danny Casolaro," *The Nation*, 28 October 1991, 511.

98. Transcript, "Plugging the Leaks," CBS's newsmagazine "60 Minutes," Steve Kroft, correspondent, and Richard Bonin, producer, CBS News, 3 November 1991.

Chapter Four

1. "Why Capital City is Sitting Pretty," *Business Week*, 21 March 1983, 121; Doug Henwood, "Capital Cities/ABC: No. 2, and Trying Harder." *EXTRA!*, March/April 1990, 8.

2. Congress, Senate, Committee on Commerce, *On Nomination of James H. Quello, to be a Member of the Federal Communications Commission*, 93rd. Cong., 2nd sess., 120. It has been reported that James Quello was "kicked upstairs" by Capital Cities when the profits of WJR started to lag in the early 1970s. See Andy Boehm, "The Seizing of the American Broadcasting Company," *L. A. WEEKLY*, 20-25 February 1987, 40.

3. "Battle Lines Form on Marshall Reappointment," *Broadcasting*, 16 September 1991, 21; "Quello, Rivera Get Reagan Nods," *Broadcasting*, 8 June 1981, 35.

4. Leonard J. Goldenson, *Beating the Odds: The Untold Story Behind the Rise of ABC* (New York: Scribner's, 1991), 421-25.

5. Ibid., 426.

6. Ibid., 423-24; Huntington Williams, *Beyond Control: ABC and the Fate of the Networks* (New York: Atheneum, 1989), 188-89.

7. Williams, *Beyond Control*, 82, 119.

8. Ibid., 209-14.

9. See Holly Sklar, ed. *Trilateralism: The Trilateral Commission and Elite Planning for World Management* (Boston: South End Press, 1980)1-2, 197-211; and Jerry Fresia, *Toward an American Revolution: Exposing the Constitution and Other Illusions* (Boston: South End Press, 1988), 131; Noam Chomsky, *Necessary Illusions: Thought Control in Democratic Societies* (Boston: South End Press, 1989), 2,3,5.

10. Williams, *Beyond Control*, 116-18.

11. Ibid., 140-41.

12. Ibid., 138-42.

13. Ibid., 141-42.

14. Ibid., 128.

15. Ibid.

16. Ibid., 156.

17. Flom was hired in 1984 to "protect" CBS from a takeover. See Goldenson, *Beating the Odds*, 456; Auletta, *Three Blind Mice*, 585.

18. Tisch eventually was able to take over CBS in 1985 by gradually buying up shares while all the time denying reports that he wanted to acquire full control of the company. See also Williams, *Beyond Control*, 155-56; Peter Boyer, *Who Killed CBS? The Undoing of America's Number One News Network* (New York: St. Martin's Press, 1989), 362-63.

19. Goldenson, *Beating the Odds,* 455

20. Dave Kaufman, "ABC Scolds Spendthrifts; Bankers, Investors, Public Resisting Crazy Film Costs," *Variety,* 16 January 1982, 5; and Williams, *Beyond Control,* 156.

21. "But as Robert Horwitz, an expert on U. S. regulatory reform, has pointed out, deregulation during this era was a *political* process [author's emphasis]...[It] certainly does not mean a democratization of industry." Deregulation, over the long term, tends to lead to even further concentration of ownership, and in many ways, "constitutes a retreat from democratic processes." See Robert Britt Horwitz, *The Irony of Regulatory Reform: The Deregulation of American Telecommunications* (New York: Oxford University Press, 1989), 264-65, 278-82, 284.

22. Ibid., 454-55; Williams, *Beyond Control,* 174-76.

23. Ibid., 454-55.

24. Garry Wills, *Reagan's America: Innocents at Home* (Garden City, N.Y.: Doubleday, 1987), 270.

25. Goldenson, *Beating the Odds,* 455.

26. Steven R. Weisman, "Administration Mounts Drive to Counter Atomic War Film," *The New York Times,* 19 November 1983, A-1.

27. Todd Gitlin, "Invaders from ABC: A Study in the Pathology of Network Television," *Mother Jones,* January 1987, 34; Williams, *Beyond Control,* 187.

28. Williams, *Beyond Control,* 220-21; "Who Bought Those 100,000 CBS shares?" *Broadcasting,* 26 July 1965, 80; Boyer, *Who Killed CBS?,* 236-37.

29. Boyer, *Who Killed CBS?,* 236-37.

30. Williams, *Beyond Control,* 199.

31. Mark Dowie, "How ABC Spikes the News: Three Reagan Administration Scandals that Never Appeared on World News Tonight," *Mother Jones,* November/December 1985, 33.

32. Williams, *Beyond Control,* 205-207; Goldenson, *Beating the Odds,* 458.

33. Williams, *Beyond Control,* 199-203.

34. Ibid., 218.

35. Ibid., 204; Goldenson, *Beating the Odds,* 457-58.

36. Goldenson, *Beating the Odds,* 457-58

37. Williams, *Beyond Control,* 204-205, 210, 222, 229; Goldenson, *Beating the Odds,* 459.

38. The appearance of these two articles seemed to follow a pattern. In 1965, one year before Capital Cities first began trading on the New York Stock Exchange, *Television Magazine,* a leading broadcasting trade magazine, published a highly favorable, 10-page report on Capital Cities as an effective and skillful manager of broadcast properties. The article played a major role in establishing Capital Cities as broadcast leader on Wall Street and in Washington, just as the 1983 articles did prior to its takeover of ABC in 1985. "The Numbers Speak for Themselves," *Financial World,* 31 March

1983, 36; "Why Cap Cities Is Sitting Pretty," *Business Week,* 21 March 1983, 121.

39. Goldenson, *Beating the Odds,* 459.

40. Ibid., 460-62.

41. Williams, *Beyond Control,* 217.

42. Goldenson, *Beating the Odds,* 463.

43. Doug Henwood, "Capital Cities/ABC: No. 2, and Trying Harder," *EXTRA!,* March/April 1990, 8.

44. Williams, *Beyond Control,* 221.

45. L.J. Davis, "What's Happened to ABC Since It's Become Murph's Turf," *Madison Avenue,* December 1986, 11.

46. Hilary Rosenberg, "Capital Cities ABC to Merge: And on Wall Street,'Networking' is Suddenly In," *Barron's,* 25 March, 1985, 36.

47. "Head of FCC Indicates No Bar to Merger," *The New York Times,* 21 March 1985, C-30.

48. Auletta, *Three Blind Mice,* 43-44; Dowie, "ABC Spikes the News," 33.

49. Williams, *Beyond Control,* 229; Auletta, *Three Blind Mice,* 42-43

50. "Warren Buffett: From Carrier Boy to Media Investor," *Editor & Publisher,* 30 March 1985, 14; Auletta, *Three Blind Mice,* 39-45.

51. "Warren Buffett," *Editor & Publisher,* 14.

52. Investors who had become participants in Buffett's first investment fund by putting in an initial $10,000 in 1956, had received a most impressive return of $300,000 by 1969. See Ann Hughey, "Omaha's Plain Dealer," *Newsweek,* 1 April 1985, 56; and Auletta, *Three Blind Mice,* 39.

53. Ibid.

54. Auletta, *Three Blind Mice,* 39-42, 58, 62.

55. "Mortgaging the Future: Goldenson Warns Against Takeovers," *Broadcasting,* 7 April 1986, 35.

56. "Current Merger Activity Threatens Financial Stability, Innovation Stability by Broadcasters," *Television/Radio Age,* 14 April 1986, 73.

57. Peter Hall, "Media Madness," *Financial World,* 17 April 1985, 12; Goldenson, *Beating the Odds,* 450-67; Williams, *Beyond Control,* 205-25; and Davis, "Murph's Turf," 8.

58. Goldenson, *Beating the Odds,* 1, 454-55, 461.

59. Ibid., 457-58. In an interview publicizing his book, Goldenson reported that he had chosen not to utilize the publishing arm of Capital Cities/ABC to publish *Beating the Odds,* but was not specific about why. See Goldenson, *Beating the Odds,* an interview on C-SPAN's "Booknotes," 17 March 1991 (Washington, D. C.: C-SPAN, 1991). See also Leonard Goldenson, *Beating the Odds,* 459-61; and Davis, "Murph's Turf," 10.

60. Andy Boehm, "The Seizing of the American Broadcasting Company," *L A WEEKLY,* 20-26 February 1987, 14.

61. Ibid.

62. "Ministries of Truth: Psywar at Home," *Covert Action Information Bulletin,* Winter 1991-92, 61.

63. Edward S. Herman and Noam Chomsky, *Manufacturing Consent: The Political Economy of the Mass Media* (New York: Pantheon, 1988), 1-14.

64. Gary Sick, *October Surprise: America's Hostages in Iran and the Election of Ronald Reagan* (New York: Times Books, 1992), 226-28.

65. Susan B.Trento, *The Power House: Robert Keith Gray and the Selling of Access and Influence in Washington* (New York: St. Martin's Press, 1992), 252.

66. Goldenson, *Beating the Odds,* 457-66.

Chapter Five

1. During 1990, the share price of Capital Cities/ABC stock rose to $633, its then highest peak since the ABC takeover, as rumors continued to circulate that CC/ABC would acquire Time, Inc., or Paramount Communications. See the 1992 Capital Cities/ABC, Inc. Annual Report & Form 10-K.

2. Huntington Williams, *Beyond Control: ABC and the Fate of the Networks* (New York: Atheneum, 1989), 256; and Geraldine Fabrikant, "Not Ready for Prime Time?" *The New York Times Magazine,* 12 April 1987, 30.

3. Williams, *Beyond Control,* 257-58.

4. Ibid., 256.

5. Auletta, *Three Blind Mice: How the TV Networks Lost Their Way* (New York: Random House, 1991), 114-19, 132.

6. Ibid., 115,129.

7. Ibid., 115.

8. This policy was threatened by management at the Capital Cities/owned Kansas City newspapers, but later was dropped after widespread employee and public criticism. See "Rumbling at ABC (New Drug Crackdowns)," *Newsweek,* 20 January 1986, 56.

9. "Burke Says Drug Woes 'Serious,'" *Advertising Age,* 14 April 1986, 3; Peter J. Boyer, "ABC to Start Drug Tests," *The New York Times,* 10 July 1987, C-36.

10. Started in 1986 to coincide with the Reagan war on illegal drugs, the partnership has been run since 1989 by James Burke, the brother of Capital Cities president-CEO Daniel Burke. James had formerly been the chairperson and CEO of Johnson & Johnson, the multinational drug manufacturer. The partnership has been primarily supported by the American Association of Advertising Agencies. From 1988 to 1991, it took in $5.8 million from its top 25 contributors. In addition, it got $150,000 from Philip Morris, Anheuser-Busch, and RJR Reynolds, and $100,000 from American Brands (Jim Beam, Lucky Strike). Other major contributors were J. Seward Johnson, Sr., Charitable Trusts ($1,100,000), Du Pont ($150,000). the Procter & Gamble Fund ($120,000), the Bristol-Myers Squibb Foundation ($110,00), Johnson & Johnson (110,000), SmithKline Beecham ($100,000), the Merck Foundation ($75,000), and Hoffman-La Roche ($50,000). Besides the ob-

vious public relations benefits, nearly all the costs of the project can be regarded as *pro bono* and thus a legitimate tax deduction for participating sponsors and media operators. See Cynthia Cotts, "Hard Sell in the Drug War," *The Nation,* 9 March 1992, 300; and Thomas S. Murphy and Daniel B. Burke, "1989 Annual Report," *Capital Cities/ABC INK* (ABC in-house newspaper), 9-11.

11. Williams, *Beyond Control,* 253-54.

12. Auletta, *Three Blind Mice,* 127.

13. Eleanor Randolph, "Bitter NBC Strike Reflects Hard Times at Networks," *The Washington Post,* 9 August 1987, H-1; A.H. Raskin, "Two Media Giants Pursue Dinosaur Labor Policies," *The New York Times,* 12 September 1987, 27; and Peter J. Boyer, "A Strike Few Noticed: Why NBC Union Lost," *The New York Times,* 27 October 1987, 27.

14. Also in 1987, the U.S. networks faced strikes by the Directors Guild of America (DGA) and the Writers Guild of America (WGA). While the DGA strike lasted only a few hours, the WGA stayed out for several months. Both guilds objected to widespread cutbacks in union jurisdiction and changes in work rules. The networks and Hollywood studios, to negotiate with the DGA and WGA, formed a joint bargaining unit called, the "Hollywood Producers." The guilds, although they each negotiate a separate contract for their rank and file, face in the same calendar year (every three years) the "Hollywood Producers." Aljean Harmetz, "Directors Accept Pact as Producers Yield on Rollbacks," *The New York Times,* 15 July 1987, C-19; Peter J. Boyer, "Writer's Guild Strikes ABC and CBS Newsrooms," *The New York Times,* 3 March 1987, C-16.

15. *The Wall Street Journal,* "ABC to Implement Technicians Contract Union Won't Ratify," 21 June, 1989, B-4.

16. The case, which began in 1986 shortly after ABC was taken over by Capital Cities, was remarkable in that ABC lost the case for legal misconduct even before it was tried. The federal district judge, Royce Lamberth, found ABC and its lawyers, "[had] taken substantial and inappropriate actions to prevent the emergence of the facts." The network denied that it had done anything to conceal evidence or mislead the court. See Sharon Walsh and Michael York, "Artists Win Race Discrimination Suit Against ABC," *The Washington Post,* 16 April 1992, A-4.

17. 1992 Capital Cities/ABC Inc. Notice of Annual Meeting of Shareholders, May 4, 1992; Capital Cities/ABC, Inc., Notice of Annual Meeting of Shareholders, May 13, 1993.

18. Ibid.

19. Estimating a 1992 market value of $500 per share of Capital Cities/ABC stock. Some of these managers also receive additional shares or stock options for themselves and for members of their family through special employment compensation—thus, the use of the minimum.

20. The Nielsen broadcast ratings service decided to delete the 11:00-11:30 evening time period from all rating reports in question. See "Former KABC-TV Employee Files Suit Against CapCities/ABC," *Broadcasting,* 24 August 1987, 67. In 1991, ABC's biggest competitor in the New York local radio

market sent a letter of complaint to the radio rating service, Arbitron, charging the Capital Cities/ABC's WPLJ-FM with also trying to rig the broadcast ratings by telling its listeners repeatedly to pledge time to listening to the station. See also "Closed Circuit: Unfair Advantage?," *Broadcasting*, 28 October 1991, 10.

21. Jennings apologized to viewers again in 1991 for erroneously reporting that the Soviet Union had sold the preserved corpse of Lenin to raise cash. ABC had failed to verify the report with *Forbes FYI*, which had first printed the item. See "In Brief (Jennings Apology)," *Broadcasting*, 11 November 1991, 96; "[The Bloch Case]. . . And the Way ABC Covered It" (Editorial), *The Washington Post*, 29 July 1989, A-16.

22. Mark Fitzgerald, "Judge Upholds Charges Against PA Newspaper," *Editor & Publisher*, 4 January 1992, 5.

23. "CNN Blasts Pirates," *The Pulse of Radio: Radio's Management Resource*, 4 February 1991, 7.

24. The case involved a false report that identified a local Buffalo restaurant owner and civic leader as having been the victim of an abduction and beating by organized-crime figures. Later, WKBW-TV tried to place responsibility for the report on the Buffalo FBI field office. See also Milo Geyelein, "New York Court Upholds Libel Verdict Against Former ABC Station in Buffalo," *The Wall Street Journal*, 12 February 1993, B-5.

25. Peter Viles, "$15.5 Million WKBW-TV Judgement Overturned," *Broadcasting*, 6 December 1993, 72; "In Brief," *Broadcasting*, 10 May 1993, 65.

26. The money generated by the sale of these properties came to nearly $1 billion. See "The Other Side of the CCC/ABC Deal: $1 Billion in Spin-Offs," *Broadcasting*, 1 April 1985, 43-44.

27. Local stations have always been crucial to Capital Cities' tremendous success. At times over the years, local news has brought in 70 percent of the station's income but required just 40 percent of their outlays. One rating point in Los Angeles, for example, is said to be worth $1 million in profits to an owner. See Bill Wood, "Transiency and Accountability in TV News Broadcasting," *The Christian Science Monitor*, 29 April 1987, 11.

28. "ABC Can Keep Radio Stations," *Broadcasting*, 10 July 1989, 29-30.

29. "The Positives of Deregulation," ABC's "20/20" John Stossel, correspondent, and Lisa Kraus, producer, airdate 29 December 1989 (New York: Capital Cities/ABC, 1989).

30. Later in 1990, Reagan was hired by MCA to star in a late-night talk show, which MCA was syndicating nationally. "MCA Banks on Reagan in P.M.," *Broadcasting*, 19 November 1990, 29.

31. "Dennis Said to Be White House Choice for the FCC," *Broadcasting*, 13 January 1986, 59.

32. Auletta, *Three Blind Mice*, 192.

33. "Robert Pepper: FCC's Forward Thinker," *Broadcasting*, 28 October 1992, 87.

34. After the FCC fined Stern's employer, Infinity Broadcasting, $105,000 (one of the largest indecency penalties imposed on a broadcaster in the history of

the FCC), some listeners at the commission say Stern has backed away from launching more of his stinging on-air attacks criticizing the FCC. See "Kinder, Gentler Stern?," *Broadcasting,* 11 January 1993, 44.

35. While Quello and the other commissioners on the FCC essentially argued that political candidates were no better than commercial advertisers, politicians in Georgia filed an FCC complaint that Quello should be removed from hearings on the case of WXIA-TV (Atlanta) for his pro-industry views. See "Quello Urges Leniency in Overcharge Cases," *Broadcasting,* 7 October 1991, 68; "Politicians Say Quello Should Quit WXIA Case," *Broadcasting,* 28 October 1991, 61.

36. "In Brief," *Broadcasting,* 1 June 1992, 56.

37. "Commission May Capsize Its Ownership limit," *Broadcasting,* 23 March 1992, 5; "Dingell Wary of Lifting Radio Limit," *Broadcasting,* 2 March 1992, 6; Raising the Roof on Radio," *Broadcasting,* 9 March 1992, 4; Joe Flint, "Radio's Magic Numbers: 30-30," *Broadcasting,* 16 March 1992, 4.

38. "FCC Considers Restoring Must Carry Rules," *Broadcasting,* 22 July 1991, 32; "Networks, Affiliates Still at Odds Over Cable Cross-Ownership Ban," *Broadcasting,* 14 October 1991, 33; "FCC Paving Way to Cross-owner- ship," *Broadcasting,* 16 December 1991, 6; Randy Sukow, "Networks Work Toward Compromise with Affiliates on Cable/Network Cross-ownership," *Broadcasting,* 6 January 1992, 88; Joe FLint, "FCC Lets Networks Into Cable Ownership," *Broadcasting,* 22 June 1992, 4.

39. "James Quello: The FCC's 'Report and Order' Chairman," *Broadcasting & Cable,* 15 February, 1993, 6; "Back to the Drawing Board on Fin-Syn," *Broadcasting & Cable,* 11 January 1993, 25.

40. "Quello Makes His Mark," *Broadcasting,* 5 April 1993, 7.

41. Jube Shriver, Jr. , "FCC on the Verge of Going in a New Direction," *Los Angeles Times,* 10 April 1993, D-1.

42. "In the Nick of Time? (*Forbes Informer)*" *Forbes,* 10 July 1987, 14.

43. Ibid. These figures are supplied by First Boston, a major investment banking firm which was closely involved in the takeover of ABC by Capital Cities in 1985. See Doug Henwood, "Capital Cities/ABC: No. 2, And Trying Harder," *EXTRA!,* March/April 1990, 8.

45. Ibid.

46. Even with considerable declines in network profit levels in the late 1980s, some Wall Street analysts thought that the networks would eventually recover. See "Network TV: An $8 Billion Nonprofit Institution," *Broadcast- ing,* 8 July 1991, 23; "Broadcasting's Exclusive 'Big Three' Financial Breakdown," *Broadcasting,* 30 April 1990, 35.

47. In 1988, for example, 100 media companies earned net revenues of $66.1 billion, while ABC had net revenues of nearly $5 billion (a 7.8 percent gain over 1987). See also Henwood, "Trying Harder," 8; "Big Three's Big Surge in '89 Profits," *Broadcasting,* 30 April 1990, 35; "100 Media Companies Hit $66. 1 Billion," *Advertising Age,* 26 June 1989, S-1; Capital Cities/ABC, Inc. 1989 Annual Report & Form 10K.

48. "Closed Circuit: Room to Grow?," *Broadcasting,* 28 October 1991, 8; Geoffrey Foisie, "Capital Cities/ABC's Finances Spelled Out," *Broadcasting,* 14 December 1992, 66.

49. "Bleak Economic Forecast," *Broadcasting,* 4 November 1991, 38.

50. "One of TV's Best-Kept Secrets: How ABC, CBS, and NBC Have Taken the Bite Out of Program Costs," *Broadcasting,* 9 December 1991, 3.

51. Anthony Baldo, "Vanishing Viewers: Here's a Paradox. As Audiences Shrink, Ad Prices Rise; Capital Cities/ABC Shows Why," *Financial World,* 7 August 1990, 26.

52. Paul Noglows, "Bullish on the Bear Facts," *Broadcasting,* 14 December 1992, 65.

53. Joe Mandese, "ABC mulls major buy," *Advertising Age,* 14 December 1992, 2; "Briefly: Capital Cities/ABC looking for Acquisition," *Los Angeles Times,* 9 December 1992, D-2.

54. "Cable Firm Stake Might Be Bought by Capital Cities," *The Wall Street Journal,* 12 March 1992, B-8; Daniel Pearl and Linda Tandro, "Turner's Search for a Partner Includes ABC," *The Wall Street Journal,* 12 February 1993, B-1.

55. See Geoffrey Foisie, "ABC's ad time is money. . . literally," *Broadcasting,* 22 March 1993, 32; "In Brief," *Broadcasting & Cable,* 6 December 1993, 109.

56. Brian Lowry, "ABC Prods. tests wings," *Variety,* 16 March 1992, 28.

57. Rick Du Brow, "ABC Sells a TV Movie to Air on CBS," *Los Angeles Times,* 16 August 1991, F-1; "Marketing & Media: Time-Warner Inc.," *The Wall Street Journal,* 13 December 1991, B-5.

58. Joe Mandese, "ABC program deals may be a boon, " *Advertising Age,* 24 June 1991, 26; "ABC Gets Cable Friendlier," *Broadcasting,* 17 June 1991, 45.

59. "ABC Deal for Cable Special," *The New York Times,* 27 November 1992, D-15.

60. Mandese, "Deals," 26.

61. Sharon D. Moshavi, "Lifetime finds niche in advertiser co-production," *Broadcasting & Cable,* 22 March 1993, 42.

62. Ibid.

63. *Reader's Digest,* a conservative summary of stories appearing in other print sources, claims a worldwide circulation of up to 25 million each month. See "ABC Pact with Reader's Digest," *The New York Times,* 29 April 1993, C-18.

64. Steve McClellan, "ABC's of Home Shopping," *Broadcasting,* 2 November 1992, 47.

65. "Closed Circuit: Home Shopping on Hold," *Broadcasting & Cable,* 25 January 1993, 10; "Closed Circuit: Talking Shop," *Broadcasting & Cable,* 15 March 1993, 79.

66. Christopher Stern, "ABC soap cleans up on QVC," *Broadcasting,* 2 August 1993, 44.

67. "ABC's Next Hit?" (Editorial), *Advertising Age*, 10 February 1992, 6.

68. Richard Sandomir, "ABC's Bunny Hop Cheapens 'World'", *The New York Times*, 26 November 1991, B-12.

69. "Addenda: Miscellany," *The New York Times*, 21 April 1992, D-23.

70. "ABC Roadblock: Pull Over, Deal!," *Mediaweek*, 27 July 1992, 5.

71. "Marketing & Media: ABC, Penney Plan Network," *The Wall Street Journal*, 20 August 1992, B-8; "J. C. Penney in Joint Venture to Provide Video in Stores," *The New York Times*, 20 August 1992, D-4.

72. "FTC Says ABC-ESPN Deals With CFA Violate Law," *Broadcasting*, 10 September 1990, 25.

73. "Football Ruling Takes Good Bounce for ABC, CFA," *Broadcasting*, 12 August 1991, 27.

74. The PPV games cost $8.95 per game or a season ticket price for eleven dates of $59.95. The PPV games will be broadcast in their entirety with commentary to be provided by ABC Sports announcers.

75. Steve McClellan, "ABC Affil To Promote PPV," *Broadcasting*, 24 August 1992, 19; Steve McClellan, "ABC, Showtime Encouraged by PPV Results," *Broadcasting*, 23 November 1992, 9; Rich Brown, "ABC, Showtime Get Ready to Pay Ball," *Broadcasting*, 10 August 1992, 46.

76. Joe Flint, "For broadcasters, it's retrans free," *Broadcasting & Cable*, 23 August 1993, 10; Mark McLaughlin, "Prime Times at ESPN," *New England Business*, October 1988, 62.

77. A&E, (along with non ABC/Hearst owned Discovery Channel,) has been dubbed "the Hitler Channel" by some. In 1992, both had at least six hours of military programming in prime-time every week (more if you count re-runs, specials, movies, and other offerings), much of it from the Second World War. Within the current "network mania" for cutting costs, WWII documentaries and archival footage--much of it presenting outdated historical information that costs next to nothing (or in some cases, nothing at all)--can be re-packaged into what seem to be new productions. A&E's historical programming focus has become so popular that in April 1993 the cable network launched a new "History TV channel," a 24-hour service featuring history-related documentaries, dramas, miniseries, and movies. Another question A&E's critics have raised is that by utilizing archival sources from twenty and thirty years ago, many historical facts coming to light recently are forgotten or ignored. "Fifth Estater: Raymond Ernest Joslin," *Broadcasting & Cable*, 1 March 1993, 67; "Hearst Puts Cable on Page One," *Broadcasting*, 19 May 1990, 38; Rich Brown, "Arts & Entertainment to make history," *Broadcasting & Cable*, 19 April 1993, 27; Mark Schone, "The Hitler Parade," *The Village Voice*, 5 May 1992, 56; *The Heroes of Desert Storm*, a prime-time broadcast on the A&E network, airdate: 26 December 1991.

78. Sikes was hired to head Hearst's New Media and Technology Group, which was to explore new business possibilities between computers, telephones, and satellites, and Hearst's broadcast, cable, and print properties. See Joe Flint, "Sikes heading Hearst's new media group," *Broadcasting & Cable*, 22 March 1993, 37.

79. Bruce Alderman, "ABC Spells Out Euro Strategy," *Variety,* 4-10 October 1989, 1.

80. While A&E's ratings are small compared to those of the broadcast networks, the disposable income levels of its viewers are high, making the channel very attractive to upscale advertisers. In February 1993, it had an average audience rating of 532,000 U.S. households during prime time (Monday-Sunday 8 pm -11 pm ET), according to A. C. Nielsen. Rich Brown, "Programming Investment Provides Boost for A&E," *Broadcasting* & Cable, 1 March 1993, 24.

81. "CapCities Makes UK Buy," *Broadcasting,* 27 May 1991, 48.

82. Meredith Amdur, "Multimedia talks abroad," *Broadcasting & Cable,* 29 March 1993, 19.

83. Elizabeth Guider, "Cap Cities/ABC Buys into Europe, Invests in Munich's Tele 5," *Variety,* 22 February 1989, 407.

84. "Capital Cities/ABC to Form Unit to Make and Distribute Videos," *The Wall Street Journal,* 11 November 1992, C-20.

85. Capital Cities/ABC already has a sizable financial interest in the successful Broadway plays "Cats," "Les Miserables," "Phantom of the Opera," and "Miss Saigon. " If the two media giants were to join together, a future scenario could have ABC produce first-run theatre productions, airing them on an exclusive pay-per-view hook-up via Paramount PPV's network, and then be broadcast later by ABC on one of its several cable networks, such as Lifetime or A&E. Kevin Goldman, "Paramount, Capital Cities/ABC Units Set Pay-per-View Television Venture," *The Wall Street Journal,* 13 December 1991, B-5; Sharon D. Moshavi, "ABC, Garden Announce PPV Plan," *Broadcasting,* 16 December 1991, 10.

86. Juanita Darling, "Mexico TV Monopoly Challenged," *Los Angeles Times,* 22 March 1993, D-1.

87. Geraldine Fabrikant, "An $8. 2 Billion Merger to Create Viacom-Paramount Media Giant," *The New York Times,* 13 September 1993, 1-A.

88. Kevin Goldman, "ABC Weighs Cutbacks in News Operation and Puts on Hold Overnight Broadcast," *The Wall Street Journal,* 15 October 1990, B-7.

89. David Lieberman, "Right-wing views to get more airtime: Peter Jennings." *TV Guide,* 9 October 1993, 37.

90. Randall Rothenberg, "If You Liked Him in the War, You'll Love Him in the Video," *The New York Times,* 15 March 1991, D-5.

91. *Post* critic Tom Shales asked, "Who was leading the U. S. off to war, Bush or the networks? They talk more of war and less of peace. " See Tom Shales, "On the Air: Images and Influences in a Different Kind of War," *The Washington Post,* 15 January 1991, C-1.

92. Eleanor Randolph, "ABC's Walters Relayed Note for Iran Middleman," *The Washington Post,"* 17 March 1987, A-11.

93. "Israel Mounts Inquiry Into a Charge by ABC," *The New York Times,* 7 July 1988, A-10.

94. Steve McClellan, "Arledge-Welch talks roil news waters," *Broadcasting & Cable,* 22 March 1993, 7.

95. "'Time,' ABC team up," *Advertising Age,* 22 January 1990, 39.

96. Bill Carter, "ABC Program on PBS," *The New York Times,* 12 September 1991, C-18.

97. Tom Jarriel, "The Exorcism," ABC's "20/20," Rob Wallace, producer, Tom Jarriel, correspondent, airdate: 5 April 1991 (New York: Capital Cities/ABC, Inc. , 1991); Bill Carter, "'20/20' Faces Accusation of Avoiding Nuclear Topics" The New York Times, 20 December 1993, B-4.

98. "ABC to Launch Overnight News," *Broadcasting,* 15 July 1991, 12.

99. Richard L. Bure, "Why Forecasts By Newscasters Will Be Similar," *The New York Times,* 4 November 1992, A-13.

100. Subscribers pay a fee of $31,000 but a higher pay scale is arranged for larger broadcast networks. This service helps many news organizations to maintain a Washington presence without the cost of running a bureau. Edward Connors, "They Still Call It Radio News," *Washington Journalism Review,* May 1991, 39.

101. Ibid.

102. "In-Brief," *Broadcasting,* 1 April 1991, 88.

103. Peter Viles, "ABC Radio Launches Wire with Reuters, Gannett," *Broadcasting,* 22 June 1992, 28; and Thomas Hoffman, "ABC Radio Seeks Parity for IS Teams," *Computer World,* 3 August 1992, 74.

104. Martin A. Lee and Norman Solomon, *Unreliable Sources: A Guide to Detecting Bias in News Media* (New York: Carol Publishing Group, 1990), 66.

105. More than half of WTN footage (as well as that of its only real competitor, Visnews, Ltd.) is shot by their own crews, while coverage in more than 70 countries comes from freelance crews. WTN and Visnews provide raw video material of world news events to broadcast customers in 84 countries. Neither agency receives screen credit for its contribution so, it is almost impossible for WTN's viewers to know where the film comes from or who paid for it. Teresa L. Waite, "As the Networks Stay Home, Two Agencies Roam the World," *The New York Times,* 8 March 1992. F-5; and L. Carol Christopher, "Visnews: World News," unpublished research paper, Department of Communication, University of California, San Diego, 28 July 1992.

106. Ibid.; The actual costs of all this are quite interesting. For a third world broadcaster, WTN might charge in the low tens of thousands dollars per year for one air-shipped videocassette per week. A U.S. network might pay several millions per year for more regular service from satellite delivery (nothing if it owns the service). Most of this coverage is gathered by freelance crews and journalists for whom traditional benefits of employment are nonexistent. They have no job security, health insurance, paid sick leave, paid vacation time, unemployment insurance or worker's compensation if hurt on the job.

107. "Video News Releases," *Broadcasting,* 25 September 1989, 51.

108. Randall Rothenberg, "Promotional News Videos Gain Support," *The New York Times,* 11 September 1989, D-12. See also David Lieberman, "Fake News," *TV Guide,* 22 February 1992, 10.

109. "ABC, BBC form world news team," *Broadcasting & Cable,* 29 March 1993, 13.

110. At the time of the announcement of their joint partnership with Discovery, ABC News officials refused to comment on how much it was making by selling "old news." Jonathan Walters, "Cable Can't Lose Recycling Network News," *Washington Journalism Review,* July/August 1991, 15.

111. "The Cablers: ABC pulls into truck stop," *Variety,* 28 September 1992, 26.

112. 1992 Capital Cities/ABC, Inc. Annual Report & Form 10-K.

113. "Capital Cities/ABC realigns radio networks," *Broadcasting,* 21 May 1990, 32.

114. Peter Viles, "ABC Radio Moves Some Functions to Dallas," *Broadcasting,* 21 September 1992, 42.

115. Originally the ABC radio networks provided mostly news, sports and other information services to some 1800 stations, until ABC purchased the Satellite Music Network. SMN provides twenty-four hour music and news programming in eight formats for local stations. Station monthly subscriber fees average $750 for SMN, in addition ABC retains the right to sell off several minutes of national spots per hour to advertisers. "Satellite Music Network Improves Standing with ABC Tie, Hot New Format," *Television-Radio Age,* 7 March 1988, 111; "Satellite-Delivered Formats: Local Programming from the Sky," *Broadcasting,* 6 August 1990, 47.

116. "ABC and ESPN to Launch ESPN Radio Network," *Broadcasting,* 9 September 1991, 22.

117. Such a radio network, however, would require a substantive change in U. S. broadcasting ratings services since Arbitron and RADAR, the U. S. ratings companies, do not measure the size of radio audiences of children under twelve. "ABC, Disney in Kids Network Talks," *Broadcasting,* 19 October 1992, 26.

118. See Peter Viles, "ABC invests in UK satellite service, " *Broadcasting & Cable,* 19 April 1993, 60.

119. "Riding Gain: ABC Radio Hooks Up with In-Flight," *Broadcasting,* 22 February 1993, 42.

120. Mike Hoyt, "Talk Radio: Turning Up the Volume," *Columbia Journalism Review,* November/December 1992, 45.

121. Lewis Grossberger, "The Rush Hours," *The New York Times Magazine,* 16 December 1990, 58.

122. "Limbaugh Even Louder," *EXTRA!,* January/February 1993, 13.

123. Peter Viles, "Limbaugh Re-Ups with EFM Media," *Broadcasting,* 7 September 1992, 26.

124. "Limbaugh Even Louder," *EXTRA!,* Jan./Feb. 1993, 13.

125. Ibid. ; "The Rush Limbaugh Program," 23 November 1991 and 9 December 1991 (New York: EFM Media Management, 1991).

126. Accompanying Limbaugh to the White House in June 1992 was Roger Ailes, Bush's 1988 media adviser who created the "Willie Horton" commercial, a largely fictional and exploitative political attack on prison work furlough

programs in Massachusettes during Bush's presidential campaign against Democrat Michael Dukakis. Ailes, who later became the executive producer of Rush Limbaugh's nationally-syndicated television program, was a behind-the-scenes advisor within Bush's 1992 re-election campaign. In 1992, Limbaugh's television program rose to the number three position in nationally syndicated late-night programming, behind "Nightline" and "The Tonight Show," but ahead of "Late Night with David Letterman" and "The Arsenio Hall Show." See Daniel Cerone, "The Rush is On," *Los Angeles Times,* 28 January 1993, F-1.

127. "Limbaugh," *EXTRA!,* 13.

128. Political support for conservative candidates nationwide is also coordinated through "The Limbaugh Letter," a monthly newsletter containing the opinions of Limbaugh. Some 85,000 listeners already subscribe to this newsletter, which sells for $29.95 per year and has generated nearly $3 million in revenue since September, 1992. See also "Riding Gain: Reading Rush," *Broadcasting,* 23 November 1992, 32. *The Rush Limbaugh Program,* 4 June 1992 and 21 September 1992, (New York: EFM Media Management, 1992); Hoyt, "Talk Radio," 45.

129. "Limbaugh," *EXTRA!* 13.

130. Cerone, "The Rush is On," F-1.

131. Following Limbaugh on WABC(AM) is Bob Grant who continues Limbaugh's tirades against "bleeding heart" liberals into the afternoon and early evening hours. Grant once called New York's black mayor, David Dinkins, a "washroom attendant." On another program, Grant told a Newark N. J. police officer during an on-air interview that he hoped young blacks who steal cars in the inner city would be maimed or killed in the commission of their crimes. "Put them in the morgue, where they won't bother anybody anymore," Grant is reported to have said. See also Hoyt, "Talk Radio," 45.

132. The Barry Farber Show, Daynet Radio Network, 21 December 1991, 2:15-2:30 pm PST, broadcast on KYOS-AM, Merced, California.

133. Capital Cities/ABC, Inc. 1989 and 1990 Annual Report and Form 10-K.

134. Dennis Kneale, "Murphy & Burke: Duo at Capital Cities Scores a Hit, but Can Network Be Part of It?", *The Wall Street Journal,* 2 August 1990, A-1.

135. Robert Lenzner, "Warren Buffett's idea of heaven: 'I don't have to work with people I don't like,'" *Forbes 400,* 18 October 1993, 40.

136. "Greenspan vs. Buffett: On the Issue of Price Stability, We'll Pay the Latter Greater Heed," *Barron's* (Editorial), 3 April 1989, 9.

137. Floyd Norris, "Buffett Urges Tougher Savings Capital Rules," *The New York Times,* 31 May 1989, D-13.

138. George Anders, "Buffett, Known for Patient Investing Finds Benefits in Takeover Arbitrage," *The Wall Street Journal,* 30 March 1987, 24.

139. Carol J. Loomis, "The Inside Story of Warren Buffett," *Fortune,* 11 April 1988, 28.

140. In the Gillette deal, Buffett reportedly suffered a loss of windfall profits of $200 million due to the Iraqi invasion of Kuwait. "Close Call," *Forbes,* 12 November 1990, 350; Buffett's investment skills were also linked to those

of Laurence Tisch, Chairman of CBS. Inc. Both men became white knights to Champion, Inc. by buying up to 30 percent control in the corporation. "Tisch and Buffett May Help Champion Turn the Page," *Business Week*, 22 October 1990, 36.

141. Linda Sandler, "Buffett's Savior Role Lands Him Deals Other Holders Can't Get," *The Wall Street Journal*, 14 August 1989, C-1.

142. Jonathan Fuerbringer, "Salomon Chairman Pursuing a Tell-all Strategy," *The New York Times*, 21 September 1991, 34.

143. Andy Boehm, "The Seizing of the American Broadcasting Company," *L.A. WEEKLY*, 20-26 February 1987, 14.

Chapter Six

1. Edward S. Herman, *Beyond Hypocrisy: Decoding the News in An Age of Propaganda* (Boston: South End Press, 1992), 12-13; Noam Chomsky, *Necessary Illusions: Thought Control in Democratic Societies* (Boston: South End Press, 1989), 19-20.

2. Ben H. Bagdikian, "The Great Media Sell-Out to Reaganism," *The Ten Best Censored Stories of 1992*, Project Censored, Carl Jensen, Ph. D, Director, Sonoma State University, Rohnert Park, CA. 94928; See also Ben H. Bagdikian, *"Journalism of Joy,"* *Mother Jones*, May/June 1992, 48.

3. Ben H. Bagdikian, *The Media Monopoly*, 4th ed. (Boston: Beacon Press, 1992), ix.

4. S. Hall, I Connell and L. Curti, "The 'Unity' of Current Affairs Television," *Working Papers in Cultural Studies* (9) 1976, 92; quoted in James Curran, "The Different Approaches to Media Reform," in *Bending Reality: The State of the Media*, James Curran et al., eds. (London: Pluto Press, 1986), 97.

5. Herman, *Beyond Hypocrisy*, 140.

6. Sean McBride ed., *Many Voices, One World: Towards a New More Just and Efficient World Information and Communication Order* (New York: UNESCO, 1980), 166.

7. Ibid., 167, 173.

8. Curran, *Bending Reality*, 104.

9. Nader interviewed on *Pozner & Donahue*, nationally syndicated interview program, 3 April 1992 (New York: Multimedia, 1992).

10. Robert W. McChesney, "The Battle for the U.S. Airwaves, 1928-1935," *Journal of Communication*, Autumn 1990, 31.

11. ———. *Telecommunications, Mass Media, and Democracy: The Battle for Control of U.S. Broadcasting, 1928-1935* (New York: Oxford University Press, 1993), 5.

12. Ralph Nader and Claire Riley, "Oh Say Can You See: A Broadcast Network for the Audience," *The Journal of Law and Politics (University of Virginia)*, Fall 1988.

13. Ralph Nader, "The Audience Network: Time for the People," Center for Responsive Law Bulletin, P.O. Box 19367, Washington D.C., 20036.

14. Phil Fahir, "Cable Operators Pan Markey's Plan for People Power," *The Washington Post*, 26 March 1992, B-10.

15. Cindy Mitlo-Shartel, "Homegrown TV in Austin, Texas," *Building Economic Alternatives*, Spring 1988, reprinted in *Utne Reader*, July/August 1990, 78.

16. Nina Eliasoph, "Routines and the Making of Oppositional News," *Critical Studies in Mass Communication*, 5 (1988), 313.

17. George Gerbner, "The Cultural Environment Movement: A Prospectus," unpublished draft for comment via Internet, 29 September 1991.

18. Wendy Carson,"How Media Literacy is Taught," *Education Forum: The Magazines for Secondary School Professionals*, Winter 1989, reprinted in *Utne Reader*, July/August 1990, 72.

19. Dona Adams & Arlene Goldbard, "Steal this TV: How Media Literacy Can Change the World," *The Independent Film & Video Monthly*, August/September 1989, in *Utne Reader*, July/August, 1990, 68.

20. For more information on media literacy education for students, activists, and teachers, see "Decoding Media at Media Literacy Workshops," *EXTRA!*, March/April 1994, 27.

21. Erik Barnouw, *The Image Empire: A History of Broadcasting in the United States* (New York: Oxford University Press, 1970), 338-39.

22. Ibid., 71.

23. Ibid., 339.

24. Ibid.

25. "Uneasy Listening: What happened to the public of public radio?" *Whole Earth Review*, Winter 1992, reprinted in *Utne Reader*, May/June 1993, 105.

26. Martin A. Lee and Norman Solomon, *Unreliable Sources: A Guide to Detecting Bias in News Media* (New York: Lyle Stuart, 1990), 84-85.

27. Sharon Bernstein, "PBS Policy on Sponsors Questioned," *Los Angeles Times*, 2 April 1992, F-1.

28. Ibid.

29. Lee and Solomon, *Unreliable Sources*, 87-88

30. Ibid., 84-92; "The Right Wing Targets Public TV," *UTNE Reader*, May/June 1992, 45.

31. CPB tried to hold funding for three years which amounted to $1.2 billion, and instituted a plan which includes a toll-free number for listeners and viewers who wish to respond to programming. CPB also called for "town meetings" on PBS programming to begin in the summer of 1993 and a "national workshop on editorial integrity" to be held later in the fall. The corporation will then consult with broadcasters about program content. If it finds bias in coverage of an issue, it may finance other programs to address the perceived imbalance. Sandy Tolan, "Dial 1-800-Censor," *The New York Times*, 7 May 1993, A-17.

32. Ibid.

33. Lou Prato, "Politics in the Raw," *Washington Journalism Review*, September 1992, 35.

34. C-SPAN Advertisement Announcing its Board of Directors, *Broadcasting & Cable*, 20 September 1993, 24-25.

35. At the time, Cox Broadcasting purchased a Pittsburgh television station for $20.6 million, only $3.8 million of which represented the station's assets. The other $16.8 million represented the market value of the Pittsburgh airspace in which the television station operated. See also "Should FCC be abolished?" *Broadcasting*, 29 November 1965, 59.

36. Barnouw, *The Image Empire*, 295.

37. "Fowler stresses fee trade-off for deregulation," *Broadcasting*, 27 September 1982, 33.

38. "In Brief," *Broadcasting*, 12 August 1991, 72.

39. R. Craig Endicott, "100 Media Companies Hit $66. 1 Billion," *Advertising Age*, 26 June 1989, S-1.

40. R. Craig Endicott, "Top 100 take it on the chin, feel biggest drop in four decades," *Advertising Age*, 23 September 1992, 69.

41. "Washington Watch," *Broadcasting*, 1 March 1993, 48.

42. D.C. Mayor Pratt-Kelly's plan to tax advertising was based on similar plans in Hawaii, New Mexico, and Washington state. These three states currently tax the gross receipts of advertising agencies and public relations companies, using a measure comparable to a corporate income tax. However, these states do not tax corporate sponsors directly. See also Nell Henderson, "Kelly Plans for Taxes Assailed," *The Washington Post*, 5 March 1993, D-5; Nell Henderson, "Businesses Say They'd Leave D.C.," *The Washington Post*, 4 March 1993, B-5.

43. Sharon D. Moshavi, "When Sold Out is Not Enough," *Broadcasting*, 9 November 1992, 44.

44. George Orwell, *1984*, 4th ed. (New York: Penguin, 1981), 204.

SELECTED BIBLIOGRAPHY

This selected bibliography lists research materials that were not cited in chapter endnotes. All of these sources assisted me in writing this book.

Books

Agee, Philip. *Inside the Company*. New York: Bantam, 1975.

Bennett, James R. *Control of Information in the U.S.: An Annotated Bibliography*. Westport, Connecticut: Meckler, 1987.

_____. *Control of the Media in the United States: An Annotated Bibliography*. New York: Garland Publishing Inc., 1992.

Cohen, Jeff and Norman Solomon. *Adventures in Medialand: Behind the News, Beyond the Pundits*. Monroe, Maine: Common Courage Press, 1993.

Craft, Christine. *Too Old, Too Ugly, and Not Deferential to Men: An Anchorwoman's Courageous Battle Against Sex Discrimination*. Rocklin, Ca.: Prima Publishing, 1988.

Eliot, Marc. *Walt Disney: Hollywood's Dark Prince*. New York: Birch Lane Press, 1993.

Friendly, Fred W. *Due to Circumstances Beyond Our Control*. New York: Random House, 1967.

Galbraith, John Kenneth. *The New Industrial State*. 4th ed. New York: New American Library, 1985.

Gans, Herbert J. *Deciding What's News: A Study of CBS Evening News, NBC Nightly News, Newsweek, and Time*. New York: Vintage Books, 1979.

Garson, Barbara. *The Electronic Sweatshop: How Computers Are Transforming the Office of the Future into the Factory of the Past*. New York: Simon & Schuster, 1988.

Geoghegan, Thomas. *Which Side Are You On? Trying to Be for Labor When It's Flat on its Back*. New York: Farrar, Straus, & Giroux, 1991.

Gitlin, Todd. *Inside Prime Time*. New York: Pantheon, 1983.

Gross, Bertrand. *Friendly Fascism: The New Face of Power in America*. New York: M. Evans and Company, 1980.

Halberstam, David. *The Powers That Be*. New York: Knopf, 1979.

Hertsgaard, Mark. *On Bended Knee: The Press and the Reagan Presidency*. New York: Farrar, Straus, and Giroux, 1988.

Lapham, Lewis H. *The Wish for Kings: Democracy at Bay*. New York: Grove Press, 1993.

Lernoux, Penny. *In Banks We Trust*. Garden City, New York: Doubleday, 1984.

Lutz, William E., ed. *Beyond Nineteen Eighty-Four: Doublespeak in a Post-Orwellian Age*. Urbana, Illinois: National Council of Teachers, 1989.

Moldea, Dan E. *Dark Victory: Ronald Reagan, MCA, and the Mob*. New York: Viking, 1986.

Navasky, Victor S. *Naming Names*. New York: Penguin, 1980.

Parenti, Michael. *Inventing Reality: The Politics of Mass Media*. New York: St. Martin's Press, 1986.

_____. *Democracy for the Few*. 5th ed. New York: St. Martin's Press, 1988.

Persico, Joseph E. *Edward R. Murrow: An American Original*. New York: McGraw-Hill, 1988.

Phillips, Kevin. *The Politics of Rich and Poor: Wealth and the American Electorate in the Reagan Aftermath*. New York: Random House, 1990.

Postman, Neil. *Amusing Ourselves to Death: Public Discourse in the Age of Show Business*. New York: Penguin Books, 1985.

Sampson, Anthony. *The Sovereign State of ITT*. New York: Stein, 1973.

Schiller, Herbert I. *Mass Communication and American Empire*. Boston: Beacon Press, 1969. (Reprinted in Boulder, Col.: Westview Press, 1992).

_____. *Culture, Inc.: The Corporate Takeover of Public Expression*. New York: Oxford University Press, 1989.

Shirer, William L. *20th Century Journey: A Native's Return, 1945-1988*. Boston: Little, Brown and Co., 1990.

Spence, Gerry. *With Justice for None: Destroying an American Myth*. New York: Random House, 1989.

Squires, James D. *Read All About It! The Corporate Takeover of America's Newspapers*. New York: Times Books, 1993.

Stockwell, John. *Praetorian Guard: The U.S. Role in the New World Order*. Boston: South End Press, 1991.

Stoler, Peter. *The War Against the Press: Politics, Pressure and Intimidation in the 1980s*. New York: Dodd, Mead, and Company, 1986.

Tunstall, Jeremy. *Communications Deregulation: The Unleashing of America's Communications Industry*. New York: Basil Blackwell, 1986.

Journals, Periodicals, and Newspapers

Aufererheide, Pat. "Free Speech for Broadcasters Only." *The Nation*, September 1984, 140.

Brown, Les. "Who's Really Running the FCC—And Is It Legal?" *Channels*, January/February 1984, 38.

Caranicas, Peter. "American TV Tightens Its Grip on the World." *Channels*, January/February 1984, 27.

Clogher, Rick. "Weaving Spider Come Not Here, Bohemian Grove: Inside the Secret Retreat of the Power Elite." *Mother Jones*, August 1981, 28.

Massing, Michael. "Ted Koppel's Neutrality Act." *Columbia Journalism Review*, March/April 1989, 30.

Morris, Roger. "Casey's Past Told Us the 'Fixer' Would Get Us into a Fix." *Los Angeles Times*, 28 August 1987, II-7.

"Nightline's Bias." *The Progressive* (editorial), April 1989, 9.

Nossiter, Bernard D. "The F.C.C.'s Big Giveaway Show." *The Nation*, 26 October 1985, 402.

Schanberg, Sydney H. "Censoring for Political Security." *Washington Journalism Review*, March 1991, 23.

Schiller, Herbert I. "World Information Cartel: Behind the Media Merger Movement." *The Nation*, 8 June 1985, 696.

Talbot, David. "Frontlines: David Rockefeller & Other Pinstriped Revolutionaries (Defunding the Left)." *Mother Jones*, November 1982, 10.

Turner, Richard. "Changes Made in a Toxic Leak Film by ABC." *TV Guide*, 22 February 1986, A-2.

Radio, Television, Video

Clark, Ramsey. "Media Coverage of Gulf War." A radio interview broadcast on "Peacewatch with Dennis Bernstein," KPFA(FM), Berkeley, California, 8 April 1991.

Moyers, Bill. "The Propaganda Battle." PBS's "A Walk through the Twentieth Century with Bill Moyers." Released on videocassette. New York: Corporation for Entertainment and Learning, 1984.

_____. "The Image Makers." PBS's "A Walk Through the 20th Century with Bill Moyers." Released on videocassette. New York: Corporation for Entertainment and Learning, 1987.

_____. "Consuming Images." PBS's "The Public Mind with Bill Moyers," produced by Gail Pellett. Original air date: 8 November 1989. Washington, DC: WETA-TV, 1989.

_____. "Illusions of News." PBS's "The Public Mind with Bill Moyers," produced by Richard M. Cohen, reported by Bill Moyers. Original air date: 22 November 1989. Washington: D.C.: WETA-TV, 1989.

_____. "High Crimes and Misdemeanors." PBS's "Frontline," produced and directed by Sherry Jones. Original air date: 27 November 1990. Boston: WGBH-TV, 1990.

_____. "The Top 10 Censored News Stories of 1990." PBS's "Project Censored," February 1991. New York: WNET-TV, 1991.

"The Real Life of Ronald Reagan." PBS's "Frontline," produced by Martin Smith, written by Martin Smith, Godfrey Hodgson, and Garry Wills. Original air date: 18 January 1989. Boston: WGBH-TV, 1989.

Stockwell, John. "Secret Wars of the CIA." A speech at American University, Washington, D.C., telecast on C-SPAN, 27 December 1989. Washington, D.C.: C-SPAN, 1990.

Index

A

B

Mary Carter Paint Company, 3-4, 57-58.
See also Resorts International
Masters of Deceit (Hoover), 41
"Maverick," 36
Mazzocco, Dennis: education, 9-10; internship, 11-12
MCA. *See* Music Corporation of America
Media Monopoly, The (Bagdikian), 5, 71
Media Unlimited, 173n65
Meir, Golda, 39
Mergers (1980s), 1-2, 53, 91. *See also*
Capital Cities/ABC merger (1985)
Metropolitan Insurance Company, 32, 44
"Mickey Mouse Club," 34
Missing (Gravas), 18
Mitofsky, Warren J., 131
Monogram Industries, 46
Morgan Company, 70
Moyers, Bill, 155
Multimedia, 126-27
Murdoch, Rupert, 37, 132, 170n17
Murphy, Henry, 59
Murphy, Thomas S., 52, 53, 59, 71, 176n34; and Burke, 66, 67; and Capital Cities/ABC merger, 90-91, 103; compensation, 108
Music Corporation of America (MCA), 83, 184n30

N

NAB. *See* National Association of Broadcasters
NABET. *See* National Association of Broadcast Employees and Technicians
Nader, Ralph, 145-46, 147
"Naked City," 35
National Association of Broadcast Employees and Technicians (NABET), 12-14, 105, 106-7
National Association of Broadcasters (NAB), 159
National Broadcasting Company (NBC), 14, 23, 37, 170n15; Blue Network, 29, 30, 169n4; General Electric takeover, 1, 106; NBC News scandal, 129
National Public Radio, 153, 155

NBC. *See* National Broadcasting Company
Nestle Beverage Company, 120-21
Network power: and deregulation, 142-43; and elite management, 141-42; and interlocking corporate ownership, 70-71; limits on, 30, 169n7; and Republican administrations, 2-5; Third World, 16-17; warnings about, 5-6. *See also specific topics*
Neufeld, Victor, 130
New York Magazine, 88
New York Times, The, 43
News Limited, 37
News-Democrat (Belleville), 69-70
Newsreels, 39, 172n46
Nicaragua, 61-62
Nickolodeon, 117-18
Nielsen, 11, 183n20
"Night Beat," 172n45
"NiteCap," 119-20
Nixon, Richard, 57. *See also* Nixon administration
Nixon administration, 46; attacks on media, 3, 84; deregulation under, 77, 82; Watergate scandal, 10, 58-59
Noble, Edward J., 29, 30-32, 35-36, 40, 169n8, 169n9, 171n32
North, Oliver, 61-62, 136

O

Oakland Press, 69
O'Connor, John, 130
October Surprise, 62
Odyssey, 62
Office of Strategic Services (OSS), 56, 60, 61
Olympics, 19, 22
"On the Corner," 169n12
On Strike! Capital Cities and the Wilkes-Barre Newspaper Unions (Keil), 71
Organized crime, 4, 169n13; and U.S. intelligence agencies, 57, 58, 61, 172n54
Orwell, George, 166
OSS. *See* Office of Strategic Services
Ownership limits, 53, 113; and Capital Cities, 69, 77, 78, 92, 178n74; democratic media proposals, 162-63

About South End Press

South End Press is a non-profit, collectively run book publisher with over 180 titles in print. Since our founding in 1977, we have tried to meet the needs of readers who are exploring, or are already committed to, the politics of radical social change.

Our goal is to publish books that encourage ciritical thinking and constructive action on the key political, cultural, social, economic and ecological issues shaping life in the United States and in the world. In this way, we hope to give expression to a wide diversity of democratic social movements and to provide an alternative to the products of corporate publishing.

Through the Institute for Social and Cultural Change, South End Press works with other political media projects—*Z Magazine;* Speak Out!, a speakers bureau; the New Liberation News Service and the Publishers Support Project—to expand access to information and critical analysis. If you would like a free catalog of South End Press books or information about our membership program, which offers two free books and a 40 percent discount on all titles, please write to us at: South End Press, 116 Saint Botolph Street, Boston, MA 02115.

Other South End Press Titles of Interest

Necessary Illusions: Thought Control in Democratic Societies
Noam Chomsky

Prime Time Activism: Media Strategies for Grassroots Organizing
Charlotte Ryan

Media-tions: Forays Into the Culture and Gender Wars
Elayne Rapping

Stop the Killing Train: Radical Visions for Radical Change
Michael Albert

Sisters of the Yam: Black women and Self-Recovery
bell hooks